Funky Things to Draw

fairies

Paul Könye ★ Kate Ashforth

Funky Things to Draw

Fairies

INTRODUCTION

For centuries, fairies have been part of popular folklore in cultures around the world. Stories of fairy sightings have been passed down through generations and many people still believe in them. The question still remains: are fairies real or fantasy?

Perhaps you'll believe in fairies once you learn how to draw these magical beings. To capture the wonder of this unique fantasy world, let your imagination go! Imagine seeing a fairy for the first time, flitting from blossom to blossom. Picture standing at the end of a rainbow where a leprechaun keeps his pot of gold!

THINGS YOU WILL NEED

- An HB or 2B pencil (they are light and won't smudge too easily)
- A pencil sharpener and a small dish for shavings
- A4 cartridge paper or copy paper and some scrap paper for experiments
- A clean eraser
- Confidence: a positive attitude will help improve your skills
- Imagination: don't be afraid to explore your own style or ideas

Drawing guidelines

There are a few things you should be aware of when drawing your fairies.

1 These fairies are built around a skeleton, which is made up of a series of lines, shapes and joints and a backbone.
2 Begin by drawing the skeleton lightly, otherwise it will be visible in the final drawing. Where possible, rub out the skeleton with a clean eraser as you go.
3 Pay close attention to where each fairy's limbs are placed and where the cross is drawn on the head. This will help you draw them in the correct pose.
4 To draw each fairy within proportion, pay close attention to the type and the size of the shapes used to create the skeleton.
5 Carefully observe the angle at which each fairy is positioned in the first step. Look at the length and the direction of all the body parts. This will allow your fairy to be seen from the correct perspective.

Stages of drawing

A common way of drawing the human form is to begin with a basic structure called the 'skeleton'. This helps you create the physical, rounded form of a person. You will learn to draw fairies using the same method. Read each step carefully before you begin. The instructions will teach you how to draw the elements of your picture in the right order.

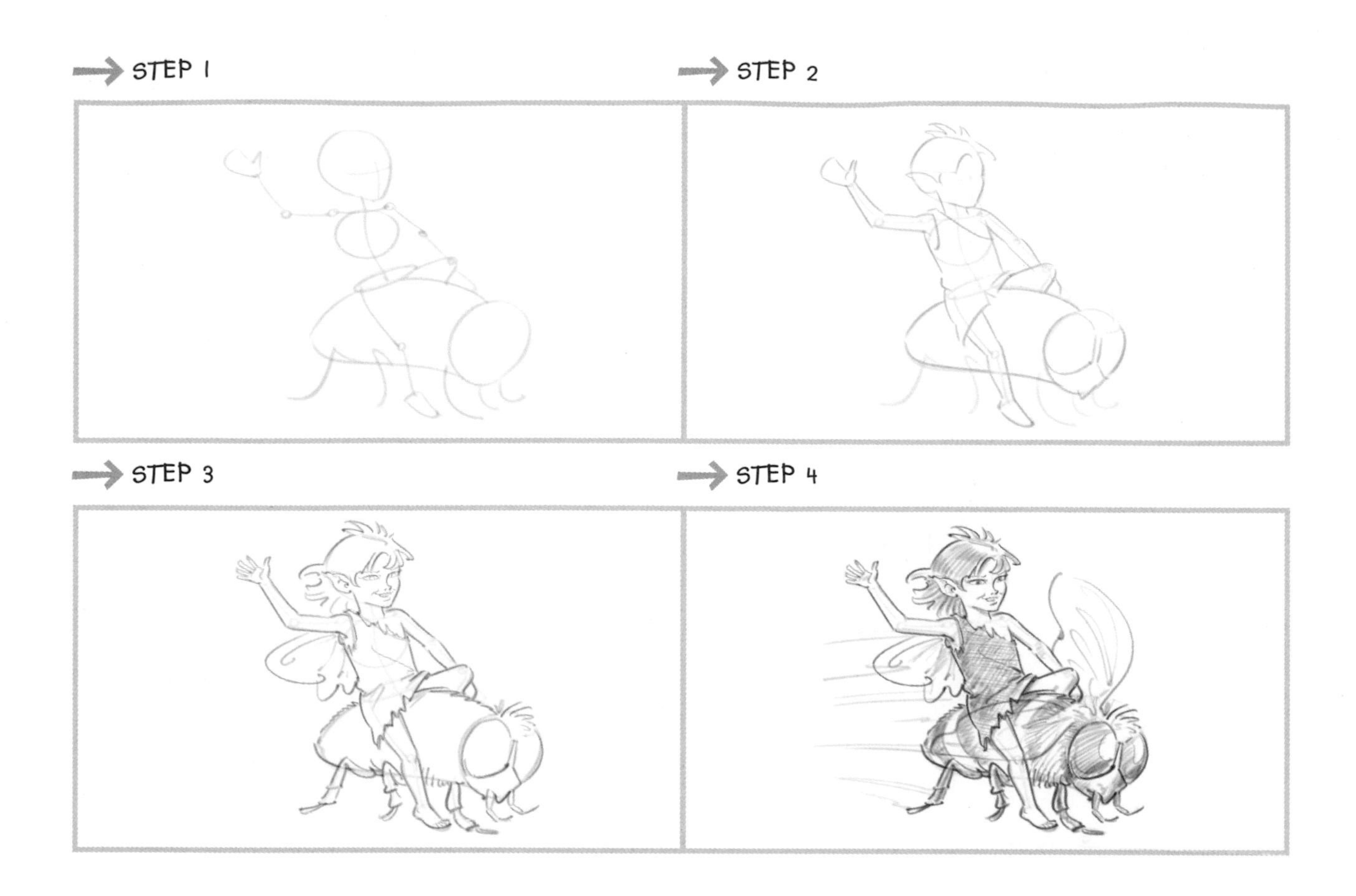

Study the structure of the skeleton. How is the fairy's body shape built around it? Observe how the drawing of the fairy changes between the steps. What type of pencil techniques have been used to create the line work for each picture? Study the pencil marks and the levels of shading, as these will add definition to your final drawing.

Skills and techniques

Here are some examples of the different art elements and techniques you will learn about.

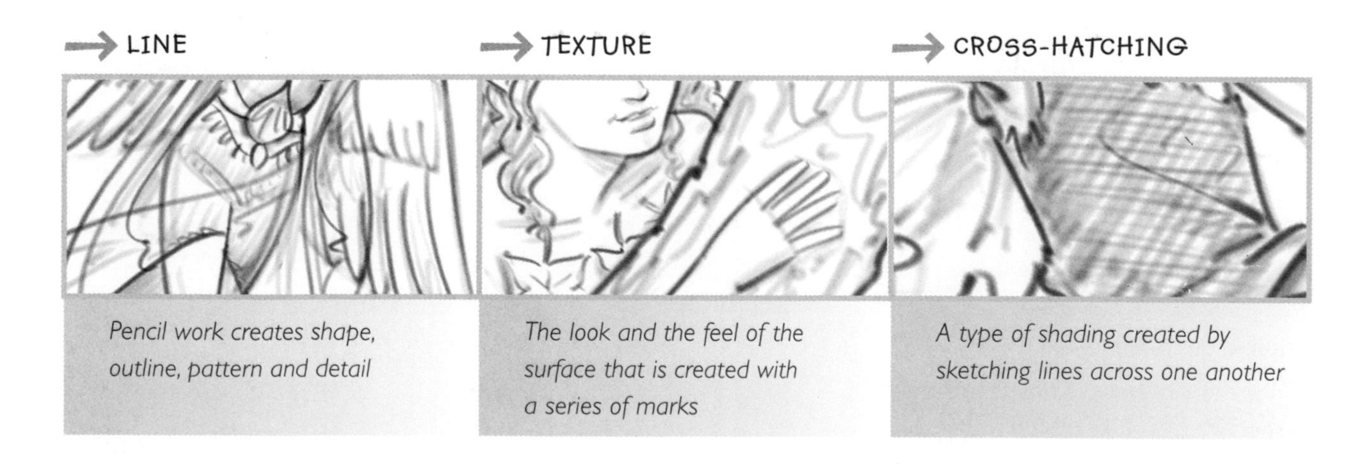

Pencil work creates shape, outline, pattern and detail

The look and the feel of the surface that is created with a series of marks

A type of shading created by sketching lines across one another

Learning to draw the human form takes time and patience. Fairies are no exception! Be confident when you practise your pencil technique and line work. Remember that practice makes perfect!

PIXIE

Pixies are little playful tricksters from Cornwall in England, where they are known as piskies. Pixies love to play tricks, such as stealing ponies at night and returning them the next morning with their manes twisted and knotted. Another trick pixies like to play is leading travellers astray in unfamiliar territory. This is called being 'pixie-led'.

Before you begin

The most important technique in the pixie drawing is the position of the legs. Create the straight leg first and then draw the right leg crossing over. Also, observe the shape and size of the head and the expression on the fairy's face in Step 4. Pay close attention to the angle of the arms and the direction the pixie is facing.

Step 1

Lightly draw a circle for the head. Add a chin and a cross on the face. Draw a line for the backbone that begins under the chin and ends at the hips. Add a shape for the chest with a collarbone across the top. Draw the straight right arm and the left arm bending around with the hand on the hip. Add a baseline half a body length below the hips. Draw the straight left leg with the foot below the line. Add the right leg and foot bending behind. Add the toadstool on the baseline with the pixie's right hand leaning on it.

Step 2

Build the pixie's form around its skeleton. Define the outline of the face and neck. Draw a hat shape above the head, paying attention to the details around the edge of the hat, such as the ear. Sketch a ring shape for the collar. Add the outline of the arms and clothes. Build a shape for the front leg and then the rear leg. Define the line work of the toadstool.

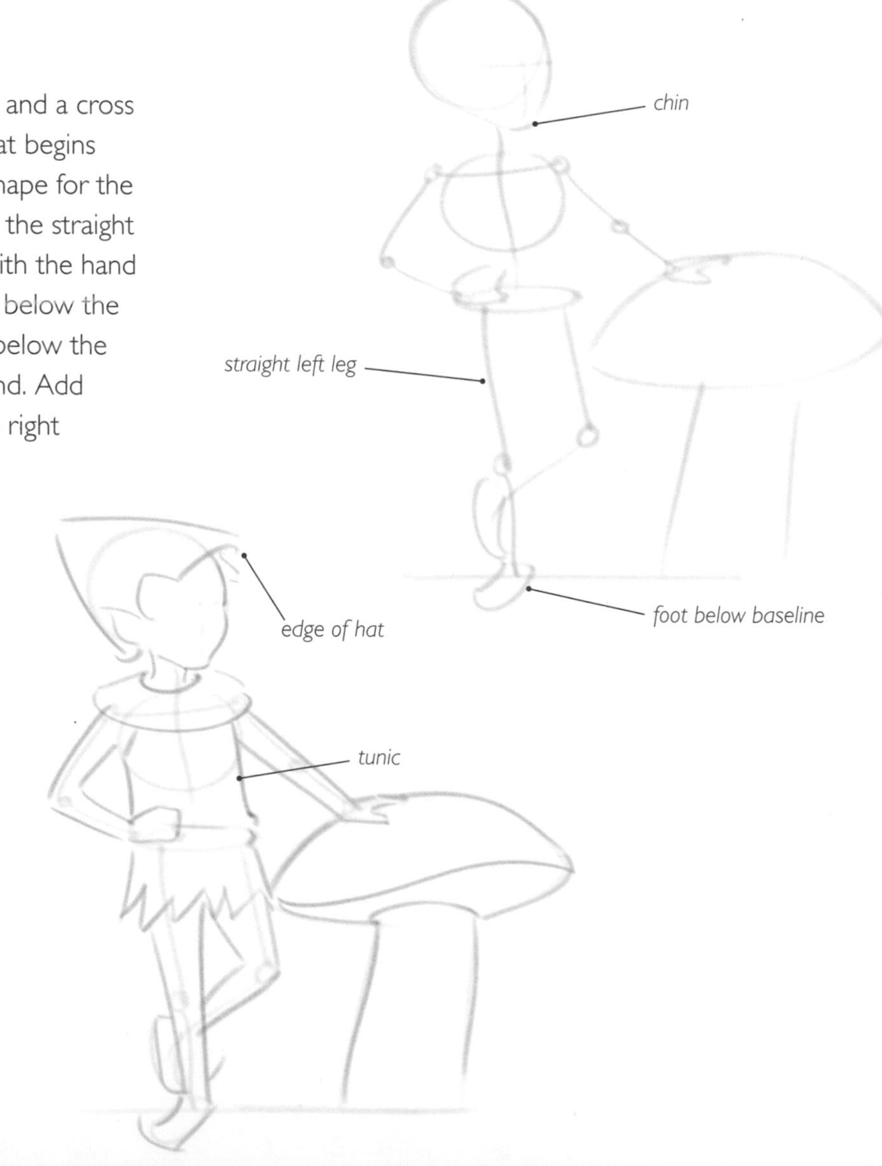

Step 3

Define, darken and smooth the line work for the whole fairy. Draw the nose and the mouth over the cross. Add eyes and brows on either side, with the eyes looking forward. Working from the top, develop the curves and details of the outline. Define the finer marks inside the clothing and wings.

DRAWING TIP

Shading is a drawing technique using pencil. Use a side-to-side drawing motion. Press softly with your pencil to create a lighter tone. To create medium to dark tones, use a medium pressure with your pencil. Keep working over an area until you reach the level of grey tone that you need.

Step 4

Darken the outline. Using a medium pencil pressure, shade a mid-grey tone over the hat, tunic and shoes. Darken the eyes and lightly shade the edges of the wing and the body.

Add a pattern to the cap of the toadstool and shade the texture underneath. Once you add the soft wildflowers and the grass in the background, your pixie is ready to play!

FAIRY FACT → Pixies sometimes leave a trail of pixie dust behind them as they fly in the air.

ELF

In Scandinavian legends, elves are said to live in the heart of the forest. They look like beautiful, fair young women, with delicate features. Elves can be found dancing through the grasslands at night under the light of the moon. People must be careful not to offend the elves, as the elves may take their revenge by afflicting them with skin diseases.

Before you begin

To draw the elf in the correct pose, carefully position the hips, legs and feet. A cone shape is created where the legs cross over. The angle of the feet is also important, as it helps the elf to be seen from the right perspective. Note how all parts of the body run off the curved backbone.

Step 1

Draw lightly at first. Sketch an oval for the head and add a cross for the face on the left side. Run a curved line for the backbone down from the chin. Add an oval for the chest in the curve of the backbone. Draw a collarbone on an angle. Add shoulders and the arms bending outward. Draw hips at the base of the backbone. Sketch the front leg bending forward and cross the rear leg at the knee, ensuring the feet are in the correct position.

Step 2

The outline of the body runs around the outside of the skeleton. First, draw the curves of the face and neck. Add the top of the shoulders and line work for the hair around the head and face. Build the arm shapes and the top of the cape. Draw a band around the hips, curves for the dress and the flowing cape.

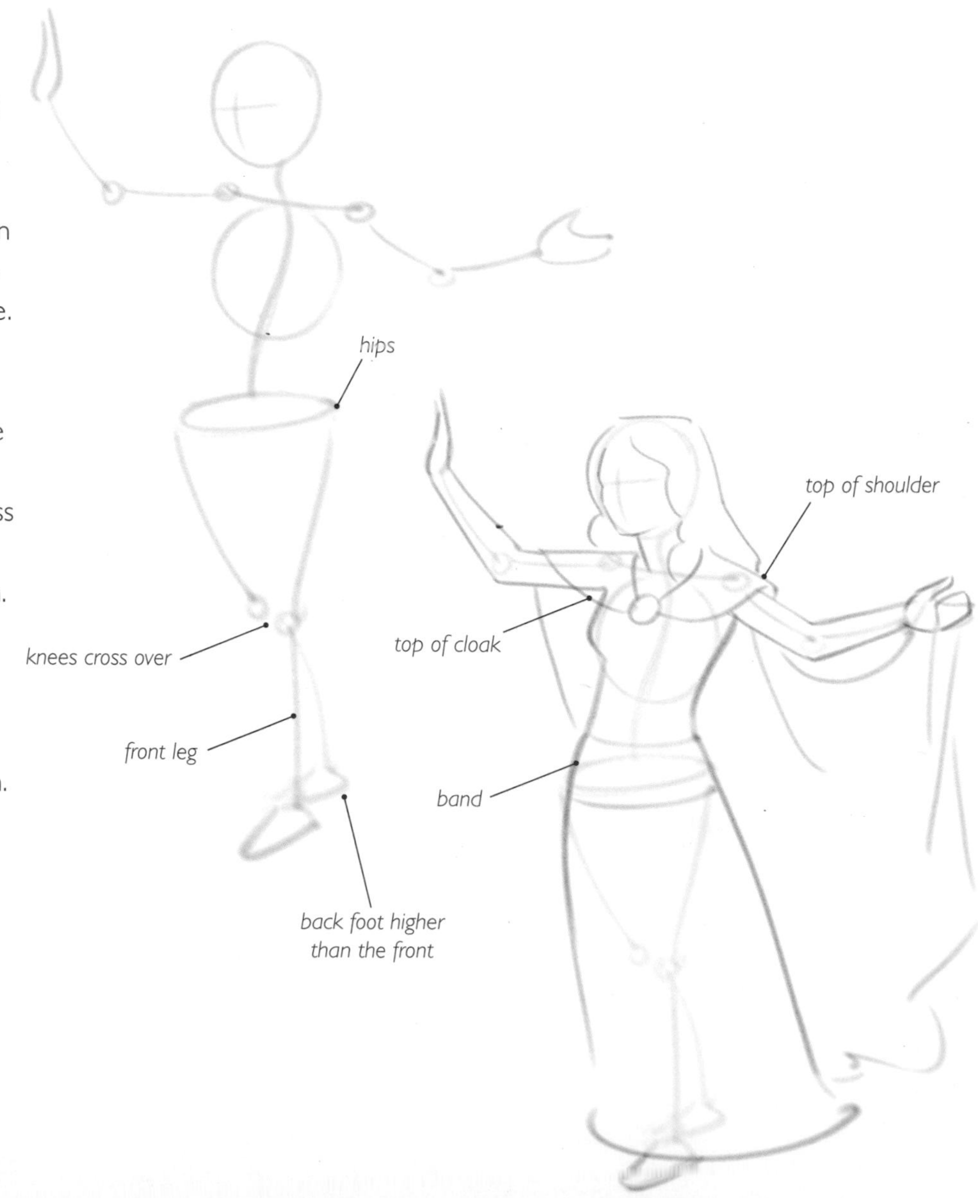

Step 3

Define and darken the outline. Draw a nose and mouth over the cross. Add eyes on either side. Sketch a brow, a head band and an ear poking out. Rub out any unnecessary line work with a clean eraser. Working around the body, add details for the clothes. Add line work for the fingers, ensuring the fingers on the right hand point upward.

DRAWING TIP

If you are having trouble coming up with ideas for a drawing, look for inspiration elsewhere. Use picture books, magazines or the internet to get your imagination going.

Step 4

With a light pencil grip, draw faint folds in the cape draped over the forearms. Add a beam of light behind the left hand. Gently shade the texture of the hair and the edges of the clothing. Darken the facial features.

To draw the column in the foreground, create an ellipse shape at the top first. Work down, drawing the vertical lines and the curves of the base. Once you add the jug, bowl and grass, your elf is ready to dance in the moonlight!

FAIRY FACT → If you find a green circle in the grass or a ring of mushrooms, it could have been made by dancing elves!

SPRITE

Sprites are mischievous, light-hearted nature spirits. Some sprites cause the leaves to change colour and fall from the trees in autumn, while others make little rainbows, reflecting off glistening water. These little creatures also play with nymphs, flying about and teasing the butterflies.

Before you begin

To draw the sprite correctly, pay special attention to the position of the head and legs. Observe how the head is curved at the back and pointed at the front. The face is drawn at the bottom part of the head. Also, study the line work used to create the limbs and clothing.

Step 1

Lightly draw a head with a cross facing down. Add a short backbone, joining to the head at the top left. The backbone should be on an angle with hips at the base. Add a curved line for the chest, running around the jaw to the back of the head. Draw a light collarbone behind the eyes. Add the arms and hands, pointing outward. Add the straight left leg and the bent right leg.

Step 2

Build the sprite's form around the skeleton. Define the shape of the face, neck and ear. Add an outline around the head for the hair. Construct the shapes of the arms and hands. Working from right to left, fan the leaf shapes of the clothing around the back of the head. Draw the shapes for the legs and the shoes.

Step 3

Define the outline, paying attention to the details of the clothes and shoes. Draw a nose and a mouth over the cross. Add the ear details and the eyes on either side of the nose, looking down.

DRAWING TIP

Different types of organic shapes can be found in nature which are great to represent in a drawing, such as leaves, starfish, shells, flowers or fruit. Next time you go outside, look around you and see what you can find.

Step 4

Add the details to the body. First, shade a dark tone over the shoes and the top of the clothing. Sketch a wavy pattern on the inside of the leafy clothing. Using a light pencil pressure, softly shade the edges of the body. Develop the facial features and add texture to the hair.

Randomly sketch leaves of different shapes and sizes around the body. Now your sprite is ready to fly through the sky!

FAIRY FACT → Sprites usually live in trees, but there are water sprites who live in ponds. Some can even change into birds.

FLOWER FAIRY

Flower fairies are born inside a budding flower. It is said that these fairies are the reason that flowers grow and bloom. As winter ends, the fairies fly to each blossom and help them to open in time for spring. You may see these fairies swinging from branches or using flowers as umbrellas!

Before you begin

To draw the fairy suspended in the air, focus on the angle and direction of the body. Observe the angle of the top of the body: it is the same as the stem. Note how the legs cross at the knees and the feet sit behind one another. Also pay attention to the position of the arms and face.

Step 1

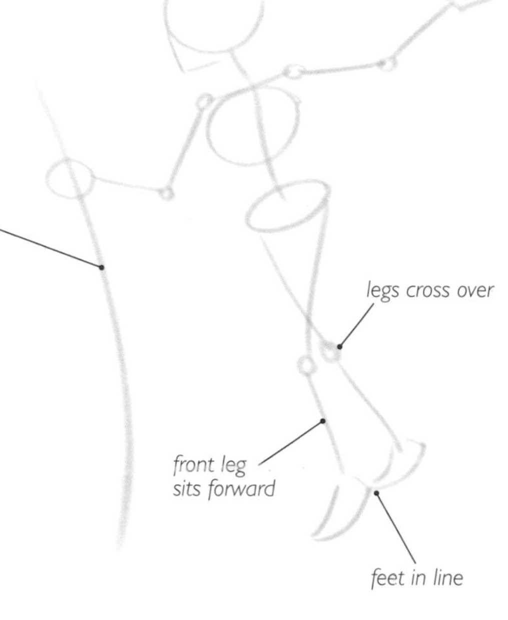

Lightly draw a curved stem on a slight angle. Sketch a head shape, with the chin pointing towards the stem. Draw a backbone behind the chin and an oval for the hips. Add a circle in the middle of the back for the chest and sketch a collarbone across the top of the circle. Draw the bent left arm with a hand holding the stem, then add the right arm and hand extending outward. Add a line to the hip for the front leg and cross the other leg behind. Sketch the pointy feet in line with one another.

Step 2

Create the line work for both flower stems. Draw a round shape for the front flower. Add an eye shape for the rear flower. Draw the wavy line over the head for the hair.

Connect the hair line and facial features. Build the shape of the neck, arms and chest around the skeleton. Draw the waistband and attach the shape for the dress sweeping behind. Construct the outline of the legs.

Step 3

Use darker line work for this step. Create curved details on the flower petals and line work for the stems. Add the shapes for the bee. Draw a garland of flowers behind the fairy's ear. Develop the facial features and wavy hair. Define the line work of the arms, hands and legs and create the butterfly-like wings. Shape the outline of the dress around the body, paying attention to its layered, wavy pattern.

Step 4

Observe the type of shading used to enhance the shapes and line work. Shade the open line work around the wings and dress using a light pressure. Gently shade the edges of the body and add texture to the hair.

Add the fine details. Shade in the darker tones to the bee, flowers and stems. Now your flower fairy is ready to flit from blossom to blossom!

DRAWING TIP

Be patient when drawing detailed pictures. Don't worry if your picture isn't perfect on your first try.

FAIRY FACT → You may find a flower fairy anywhere that flowers grow, from fields and forests to backyards and botanical gardens!

DRYAD

Dryads are the spirits of trees, most often oak trees, and are found in Greek mythology. Dryads, always female, keep watch over their own tree, as well as the forest. Dryads live for a long time, but they will die if their tree is cut down. For this reason, the Greek gods would often punish people who damaged the trees.

Before you begin

The structure of the tree and the dryad's form are both important in this drawing. This is because the dryad is part of the tree. No skeleton is used to develop the structure of this drawing; instead it's based on line work. Pay attention to the type of line work used in each step and how the texture of the hair and the bark is created.

head on angle

front branch under chin

rear branch

Step 1

Draw a shape on a slight angle for the head. Sketch the back of the head and the angled lines of the face. Add a cross on the head facing to the right and the neck below the jaw and chin. Draw rounded shoulders and the rear branch. Add the front branch running under the chin, paying attention to the angles. Draw an arm shape leaning over the front branch and add the line of the body.

Step 2

Define the bumpy outline of the front branch. Draw a nose and a mouth above the cross. Draw eyes looking to the right and brows above the eyes. Sketch a fringe around the face and leaves dangling below. Add the ear and headband. Draw a wavy hairline around the head. Shape the arm and hand.

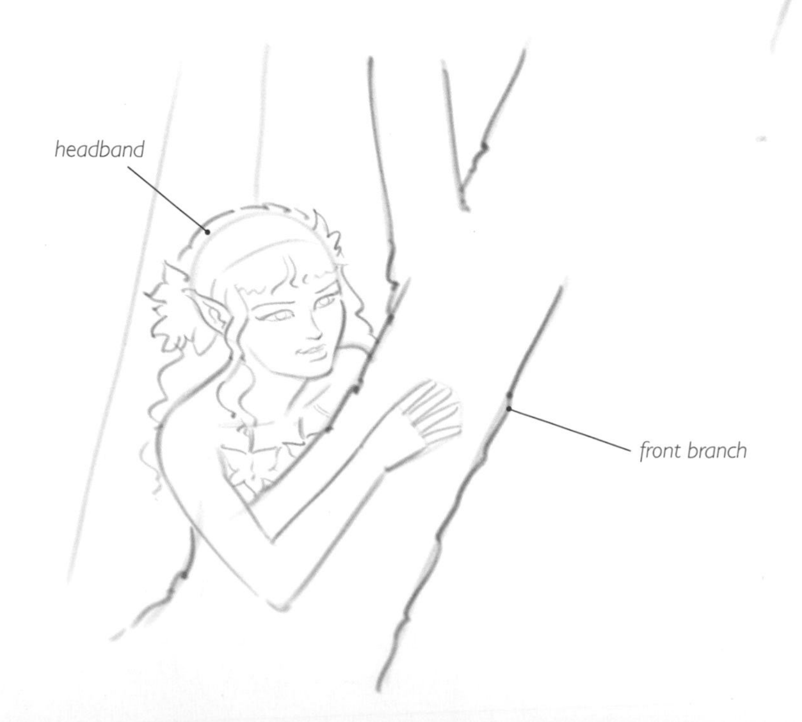

Step 3

Define the bumpy outline of the rear branch and draw shapes for the leafy headband. Using wavy open line work, draw the texture of the hair.

DRAWING TIP

Texture is the look and feel of a surface. In drawing, it is represented by a series of marks. For example, the bark of a tree could be drawn as a series of irregular deep lines and hair could be represented as a series of soft wavy lines.

Step 4

Darken the line work. Observe the texture of the tree bark and shading of the hair. Starting at the top of the branches, shade the bumpy line work of the bark. Define the eyes and facial features. Shade a mid-grey tone over the hair and darken the berries. Very lightly shade around the face and arm.

Once you add the faint outline of the trees in the background, your dryad is ready to dance in the moonlight!

FAIRY FACT → Dryads are spirits of nature. Other spirits include 'naiads' (fresh water spirits), 'oreads' (mountain spirits) and 'hesperides' (garden spirits).

PILLYWIGGIN

Pillywiggins are tiny flower fairies from Britain and Ireland. They live at the foot of oak trees among the wildflowers and are very playful. Pillywiggins are seasonal helpers who tend spring flowers by riding bees from blossom to blossom. They eat pollen, nectar and dew.

Before you begin

The most important element of this drawing is the bee. The bee supports the pillywiggin's body and helps position it correctly. Observe how the pillywiggin leans back against the body of the bee. Note the size of both figures and how the pillywiggin's legs and hips are positioned on the bee's body. Pay attention to where the arms are drawn.

Step 1

Lightly draw the structure of the bee and add the pillywiggin's hips on its back. Draw a line on an angle for the backbone and a head shape with the chin pointing down. Sketch a cross on the face. Add a circle to the middle of the backbone for the chest. Draw a front leg across the bee, hanging between the bee's legs. Add a leg curved behind and the collarbone at the top of the chest. Draw an arm thrown back in the air and a straight arm resting behind the bee's head. Don't forget the hand and foot.

Step 2

Develop the pillywiggin's form around the skeleton, starting with the hairline on the head. Define the ear, neck and face. Working your way down, build the shape of the arms, tunic and legs. Define the outline of the bee and its head.

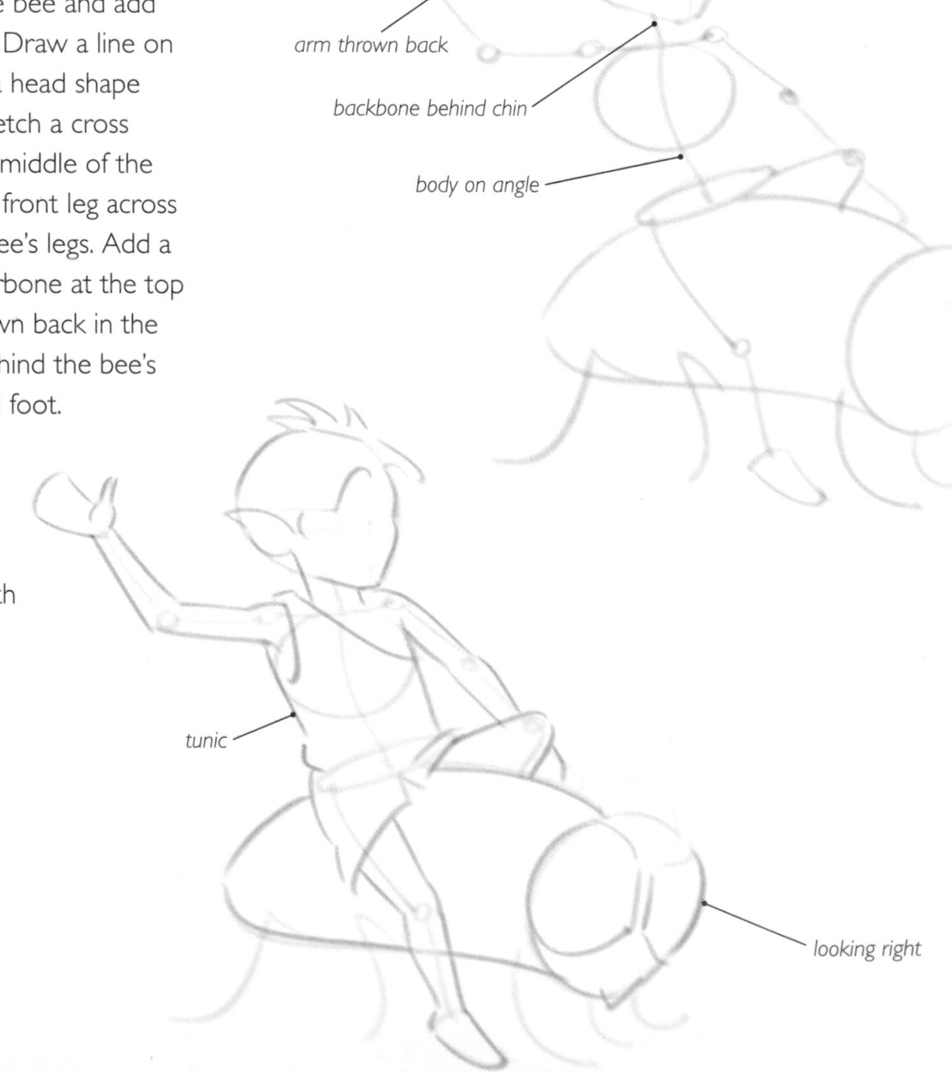

Step 3

Define and smooth the pillywiggin's outline. Beginning at the head, draw the hair blowing backwards. Add the fringe. Draw a nose and a mouth. Add the eyes on either side, making sure they are looking to the right. Add the details for the ear. Develop the jagged outline of the tunic and sketch the wings curving out behind. Define the pillywiggin's legs and foot. Build the bee's leg and antennae, then add its hairy outline.

Step 4

Observe the level of shading and the darkness of the line work. Using a medium pencil pressure, shade the pillywiggin's hair. Develop its facial features and shade the tunic with cross-hatching (lines that travel across each another). Lightly shade the edges of the pillywiggin's body and wing.

For the bee, add texture to the stripes using a series of lines. Shade a mid-grey tone across its face and legs. Add the wing above the bee's left eye and draw the transparent front wing over the length of its body. Once you have drawn the movement lines, your pillywiggin is ready to fly!

DRAWING TIP

Remember not to press too hard with your pencil when beginning to draw. Draw lightly at first; you can always add more detail as you go.

FAIRY FACT → Pillywiggins get angry when flowers are destroyed, but you just need to plant a tree or flower to make them happy.

GOBLIN

Goblins are ugly and unpleasant creatures that make their homes in creepy churchyards or among the slimy roots of ancient trees. They play malicious pranks on humans, such as hiding things and turning signposts to face the wrong way. Goblins celebrate Halloween, causing havoc with ghosts and other evil creatures.

Before you begin

The goblin is made up of many different elements. Study the size, shape, length and position of the body parts so you can draw it correctly. Notice how the head and chest shapes overlap in the first step. See where the backbone and limbs are placed and observe the details and line work that have been developed in the final step.

Step 1

Lightly draw an oval for the chest. Sketch a head shape over the top left corner of the oval. Add a cross on the head, facing up, and a curved backbone to the side of the chest. Draw the hips on an angle and extend the collarbone under the chin. Attach a bent front arm and a hand. Draw a bent rear arm above it and add a circle for the mug. Add the front leg, connecting to the backbone, and the foot pointing up. Draw the rear leg curving back, with the foot pointing down.

Step 2

Build the the goblin's body around the skeleton. Draw a hat above the head and develop the shape of the face and ears. Construct the shape of the body and the front arm. Add the neck, collar, rear arm and mug. Build the shape of the bottom and the front leg and then add the rear leg.

Step 3

Darken the goblin's outline. Define the shape of the face and ear. Sketch the nose and then mouth. Add eyes and eyebrows on either side. Define the hat, the details of the tunic and the front arm. Then focus on the back arm and the face. Develop the legs.

Step 4

Starting with the face, add a tooth and a wart, and then darken the eyes. Add hairy eyebrows and wrinkles and shade the mouth. Study the levels of shading over the clothing. Shade a dark tone across the legs and hair, and lighter grey tones over the rest of the body.

When drawing the background, see how the tree sits above the goblin's back foot. Draw the soft outline and texture of the tree, then add the other details. Now your goblin is ready to make mischief!

DRAWING TIP

When using an eraser, make sure you keep it clean. You can do this by rubbing the grey residue off its end on a separate page.

FAIRY FACT → It is thought that a goblin's ugly crooked smile can turn milk sour!

BANSHEE

Banshees appear at night to foretell or mourn the death of a member of one of the ancient Irish families, whose surnames start with 'O' or 'Mac'. Their wailing, lamenting cry is called 'keening'. They take on several forms, appearing as a cloaked hag, a young woman or a middle-aged lady. Banshees carry a comb, tearing it through their hair in anguish, like mourners did in ancient Ireland. Their eyes are red from centuries of weeping.

Before you begin

To draw the banshee from the correct perspective, focus on the direction of the back and face and the positioning of the limbs. Observe how the back and hips sit against the branch. Pay attention to the type and length of line used to construct the limbs and how the legs hang over the branch in step two.

Step 1

Draw a straight line with a crooked end for the branch, making sure it is on a slight angle. Lightly draw hips on the straight end and a curve for the backbone around. Attach a head shape with a cross facing to the right. Draw a circle below the head for the chest. Add a bent front arm next to the neck and an arm behind. Sketch a bent right leg over the branch and then a left leg crossed over it. Add shapes for the hands and feet.

Step 2

Sketch the bottom of the branch and the sharp line work for the rest of the tree. Build a curved form around the skeleton. Define the face, adding a hood over the head. Draw the back and waistband and a shape for the front arm. Add a knee line and the rear arm. Sketch the bottom of the cloak. Build the shape of the left leg, then add the right.

Step 3

Darken and define the line work. Beginning at the top, define the tree's branches. Add the structure of the owl. Sketch a nose and a mouth over the cross and eyes on either side. Define the cloak and develop the hands, including the comb. Draw the shoes. Sketch the flowing line work for the hair and run it through the comb.

DRAWING TIP

Follow drawing instructions carefully. They teach you to sketch elements of a drawing in a specific order, making it easier to develop a drawing correctly as you go.

Step 4

Observe the different levels of shading. Lightly draw the textured line work of the tree, starting at the top and moving down. Using a medium pressure with your pencil, shade the open line work across the cloak and shoes. Darken the facial features and create the texture of the hair.

Once you have drawn in the details of the owl and moon, your banshee is ready to keen!

FAIRY FACT → If you pick up the comb of a banshee, you may be cursed forever.

LEPRECHAUN

Leprechauns are Irish fairy cobblers that make shoes for other fairies. The strange thing is that they only ever make one shoe! These creatures look like little old men dressed in green with silver buckled shoes. A leprechaun owns a magical pot of gold, hidden at the end of the rainbow. If you catch a leprechaun, he will give you his treasure.

Before you begin

The most important elements of this drawing are the head, backbone and hips. Study these elements carefully, as they will help you draw the leprechaun standing in the correct pose, facing in the right direction. Pay close attention to the length of the limbs; the arms are bent and raised, as is the left leg.

Step 1

Lightly sketch a circle on a slight angle for the head. Place a cross in the right side of the circle. Add a line for the backbone and add the hips at its base. Draw a circle for the chest in the centre of the backbone. Add the collarbone across the top of the chest. Add bent arm lines to the shoulders and a bent line to the hip for the left leg. Draw the straight right leg and sketch the hand and foot shapes. Connect a tree to the left hand and a rock to the left foot. Don't forget the pot of gold!

Step 2

Pay attention to how the clothes and hair are developed over the skeleton. Draw a beard and hair around the face and add an ear. Sketch a curved hat above the head. Draw the straight edges of the jacket and trousers over the legs. Add details to the pot and shoes.

Step 3

Define the hairy edges of the beard and hair. Starting at the brow, add the face details over the cross, making sure the eyes are facing the right way. Develop the outline and details of the clothes and shoes. Beginning with the hat, define the line work and move your way down to the shoes. Don't forget the tree, rock and hands.

DRAWING TIP

Why not create your own fairyland garden for all your fairies to live in? You can also use coloured pencils when drawing your picture.

Step 4

Darken the line work. Observe the soft level of shading used on the whole figure of the leprechaun. With the side of your pencil, lightly shade the edges of the clothing, shoes and pot. Ensure the shading is darker inside the hat. Add the texture of the hair and define the details of the face.

Draw the gold inside the pot. Shade the textured line work inside the tree and rock. Once you add the leaves your leprechaun will be ready to search for more treasure!

FAIRY FACT → A leprechaun will vanish in a flash if you take your eyes off him!

KELPIE

Kelpies are water fairies that appear in the form of a horse or sometimes a human. They are found in the lakes and rivers of Scotland. Kelpies entice their victims to climb on their backs. Once the passenger is astride, the kelpie gallops into the water to drown them. To see a kelpie is a great misfortune.

Before you begin

The most important elements of this drawing are line and shape. Shape helps construct the kelpie's rounded muscular form and line gives the kelpie a sense of movement. The line of the backbone is the main element that this drawing is built around. Study the changes in each step and observe the curved line work.

Step 1

Lightly draw a flowing curve on an angle for the backbone. Add a circle for the head at the top of the curve and an oval for the rump at the bottom. Draw a larger oval for the stomach next to the dip of the backbone. Attach the nose to the bottom left of the head. Add a curved line for the chest, drawing it around the stomach and up to the hip. Create construction lines joining the stomach and hip for the legs.

Step 2

Build the shape of the front legs around the construction lines and then the shapes for the rear legs. Add line work for the forehead, ear, mouth and jaw. Draw the line work for the mane and tail, making them resemble puffy clouds. Start at the forehead and work your way down to the tail.

Step 3

With a clean eraser, rub out any unnecessary line work inside the body. Beginning at the head, define and smooth the curves of the body. Add an opening for the mouth. Draw the details of the body, ear, hooves and the eye below the brow. Develop the wavy, flowing mane and tail, then darken all the line work.

DRAWING TIP

Different types of line work are used to create a drawing. Develop your pencil technique by experimenting with curved, curly, bent, straight and wavy line work on a separate piece of paper.

Step 4

With the side of your pencil, gently shade the texture of the hair inside the mane and tail. Starting at the head, develop the shading around the edges of the body. Darken the shading of the eye, nostril, hooves and back legs.

To make your kelpie look like it is jumping through the water, make sure there is a space between its body and the surface of the water. Your kelpie is now ready to lure its next victim!

FAIRY FACT → It was thought a kelpie could be captured if someone could steal their bridle.

Funky Things to Draw

fairytale Princesses

Paul Könye ★ Kate Ashforth

Funky Things to Draw

Fairytale Princesses

INTRODUCTION

For centuries, children have lost themselves in the world of fairy tale princesses, inspired by popular stories such as Cinderella and Snow White. Imagine dressing in lavish gowns and sparkling tiaras or meeting your own prince charming in real life!

As you draw these pictures, drift off to a land far, far away filled with magic and fantasy. You could be attending a royal ball and dancing with a handsome prince. Imagine you're a knight in shining armour, protecting your kingdom. Pretend you live in an enormous castle, high on a hill.

THINGS YOU WILL NEED

- An HB or 2B pencil (they are light and won't smudge too easily)
- A pencil sharpener and a small dish for shavings
- A4 cartridge paper or copy paper and some scrap paper for experiments
- A clean eraser
- Confidence: a positive attitude will help improve your skills
- Imagination: don't be afraid to explore your own style or ideas

Drawing guidelines

There are a few things you should be aware of when drawing your fairy tale characters.

1 Drawings of people are built around a skeleton, which is made up of a series of lines, shapes, joints and a backbone.
2 Begin by lightly drawing the structure of your subject, otherwise it will be obvious in the final drawing. Where possible, rub out any unnecessary line work with a clean eraser as you go.
3 Pay close attention to where each character's limbs are placed and where the cross that indicates the position of the face is drawn on the head. This will help you draw them in the correct pose.
4 Some subjects are constructed using a series of shapes that connect to one another. Pay attention to the size and type of shapes used and how they join together.
5 Carefully observe the angle at which each subject is positioned in the first step. Focus on the length and the direction of all the body parts. This will ensure that your subject is seen from the correct perspective.

Stages of drawing

When you begin a drawing, it is always a good idea to create a basic structure. A good way to draw the human form is to start with a skeleton. Other subjects are constructed using a series of shapes. Once you have created

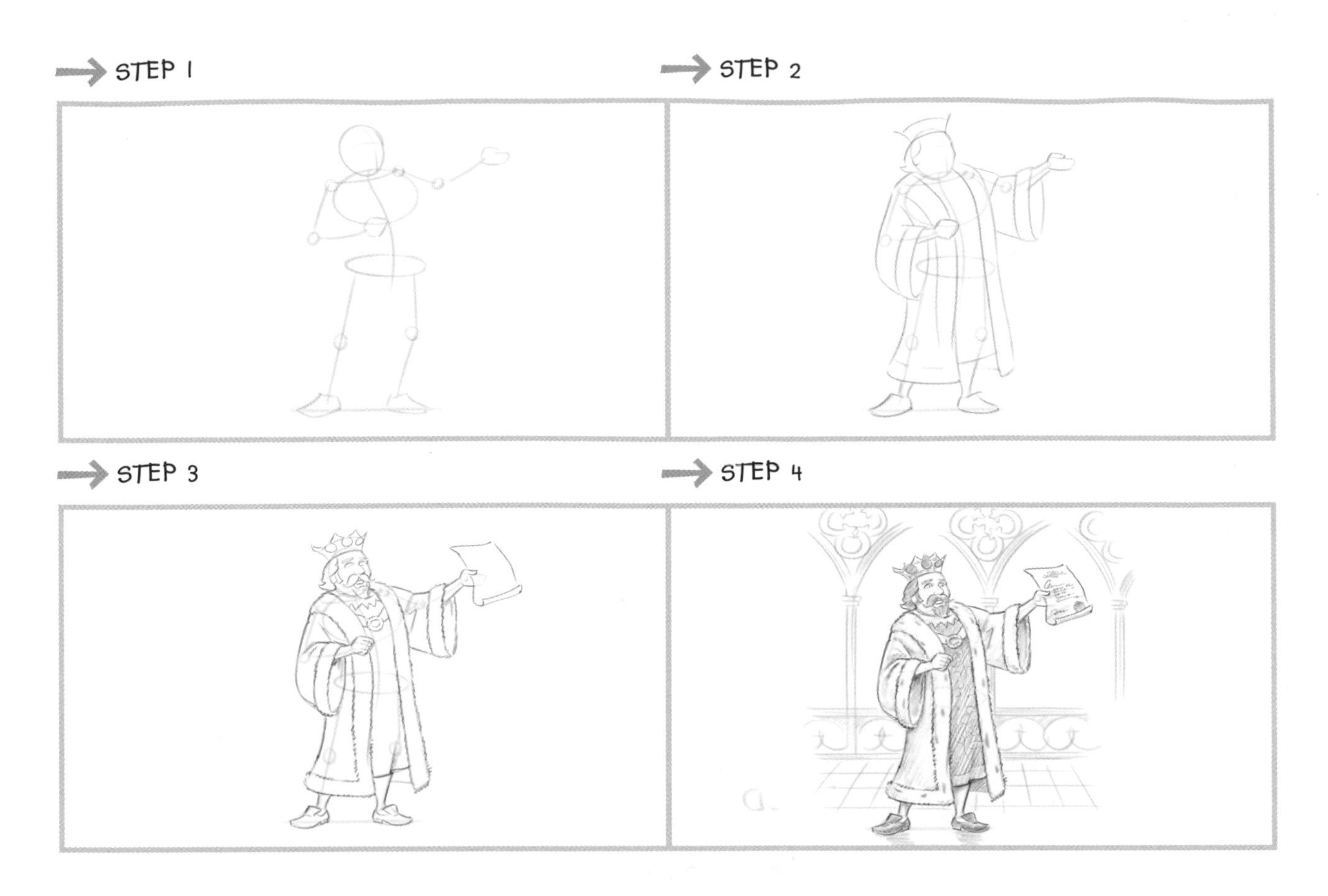

the foundation of a drawing, develop an outline to produce a subject's form (its whole shape). Read all instructions carefully before you begin a step and observe how each picture is developed.

Take your time to study the size of the shapes and the types of lines. How is each subject proportioned? What kinds of pencil lines are used to create it? Are they curved, rounded, straight or wavy? Different levels of shading are applied to give a subject dimension. How soft or dark is the shading and how is it applied? In some cases, line work and pattern are also used to add decorative details.

Skills and techniques

Here are some examples of the different techniques and art elements you will use.

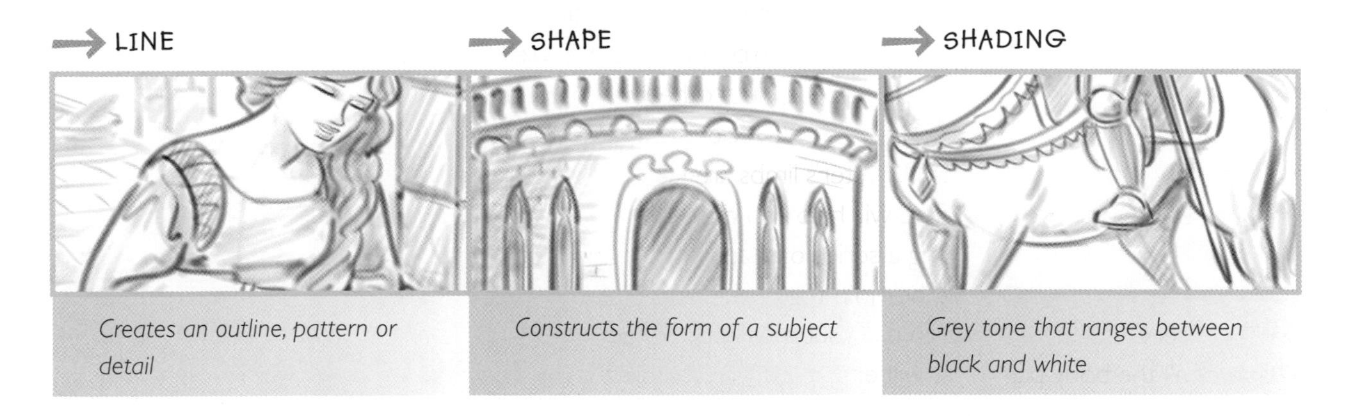

Creates an outline, pattern or detail

Constructs the form of a subject

Grey tone that ranges between black and white

People can be difficult to draw because of their different body parts and the angles of their poses. Remember that the process of drawing needs to be well planned and that there is always an element of your picture that should be drawn first. Observe, take your time and don't be afraid to experiment.

PRINCESS

A typical fairytale princess lives in a land far, far away in a beautiful palace. She wears stunning gowns dripping with diamonds and sparkling tiaras in her hair when she attends magical balls. A fairytale princess is both a heroine and damsel in distress who is often rescued by a handsome prince on a pure white horse. She'll always live happily ever after!

Before you begin

The princess is drawn around a skeleton attached to a skirt shape. It is important to draw the face, arms and backbone correctly so that the princess is standing in the correct pose. Pay attention to how the curves of the outline are built over the skeleton.

Step 1

Lightly draw a skirt shape with a fold and an ellipse at the top. Add a curved backbone with a circle in the middle for the chest and shoulders across the top. Sketch a circle for the head and a chin pointing down. Add a cross looking right for the face. Draw a bent right arm and a straight left arm hanging down. Add the joints and hand shapes.

Step 2

Build the shape of the princess's form over the skeleton. Define the curved outline of the face, shoulders, arms, hands and chest area, ensuring that the gown nips in above the oval waist. Add the hair around the head and flowing behind the shoulders. Add a half circle for the tiara.

Step 3

Define, smooth and darken the curves of the outline. Add petal details to the tiara and waves to the hair. Draw eyes on either side of the cross facing to the right and a nose and mouth. Sketch a scooped neckline, the wristbands and the fingers. Draw a v-shaped waistband with a zigzag beneath. Create a wavy hem and add marks and folds over the gown.

DRAWING TIP

Always begin your picture by drawing lightly so you are able to rub out any marks you are unhappy with.

Step 4

Study the soft levels of shading over the princess's figure. Using a light pressure with your pencil, gently shade the texture of the hair and the edges and folds of the gown. Add fine details to the tiara and develop the facial features. Define the neckline, wrists and waistband and add three stripes to the bodice of the dress.

Once you add a shadow beneath the princess, she will be ready to waltz the night away!

INTERESTING FACT

In the 19th century, a British woman claimed she was 'Princess Caraboo'. She pretended to be royalty from an exotic island, kidnapped by pirates. She spoke a made-up language and dressed strangely, but was exposed as a fraud.

PRINCE CHARMING

Prince Charming is a dashing, handsome young prince with whom every fairytale princess dreams of falling in love. He is gallant and brave, with the mission to rescue any damsel in distress. When a princess is forced to marry a villain, she dreams of being saved by her Prince Charming. In many fairytales, one kiss from Prince Charming is enough to break an evil spell!

Before you begin

The prince is drawn from a side-on perspective. Position the limbs and body parts correctly so the backbone curves over, the head faces down and the left arm bends outward. Pay attention to how the left leg is bent at the knee and the foot is side-on. The right leg is bent behind with the foot on an angle.

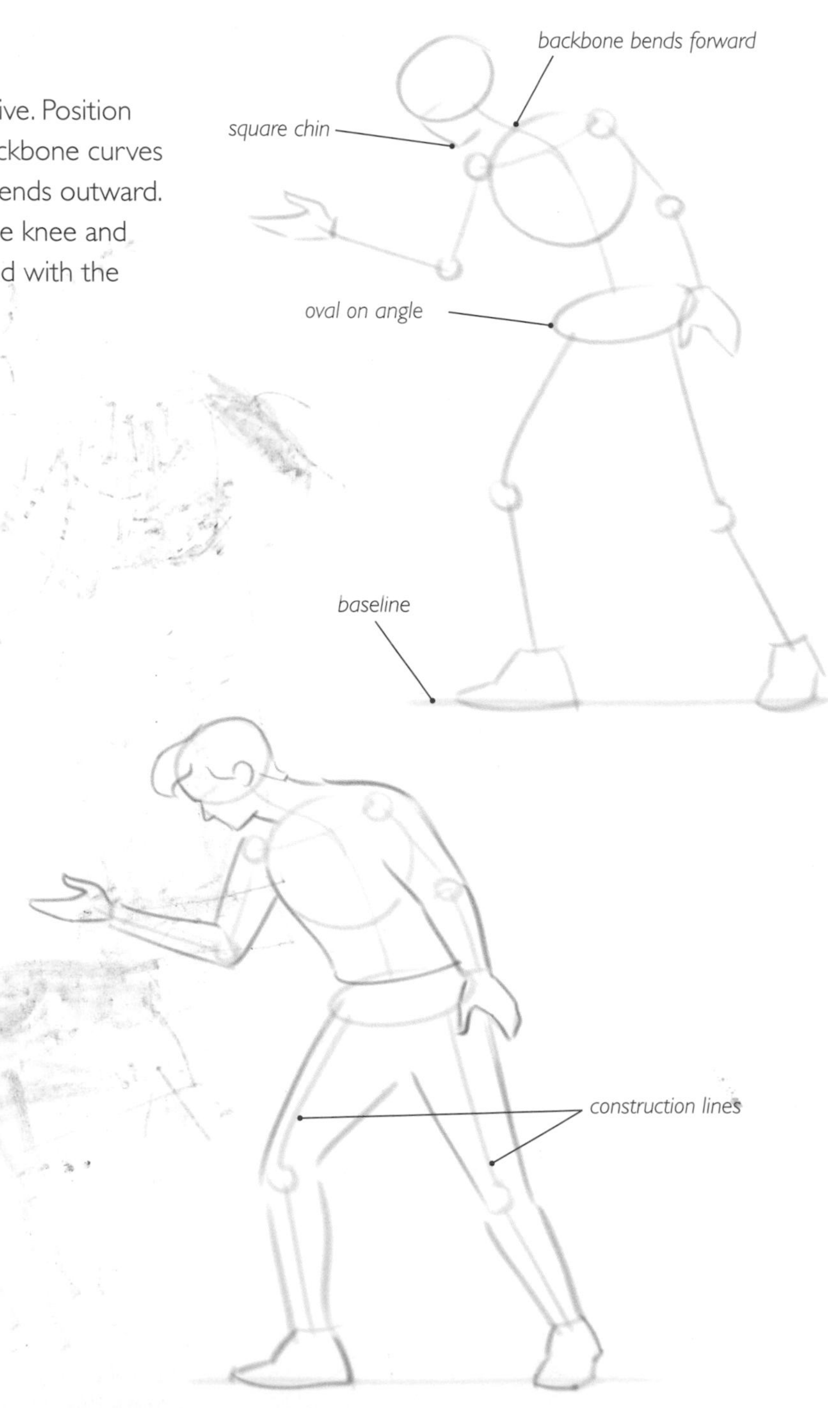

Step 1

Lightly draw a baseline and a small, slightly angled oval about a leg-length above. Sitting both feet on the baseline, draw a bent left leg with a side-on foot shape and the right leg with the foot on an angle. Above the oval, add a curved backbone bending forward. Draw a chest circle in the middle of the oval with shoulders across. Add a circle for the head, a brow line and a square chin pointing down. Sketch a bent left arm reaching out and a right arm hanging behind the body. Draw hand shapes and the joints.

Step 2

Build the shape of the prince's form over the skeleton. Starting at the head, define the shape of the face, neck, shoulder and right arm. Draw the hair around the head and construct the shape of the left arm and chest. Lightly draw the shape of the legs and feet around the construction lines.

Step 3

Define, smooth and darken the outline. Add an eye looking down to the brow line and a mouth. Develop the shape of collar and a round clasp underneath it. Draw the line of the cloak draping over and behind the shoulders and legs. Sketch the fingers, the wristbands, the waistband and the bottom of the tunic. Develop the shape of the boots.

DRAWING TIP

When drawing the scene with your prince and princess, try experimenting with coloured pencil. Grey pencil can smudge, so be careful not to colour heavily over line work.

Step 4

Study the levels of shading over the prince's body. With a light pencil, work your way from head to toe, applying a mid-grey tone over the hair, tunic, cloak and boots. Lightly shade the soft folds of the cloak and tunic and parts of the face and legs. Develop the facial features and darken the underside of the cloak.

Once you add a shadow under the boots, your prince is ready to ask the princess to dance!

INTERESTING FACT → A Prince Charming character appears in many fairy tales, including Cinderella, Sleeping Beauty, Snow White and the Frog Prince.

MEETING PRINCE CHARMING

Now you have learned to draw a fairytale princess and Prince Charming, create a magical scene where they meet for the first time. When a fairytale princess meets her Prince Charming, all her dreams come true. The handsome prince is captivated by the lovely princess's beauty and, of course, they dance into the night. The prince asks for the princess's hand in marriage and they live happily ever after.

DRAWING TIP

Before drawing this fairytale scene, observe the perspective that the picture is drawn from. The columns and tiles are drawn on the same angles and become smaller as they travel backward towards the horizon. The front columns are also higher at the top than the ones in the background. Make sure you draw the characters first and then add in the balcony and the floor, followed by the columns.

QUEEN

Many cultures have produced powerful queens who have left their imprint on history. However, not all female monarchs have the same power. A queen regnant is an heir to the throne and has all the powers that a king possesses, while a queen consort is married to a king and has no official powers. In fairy tales, the people often admire a queen for the regal qualities of strength, pride and tradition and for the elaborate costumes and jewels she wears.

Before you begin

This drawing is built around a skeleton. To achieve the right pose for the queen, draw the baseline and construction line on the correct angle. Pay attention to where the feet are placed and how the knees bend. Note how the hips sit on the construction line and how the cross for the face looks left.

Step 1

Lightly draw an angled baseline with a rounded rock shape in the middle. Draw a parallel construction line with an oval sitting above it. Add the left leg bending sharply. Draw the bent right leg. Draw rounded foot shapes on the rock shape. Sketch a backbone curving up from the oval and a circle for the head. On the head, draw a chin and a cross facing left. Add a circle for the chest with shoulders running above. Draw the left arm bending out and the right arm over the skeleton. Add the joints and hands shapes.

Step 2

Build the shape of the queen's form around the skeleton. Define the shape of the face, neck and collar. Construct the cloak and arms, followed by the hands and chest. Draw a headpiece and the shape of the hair around the face. Sketch the shape of the fabric and the knee area, and define the hem of the dress around the feet.

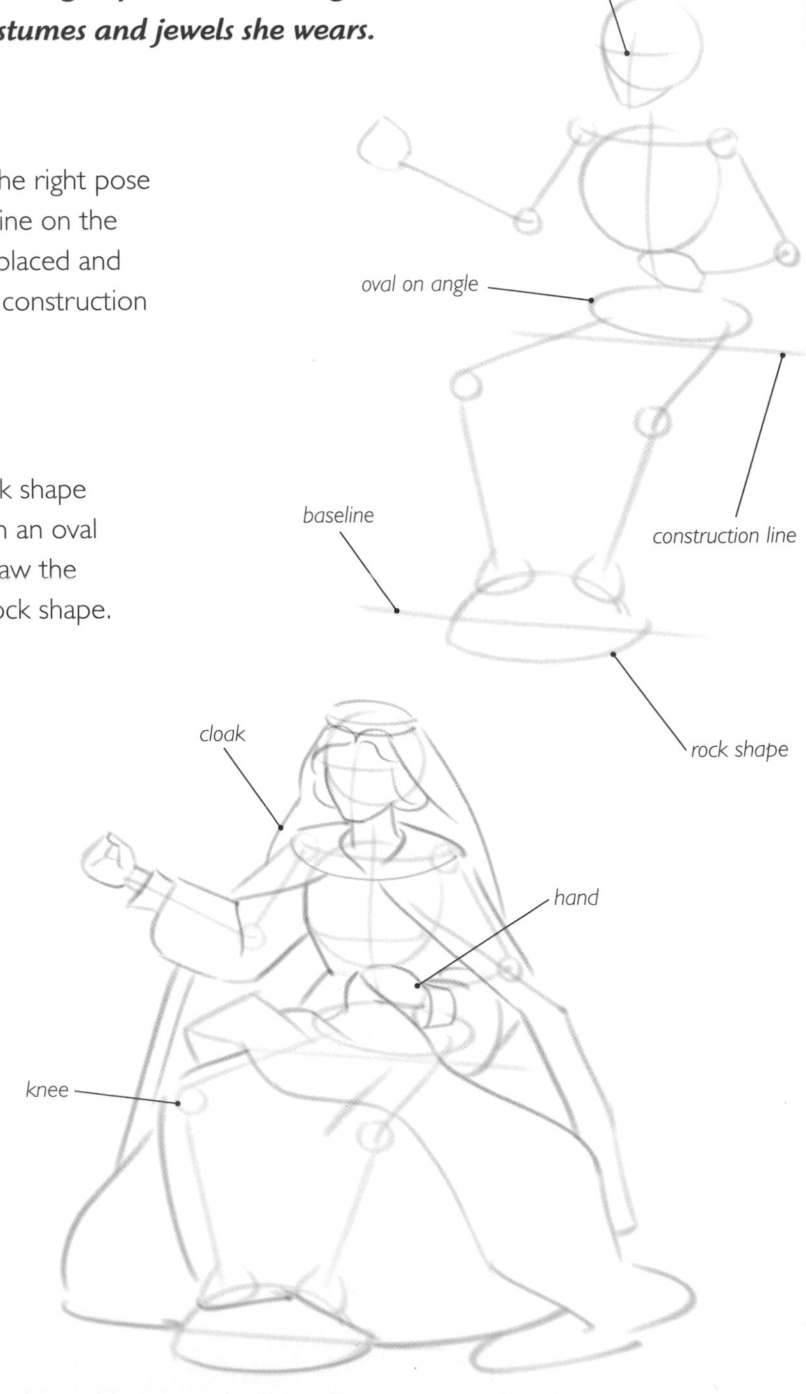

Step 3

Define, smooth and darken the outline. Starting at the head, develop the details of the crown and the folds of the veil. Draw the eyebrows and the eyes on either side of the cross. Add a nose and mouth and the details around the face. Sketch a square brooch and the folds of the cloak, sleeves, fabric and dress. Define the fingers and the cushion under the feet.

DRAWING TIP

Try turning the page as you draw to avoid smudging your work.

Step 4

Study the level of shading over the queen's form. With a light pencil, create soft levels of shading from head to toe, focusing on the folds of the cloak and dress. Add a thread between the hands, details to the brooch and chest and a pattern and tassels to the cushion.

For the faint line work of the window, draw the outside circle first behind the queen. Add the inside circle and the lines for the windowpanes. Once you draw a diamond pattern and brickwork fanning around the window, your sewing queen will be ready to rule!

INTERESTING FACT → Cleopatra VII is one of the most famous queens in the world and was the last leader of Egypt.

KING

Traditionally in fairy tales, kings rule the land with absolute power. A king inherits the throne and rules his kingdom for life. Good kings perform noble duties, rule with dignity and are admired by their subjects. They take charge of the cavalry, call upon their knights to undertake special quests and battle to protect their kingdom.

Before you begin

This drawing is built around a skeleton. To draw the king from the correct perspective, pay attention to the angle of the backbone and the arms, where the head is placed and the direction of the feet. Line work is also important when adding texture, pattern and shading.

Step 1

Lightly draw a baseline. Sketch shoes sitting on the baseline, pointing outward. Add an oval above the baseline and draw the straight left leg and the bent right leg. Sketch a curved backbone running down to the hips and an oval at the top for the chest. Above this, draw shoulders, an oval for the head and a cross looking up on the face. Sketch the left arm bending around to the chest and the right arm bent outward. Add the hand shapes and the joints.

Step 2

Build the shape of the body around the skeleton. Starting at the head, develop the shape of the face, hair and crown. Draw lines running over the shoulders and down the body for the cloak, adding in the bottom of the tunic. Sketch the lines of the sleeves around the construction lines and add the opening of the cuffs. Build the shape of the legs and arms.

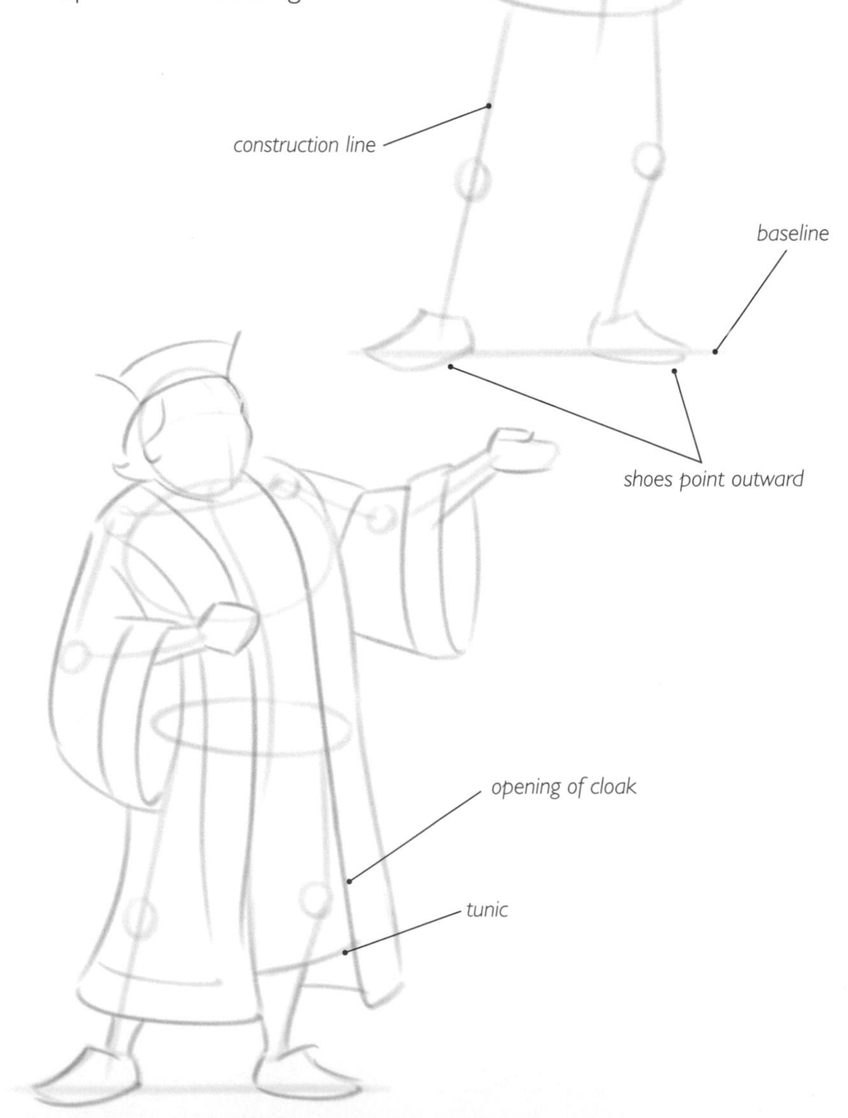

Step 3

Add eyes on either side of the cross and a nose pointing right. Add a moustache, mouth and beard. Develop the shape of the hair and the details of the crown. Create a furry-edge trim on the cloak. Build the shape of the legs, shoes and hands and add the declaration to the right hand. Add a zigzag pattern to the neckline and a sash with a brooch to the chest. Develop the tunic and the back of the coat, then darken and define the king's outline.

DRAWING TIP

Be patient as you follow each step. Take time to study the size of shapes and the types of line.

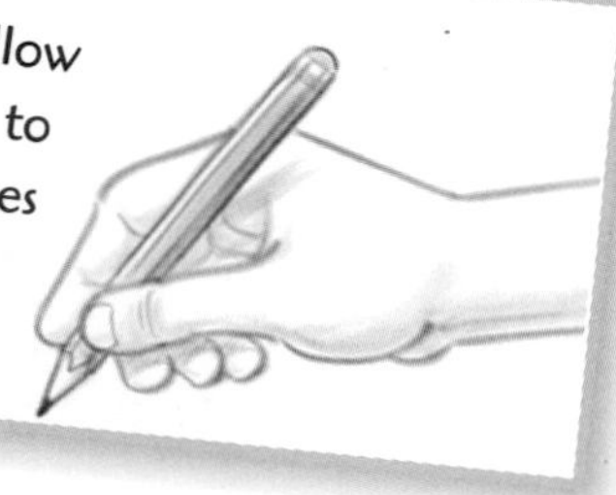

Step 4

Using a light pencil pressure, shade a mid-grey tone across the tunic, the cuffs and the beard and inside the crown. Develop the details of the face, the brooch and the declaration. Add details to the fur trim and a flowery pattern over the tunic. Darken the shoes and apply soft shading over the cloak.

Using faint line work, draw the base of the lattice in line with the left cuff and add the arches above. Once you add the line work on different angles for the floor, your king will be ready to reign!

INTERESTING FACT → One of the most well known tales about a king is the story of King Arthur and his Knights of the Round Table.

GLASS SLIPPER

When the clock strikes twelve, Cinderella flees the grand ball, leaving her glass slipper on the castle stairs. Captivated by her beauty, the prince travels throughout the land insisting that every maiden in the kingdom try on the glass slipper. Only Cinderella can fit into the slipper and they live happily ever after.

Before you begin

The drawing of the glass slipper is three-dimensional. It is drawn from the perspective of looking down on the slipper. The glass slipper is constructed using curved line work. The base is drawn first and then the rest of the shoe is constructed around it.

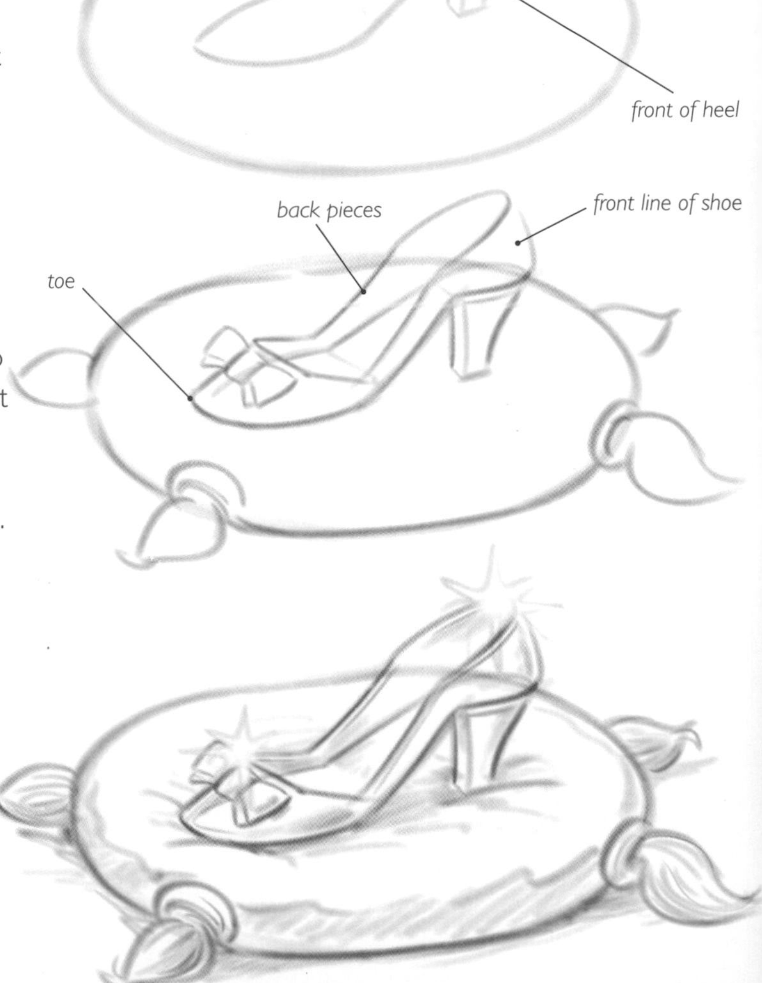

Step 1

Lightly draw an oval for the cushion. Draw the curved shape of the sole, overlapping it slightly with the top right of the cushion. Starting at the bottom and working your way up to the heel, add the front of the heel and the inside edge.

Step 2

Sketch the top of the shoe, starting at the front and working from the back of the heel and curving around to the toe area. Add the rear side of the slipper, connecting it to the toe area, the sole and the back of the shoe. Draw a bow across the toe. Sketch the front and back cushion tassels. Define the cushion and add a line around the heel.

Step 3

Draw the fine lines inside and outside the shoe. Using a clean eraser, rub out part of the heel and the bow and draw soft starbursts over the top. Add soft line work for the indents under the shoe, the edge of the cushion and for the texture of the tassels. With a light pencil, add soft shading over the cushion and slipper. Now Cinderella can try on the glass slipper!

INTERESTING FACT → Versions of Cinderella have appeared in stories from cultures around the world, dating all the way back to ancient Egypt.

PUMPKIN CARRIAGE

In the story of Cinderella, the fairy godmother transforms a pumpkin into a magnificent gold carriage to transport Cinderella to the royal ball. Cinderella makes a grand entrance when she arrives. She looks so beautiful in her dazzling gown and sparkling jewels that the prince dances with her into the night. However, she must escape before the clock strikes twelve or the coach will turn back into a pumpkin!

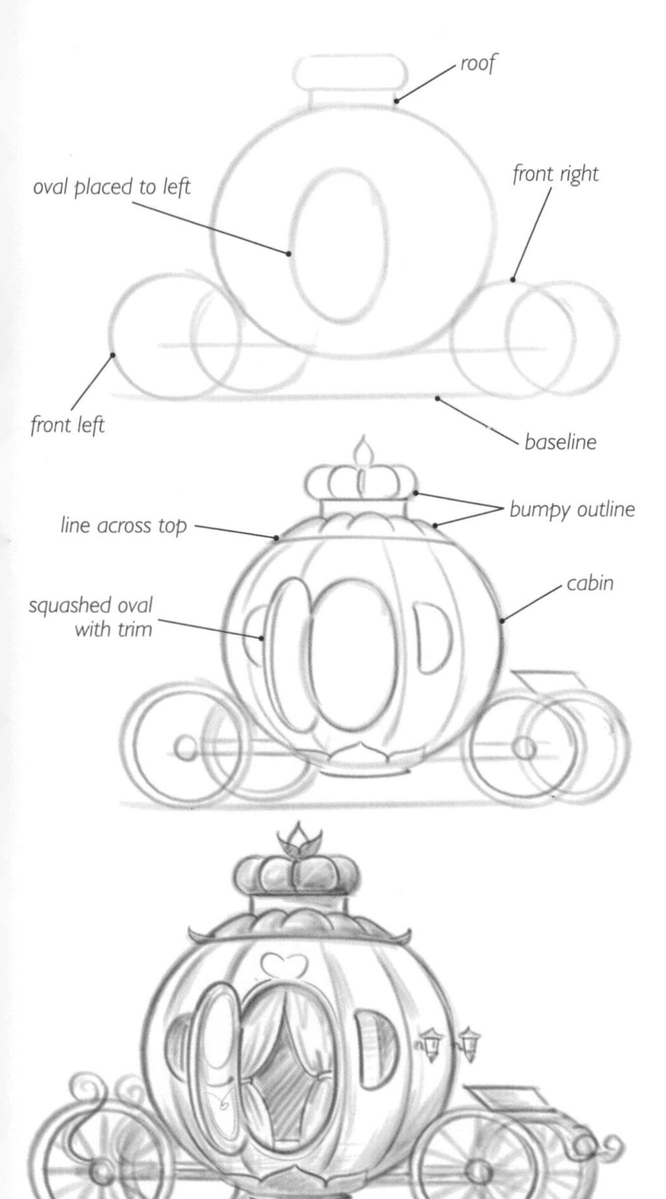

Before you begin

The most important art element of this drawing is shape. Observe how the pumpkin carriage is drawn using a series of circles. The wheels sit on the baseline and overlap.

Step 1

Lightly draw parallel baselines. Draw a large circle above with an oval shape inside, sitting to the left. Add the front left and right wheels to the carriage, sitting them on the baseline. Overlap the rear wheels and sketch the roof shapes. Draw an axle running underneath the carriage and through the wheels.

Step 2

Draw a line across the top of the cabin and define the bumpy outline of the roof and top. Attach a squashed oval to the left of the door. Add curved line work to the roof and the cabin. Sketch the tip of the roof, half circles for windows and a leaf shape for the base. Define the line work of the wheels and axle.

Step 3

Sketch the details inside and around the door and add curtains. With a light pencil, apply medium grey shading across the roof, the windows, the door and the base. Add faint lines for spokes and curly details to the wheels. Apply shaded highlights around the whole carriage.

Once you add the lanterns in front, your pumpkin carriage will transport you to the ball!

INTERESTING FACT → In the German version of Cinderella (known as *Aschenputtel*) written by the Brothers' Grimm, the heroine does not have a fairy godmother. Instead, her magical help arrives after she plants a tree on her mother's grave.

WICKED STEPMOTHER

Wicked stepmothers appear in a number of fairy tales, including Snow White and the Seven Dwarves, Cinderella and Hansel and Gretel. In these stories, stepmothers are cruel to their stepdaughter or stepchildren, either by treating them like servants or trying to lose them in the forest. The wicked stepmother is often trying to secure her own children's wealth and position, such as the case of the stepmother and ugly stepsisters in Cinderella.

Before you begin

The structure of the wicked stepmother is built around a skeleton. Observe how the skirt shape is drawn with a small oval at the top and a large one at the base. The backbone of the skeleton connects to the small oval. Study where the left arm bends over the body and how the head faces left. Pay attention to how the cloak is built over the skeleton.

Step 1

Lightly draw a large oval for the bottom of the skirt shape. Draw the outside of the skirt and a small oval at the top. Attach an angled backbone with a circle for the head. Add a chin pointing left and a cross for the face. Draw a circle in the middle of the backbone for the chest with shoulders running across. Sketch the left arm bent over the skeleton and the right arm bent outward. Add the joints and hand shapes.

Step 2

Build the shape of the cloak over the skeleton. Define the shape of the face and draw the hair around the head. Draw the top of the collar, working down to the shoulders. Sketch the top of the arms and add the triangular shapes of the open sleeves. Add a chalice in the right hand, develop the hand shapes and define the hem of the dress.

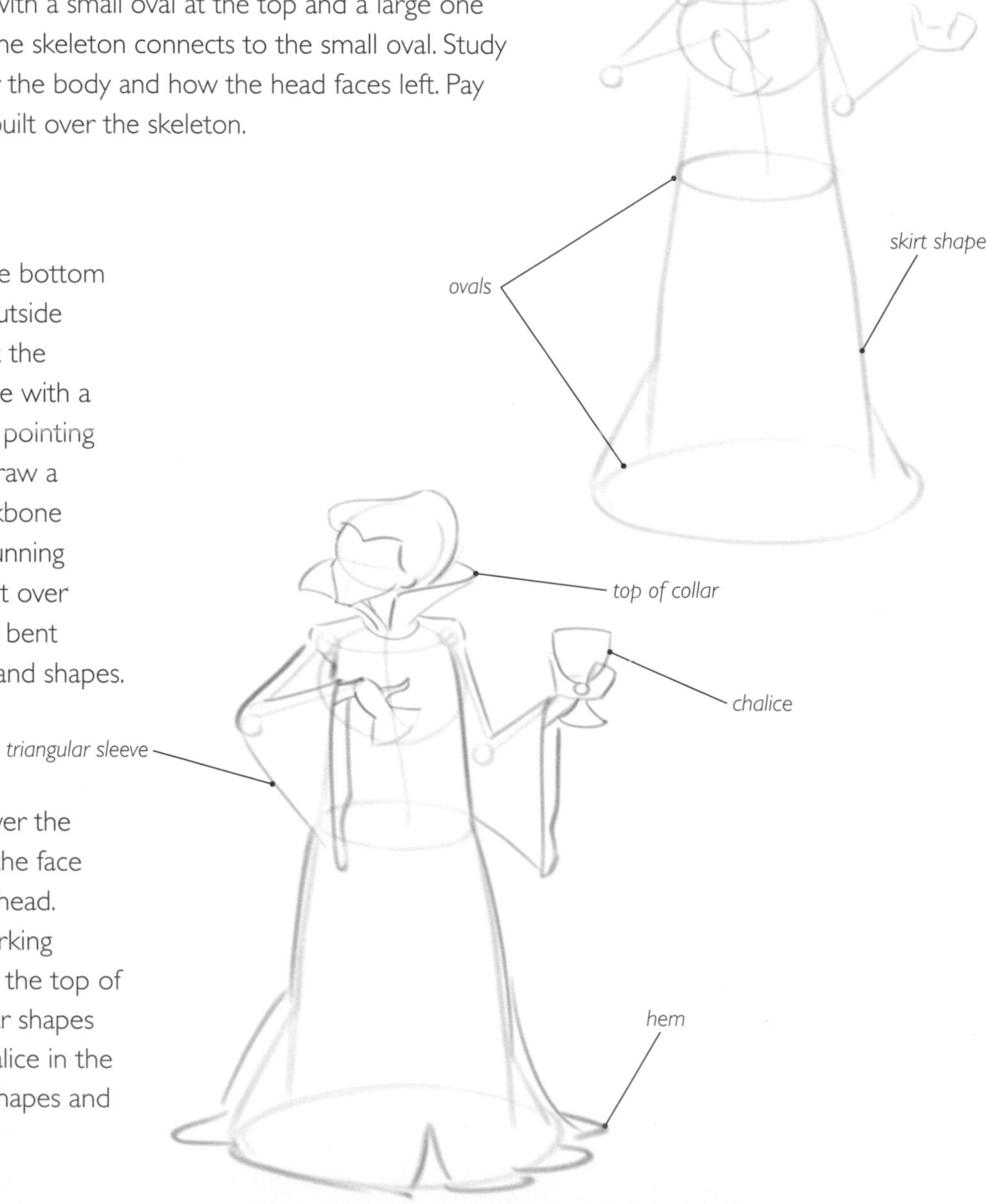

Step 3

Darken and define the outline. Draw arched eyebrows and eyes on either side of the cross, then a nose and mouth. Develop the waves of the hair, the v-shaped neckline and a round brooch. Add a strip down the front on the dress and around each sleeve. Define the fingers, the chalice and the folds of the dress.

DRAWING TIP

When using an eraser, keep it clean. Rub the grey residue off the end on a separate page.

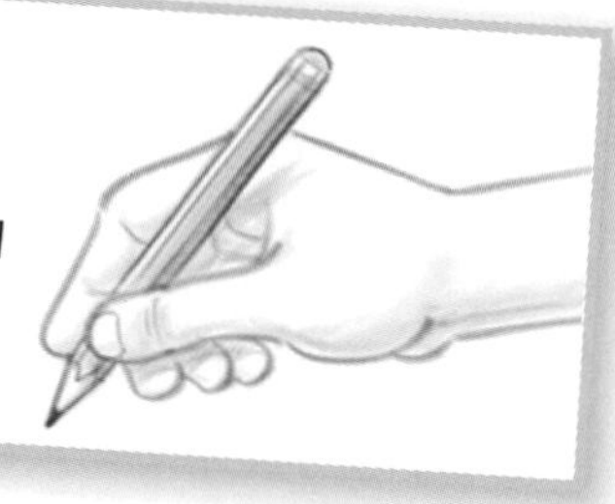

Step 4

With a light pencil, shade a medium grey tone over the hair, neckline, chalice and sleeves. Lightly shade the folds of the cloak, define the facial features and add steam coming off the potion.

For the faint details in the background, first draw the mirror and then sketch the curtain. Add brickwork around it, making sure the bottom of the bricks sits above the hem of the dress. Now your wicked stepmother is ready to do some evil deeds!

INTERESTING FACT → In many fairy stories, the original tale featured an evil mother. This was altered in later versions to an evil stepmother to make it more appropriate for children.

KNIGHT

A knight in shining armour serves under a king or lord. A fairy tale knight is a romantic at heart and performs his good deeds in the name of a lady. A knight can be a gallant hero who wanders alone throughout the kingdom performing noble, heroic acts. He has many foes in battle, such as giants, dragons or evil witches.

Before you begin

There are many elements to sketch for this drawing, so start by observing the different types of lines and shapes used for each step. To create the drawing from the correct perspective, study the angle of the baselines and where the horse's legs are positioned. The skeleton of the knight is constructed over the horse's back. Note the direction both subjects face.

Step 1

Draw two parallel baselines. Sketch the outline of the horse's form, starting at the head and working down to the hind leg. Add construction lines and joints for the horse's legs, sitting the hoofs on the baselines. Sketch the knight's hips above the horse's back and the legs hanging either side of the horse. Draw a foot shape facing left and a knee joint. Add a backbone and a chest shape with shoulders running across. Sketch a circle for the head, adding a brow line and chin. Add the left arm bending upward and the right arm bending across the backbone. Add the joints and hand shapes.

Step 2

Build the shape of the knight and the horse around the skeleton and construction lines. Beginning at the knight's head, work your way down the body, building the shapes as you go. Draw the horse's ears pointing up and add the hoofs. Add a flagpole in the knight's hand and define and smooth the outline.

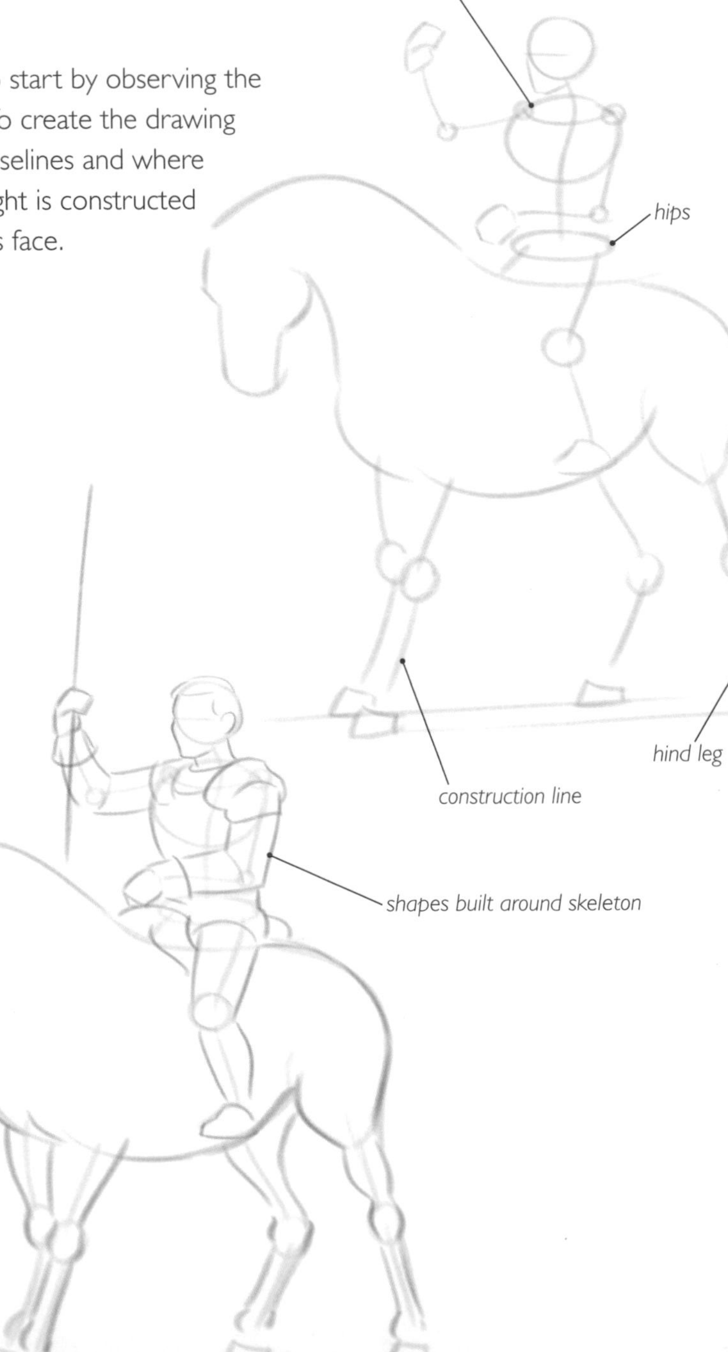

Step 3

Draw the horse's flowing mane on its neck and its tail on the hindquarters. Add a bridle to the head and reins in the knight's hand. Draw an eye, a nostril and a mouth. Sketch a sash around the chest area and a saddle under the knight's leg. Draw the knight's eyes across the brow line and a nose and mouth. Add hair and develop the details of the knight's armour. Attach a flag to the pole and a sword to the hip.

DRAWING TIP

It is important to be confident when learning to develop your drawing skills. If you doubt yourself, the results will show it!

Step 4

Study the levels of shading over the picture. With a light pencil, shade a mid-grey tone across the flag and the horse's bridle, saddle and hind legs. Shade some areas of the knight's armour to make it look shiny. Add detail to the hair and define the face and sword. Apply light shading to the horse and add soft line work for the texture of the mane and tail.

Once you add decoration to the horse's sash, your knight will be ready to rescue a damsel in distress!

INTERESTING FACT

→ In medieval times, knights competed in tournaments in events such as jousting and combat (known as the melee).

CASTLE

Castles were first built in the early Middle Ages and were used as a residence or stronghold for an aristocrat or a king. Castles were a safe haven against siege or assault from an enemy and were also a safe community for the kingdom's subjects. The magical castles of popular fairy tales are often based on real buildings. You will find castles in countries like France, Germany, Spain and England, as well as Russia, China and Japan.

Before you begin

The most important art element of this drawing is shape. Observe how the different sized square, rectangular and triangular shapes are stacked on top of each other. When drawing this picture, begin at the baseline and work your way up. Pay attention to the many patterns and types of shading and line work that adorn the castle.

Step 1

Draw a baseline with a shape for the staircase below the centre and add a curved line underneath for the moat. Sketch a rectangle above the staircase for the entrance and add a large curved balcony above it. Draw a square with small balconies in each corner and add conical roofs with triangular peaks. Sketch a shelf to the right of the large balcony and add a small conical tower. Draw the rectangular towers on the left, working from the centre out. Add the conical roofs to the towers.

Step 2

Define and smooth the castle outline, developing the line work around the tower, the conical roofs and the balconies. Build the shape of the staircase, adding an extra line below the baseline. Add a door. Draw curved arches on each side of the staircase and sketch the arched windows. Develop the shape of the peaked roof.

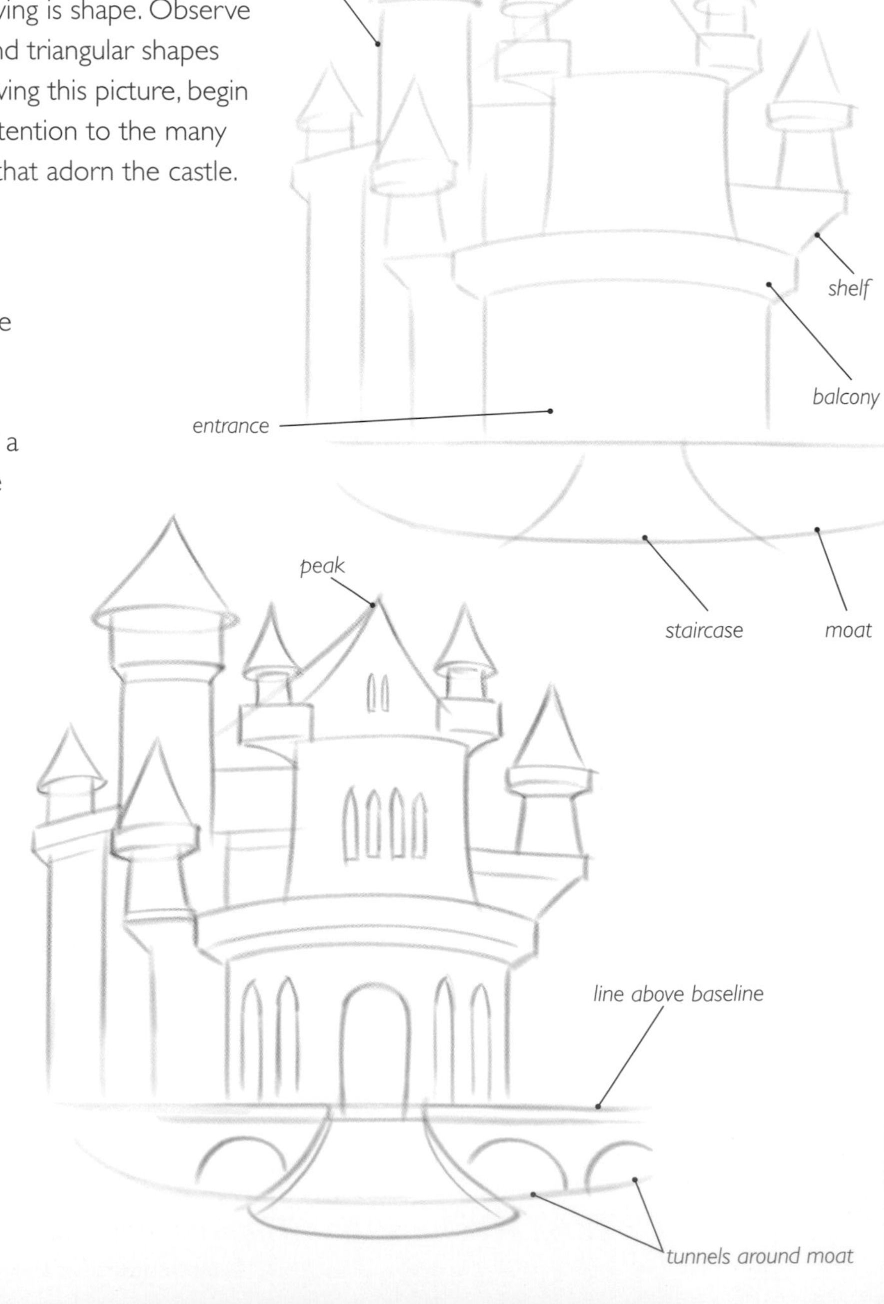

Step 3

Draw the battlement details around the conical roofs and add windows to the towers. Sketch a pattern for the stairs and develop the line work around the moat. Draw the bushes in the foreground and smaller fir trees behind.

DRAWING TIP

Using a bigger piece of paper, try drawing your castle on a larger scale. Add a more detailed background environment with hills, clouds, trees or knights galloping on horses.

Step 4

Darken the outline. Apply a faint brick pattern over the castle, leaving some areas clear white. Using a light pressure with your pencil, apply a mid-grey tone to the roofs and inside the windows and the door. Shade open line work over the brickwork, towers and trees.

Once you add details around the door and moat, your castle will protect its subjects during battle!

INTERESTING FACT

The Sleeping Beauty Castle at Disneyland in California, USA is based on the Neuschwanstein Castle in southern Germany. Several castles in France, including Château de Peirrefonds and Château d'Ussé, served as inspiration for the Cinderella Castle at Disneyworld in Florida, USA.

RAPUNZEL

Rapunzel was a beautiful girl who was taken by an enchantress after her father stole some lettuce from the enchantress's garden. Rapunzel was sent to live in a tower with no door, deep in a forest. To enter, the enchantress would shout, 'Rapunzel, Rapunzel, let down your hair', and then climb up Rapunzel's long golden plait. One day a prince heard Rapunzel singing. He learned how the enchantress entered and then rescued Rapunzel and asked for her hand in marriage.

Before you begin

The window is the most important element of this picture as it supports Rapunzel's figure. The window and figure must be drawn at the correct angle to achieve the right perspective. Observe the curved arch, the angle of the window and how the arms lean over the window sill. Pay attention to the angle of the backbone and head and how the eyes face down.

Step 1

Draw the outside line of the arch, with the bottom on an angle. Add a ledge and the inside edge of the arch. Lightly sketch a circle above the middle of the ledge for the chest and a backbone curving through it. Draw a circle for the head and a chin and cross facing down. Add shoulders across the chest and the arms sitting on the ledge, with the right arm over the ledge and the left arm leaning on it. Add joints and hand shapes, ensuring the left hand curves over the ledge.

Step 2

Build the shape of Rapunzel's form around the skeleton and define the face. Starting at the back of the head, draw the wavy outline of the hair over the shoulder and through the hands. Develop the shape of the neck, shoulders, arms and hands. Add the details of the chest area and the wristbands.

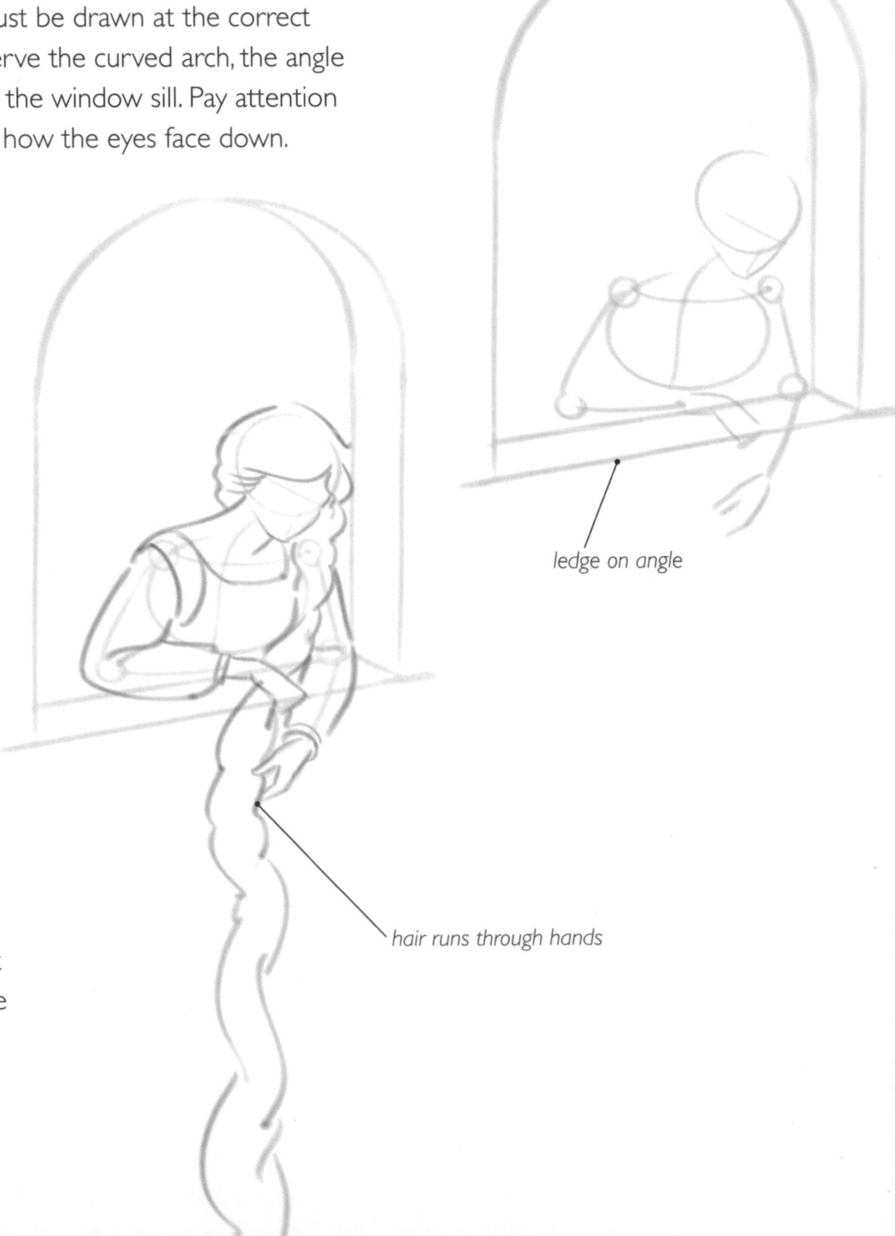

outside ledge

Step 3

Draw the outside rectangle of the ledge under the plait. Sketch the inside of the arch on an angle and the details of the brickwork fanning around the outside. Draw eyes on either side of the cross and a nose and mouth underneath. Use wavy line work to add texture to the hair and define the details of the dress.

DRAWING TIP

Texture is the feel of something. It is drawn using a series of marks, dots or lines. Hair could be represented using soft, wavy, repeating lines. For cement, use a bumpy pattern to make it look rough.

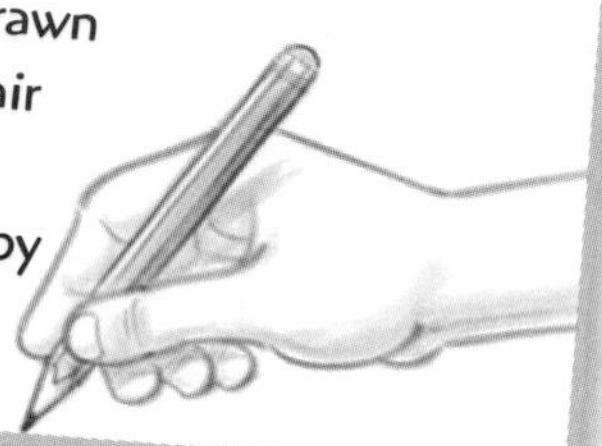

Step 4

Darken and smooth the outline. Draw soft brickwork under the ledge. Using a light pressure with your pencil, shade an open mid-grey tone across the hair, parts of the dress and inside the arch. Darken the facial features and apply light shading around the neck, dress and plait.

Once you add the faint details of the fireplace in the background, Rapunzel will be ready to let down her hair!

INTERESTING FACT

Rapunzel was named by the enchantress after the lettuce her father stole. In Germany, Rapunzel is the name of a species of lettuce, also called 'Feldsalat'.

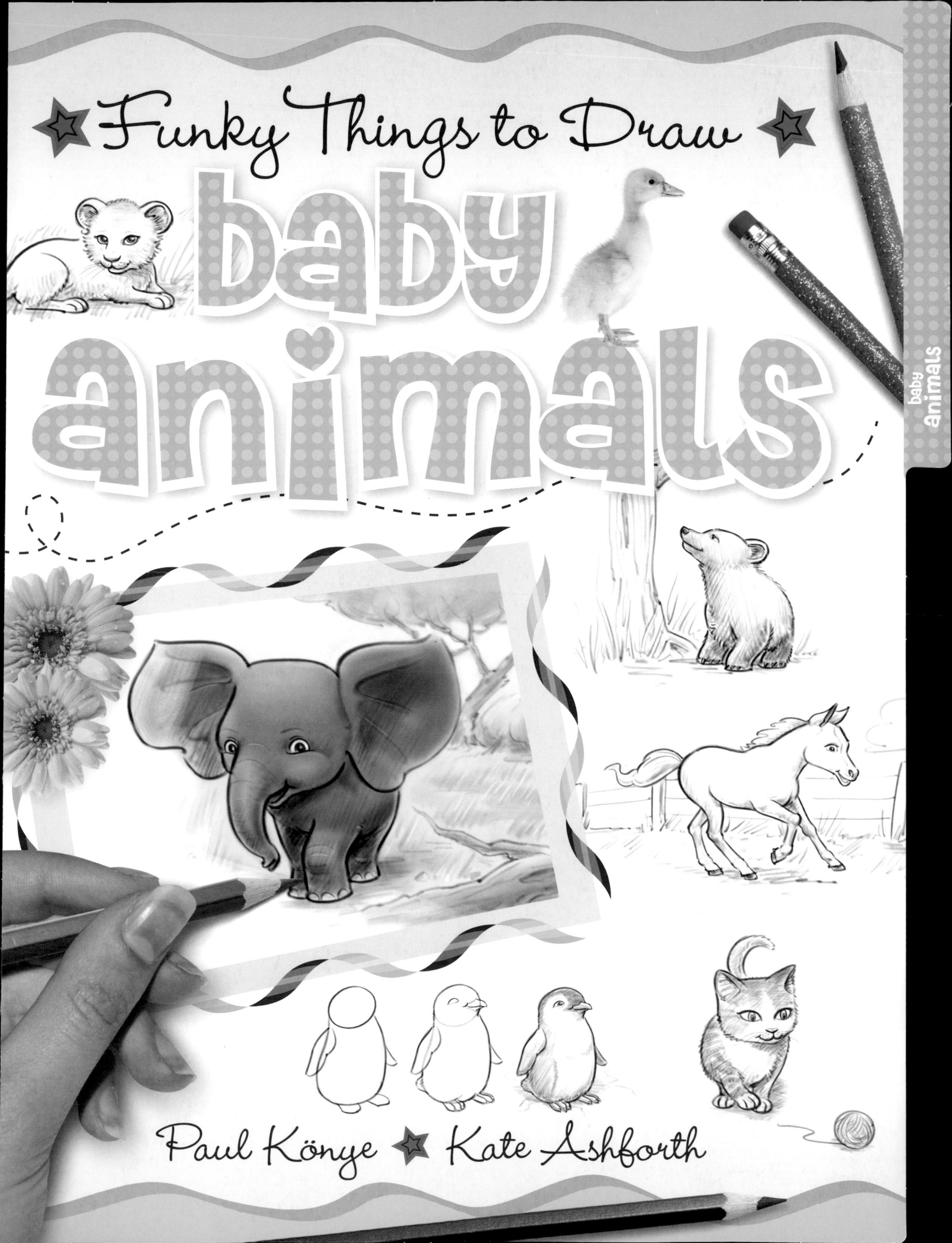
Funky Things to Draw
baby animals
Paul Könye
Kate Ashforth
baby animals

Funky Things to Draw

baby animals

INTRODUCTION

It's hard not to smile at the sight of baby animals because they look so cute and cuddly. Their distinct features make them a favourite subject of illustrators and cartoonists, as these features are easy to replicate in a drawing.

Before you learn to draw these cute creatures, try to visualise their characteristics. Think of the oversized body parts and large eyes of a clumsy puppy. Imagine you are seeing a kid goat trying to stand for the first time on its lanky legs. Perhaps you can visualise a tiny soft, feathered chick chirping in its nest!

- An HB or 2B pencil (they are light and won't smudge too easily)
- A pencil sharpener and a small dish for shavings
- A4 cartridge paper or copy paper and some scrap paper for experiments
- A clean eraser
- Confidence: a positive attitude will help improve your skills
- Imagination: don't be afraid to explore your own style or ideas

Drawing guidelines

There are a few things you should be aware of when drawing your baby animals.

1 The form of each animal is built around a series of rounded or irregular shapes.
2 The shape of some animals' limbs is constructed using lines, joints or circles.
3 It is important to position the limbs properly so you can see a subject from the correct viewpoint.
4 Line is used when defining an animals' curved outline or creating the texture of its skin or fur.
5 Use light pencil work when you begin a drawing. This means you can erase any pencil lines you don't need. You darken the line work of your picture when you are closer to finishing.

Stages of drawing

These drawings are drawn in a basic illustration style, with recognisable shapes and smooth, defined line work. You will observe that the drawings aren't overly detailed. However, you must carefully read and follow all steps so that you draw the elements of your picture correctly and in order. The instructions include guidelines on how to shade

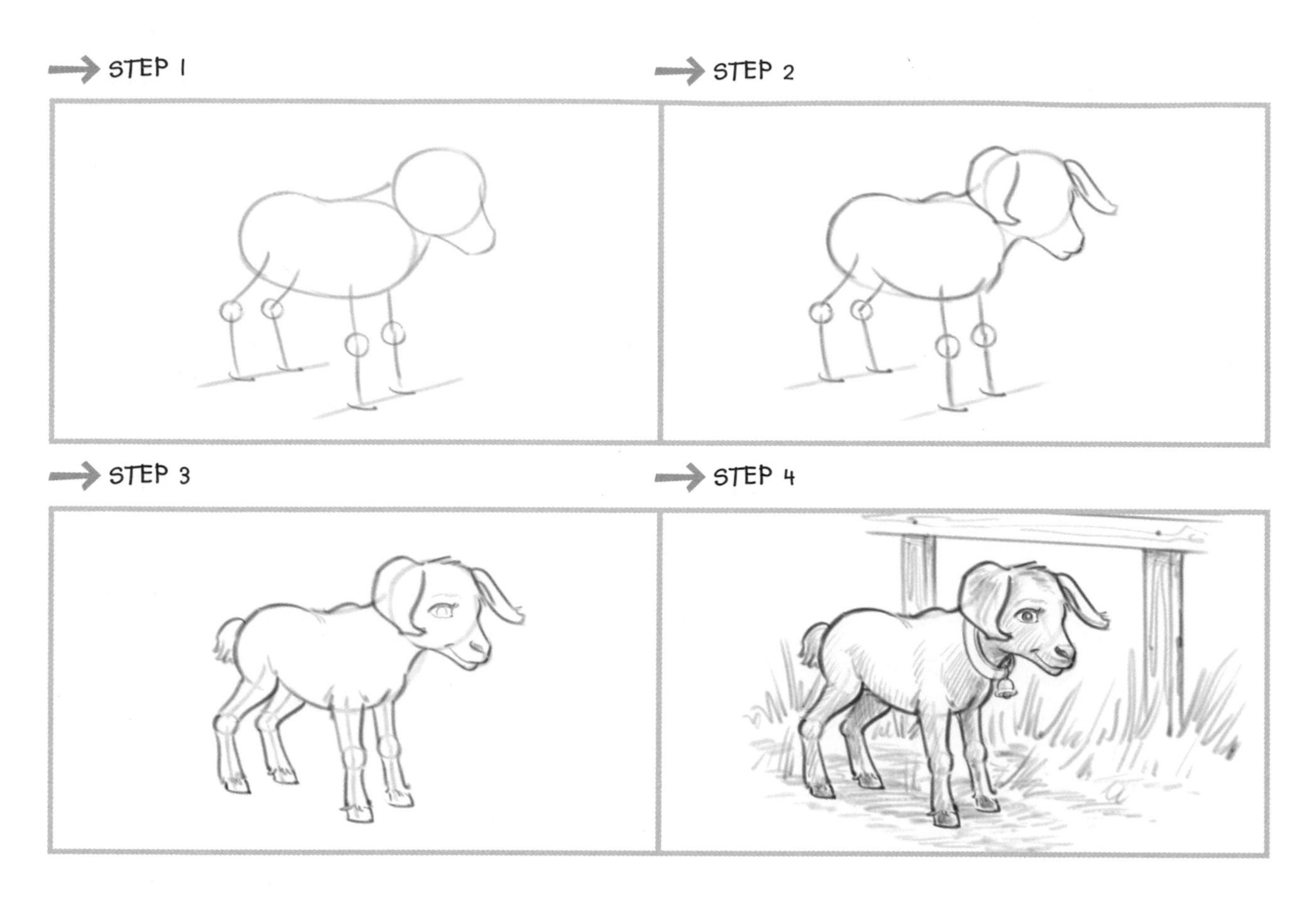

or add texture in the final stage. Study the levels of shading and the types of texture. Also, pay attention to the type of shapes and lines you are drawing. For each step, look at the proportions of each subject. What size are the body parts? Where are the lines for each limb placed and positioned?

Skills and techniques

Here are some examples of the different art elements and techniques you will learn about.

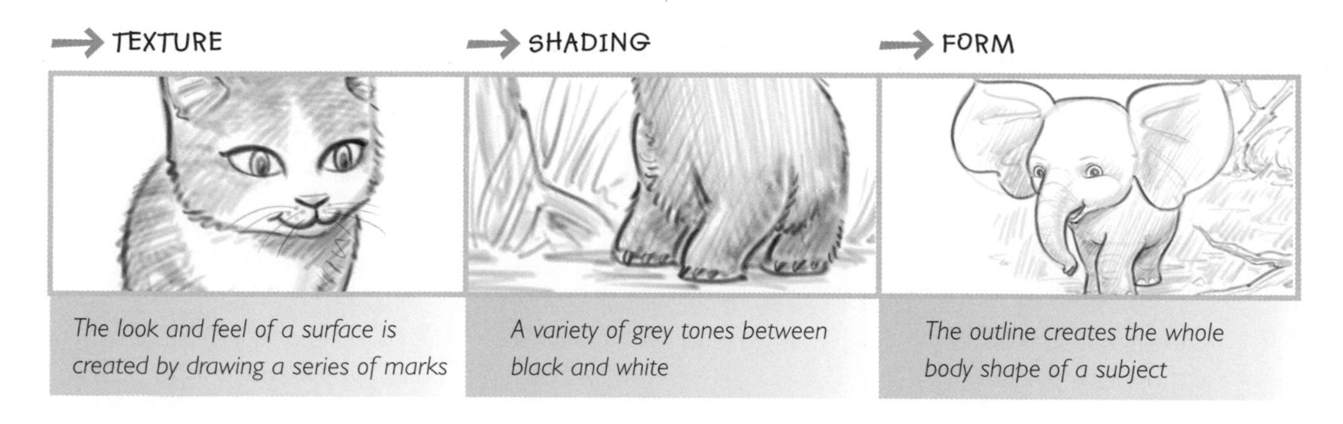

The look and feel of a surface is created by drawing a series of marks

A variety of grey tones between black and white

The outline creates the whole body shape of a subject

Practising with your pencil will help develop your drawing style. Experiment by drawing a variety of lines, shapes, textures and levels of shading so you learn to understand pencil technique. By applying yourself, your drawing skills will improve in no time!

KITTEN

Kittens are born into a litter of three to six babies on average. Their sight and hearing are very poor at birth, but develop over the first three months. During this period, kittens learn to wash themselves and play games with their siblings. Their mother's milk is very important for their growth.

Before you begin

The most important art elements in this drawing are shape and texture. Simple rounded shapes are used to create the kitten's form (its whole shape). The drawing is constructed around a circle for the body. The fur texture is created by a series of fine lines layered one over the another. Practise this on a separate piece of paper before you begin. Pay attention to the angle of the baselines, as they help you position the feet correctly. The fur texture is created using a series of fine lines layered over another. Practise creating the fur texture on a separate piece of paper before you begin.

Step 1

Using light pencil work, draw a circle for the body and baselines underneath, drawing the front one first. Add a construction line for the back leg and another for the front legs, meeting them in a point. Draw a circle for the back paw and then for the front paws, ensuring they overlap. Draw a head on top of the body, beginning with the jaw and working up to the pointy ears. Add a curve for the tail and a cross for the face.

Step 2

Build a curved shape around the construction line for the tail. Create a shape for the front left leg and then add the right leg, ensuring the left paw is on top. Draw a shape for the back paw. Add points for the inside of the ears. Define and smooth the kitten's outline.

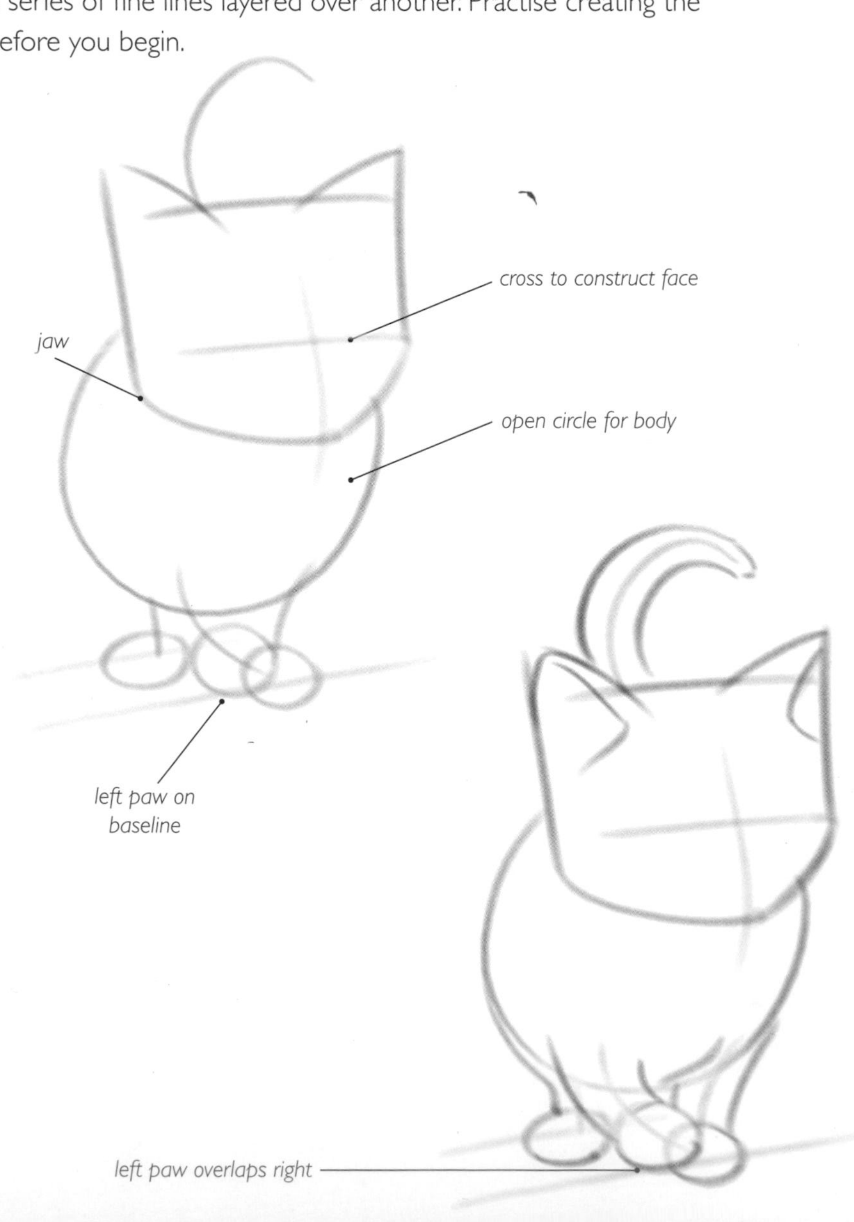

Step 3

Rub out any unnecessary line work with a clean eraser. Using a cross as a guide, draw wavy lines for the mouth and a triangle for the nose. Draw almond-shaped eyes on a slight angle on either side of the cross. Add ovals for the pupils and marks for the toes and fur.

DRAWING TIP

As you draw, try turning your page to avoid smudging your work.

Step 4

Draw a furry outline around the edges of the kitten's body. Using the side of your pencil, draw a fuzzy grey pattern to make the fur's background. Overlay this with faint lines to create the fur's texture. Use the sample boxes below as your guide.

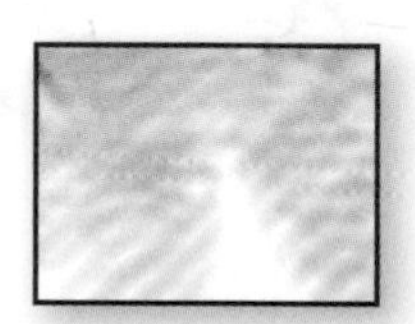

Shade the eyes and add fine lines for the whiskers and the texture inside the ears. Once you draw the shadow around the feet and a ball of wool, your kitten is ready to play!

INTERESTING FACT → Cats (and especially young kittens) love to play with string. This is probably related to their hunting instincts.

PUPPY

Puppies spend most of their first few weeks feeding and sleeping. Their eyes are closed at birth, but open around ten days after they are born. As they grow and get stronger, puppies will chase and wrestle with their brothers and sisters. A puppy can usually start training at around three months.

Before you begin

Line is the most important element in this drawing, as it gives the puppy its curved, furry, solid shape. Study each step to see the type of line work used to shape the puppy's outline and solid form (its whole body shape). Line work is also used to create the furry texture of the coat.

Step 1

Start by drawing a baseline. Using light pencil work, sketch an oval-shaped body on the baseline, paying attention to the angle. Add solid shapes for the front legs, placing them on the baseline, and the rear leg above the baseline. Draw the middle leg on an angle, with the paw below the line. Sketch a pointed jaw above the body, and add ear shapes and the top of the head.

Step 2

Define and darken the curves of the outline. Draw an outline of the snout poking out from the left side of the jaw. Add the nose shape and a mouth underneath. Attach a curved shape to the left outside leg for the tail. With a clean eraser, rub out any unnecessary construction lines.

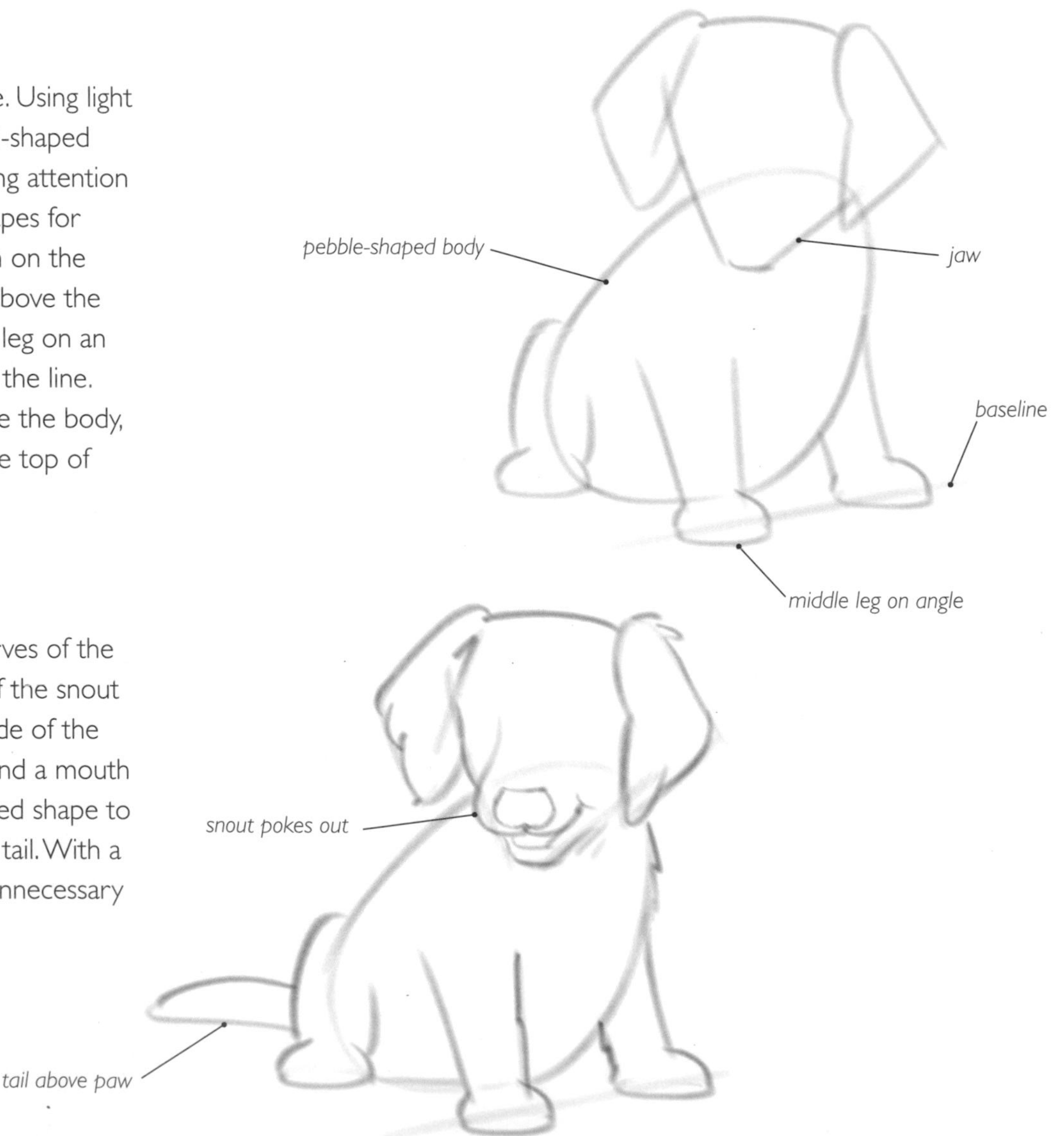

Step 3

Develop the shape of the puppy's form by adding curves to the back. Draw a furry edge on the tail and lines for the toes. Add half circles for the eyes in line with the top of the snout. Add circles for the pupils.

Step 4

Apply a mid-grey tone to the pupils, nose and mouth. Remember to leave any white areas unshaded. Add whisker details and eyebrows and lightly shade the edge of the snout. Draw pointy line work for the fur around the chest, stomach and legs. With the side of your pencil, lightly shade the edges of the whole body.

When drawing the background, make sure that the top of the bowl is an ellipse (a flattened circle). The mat is a flattened rectangle on an angle. Draw the bowl shape first and then draw the mat. Your puppy is now ready to play a game!

DRAWING TIP

Be patient and confident when drawing detailed pictures. Don't worry if your picture isn't perfect for your first try. Your skills will improve in time with practice.

INTERESTING FACT

The smaller and weaker dogs of a litter are called runts and can struggle for their position when feeding because of their size.

JOEY

Joeys are tiny when they are born (about the size of a jellybean) and are pink, blind and hairless. They stay inside their mother's pouch for the first few months, feeding off her milk. When they are big enough, they leave the safety of the pouch for short periods to learn how to feed.

Before you begin

To create the joey's distinct form, you will need to position the shapes and construction lines correctly. Study the first step to see where all elements are positioned. Also, pay attention to the size of the shapes and the types of line used.

Step 1

Lightly draw an oval-shaped body on a slight angle. Draw a head next to the side of the oval. Attach a snout shape in the bottom right corner. Add a curve for the chest and a neckline that dips in. Draw the right ear curving upward. Add the left ear, pointing out from the back of the head. Sketch short construction lines for the arms. Draw legs and long feet on an angle and a tail curving down from the back. Notice that the tail is flat on the bottom.

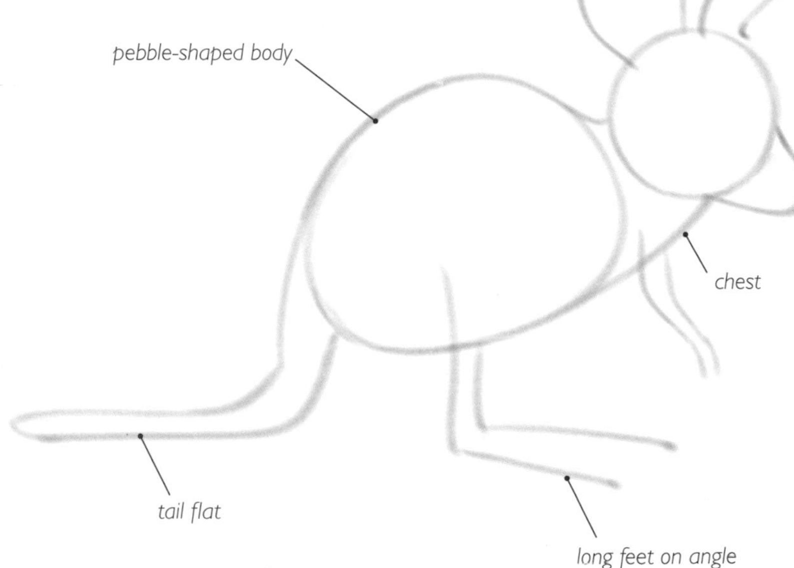

Step 2

Build shapes for the front leg and arm around the construction lines. Add the shapes for the back leg and arm. Add curves inside the ears. Define the sharper edges of the face and the curves for the rest of the body.

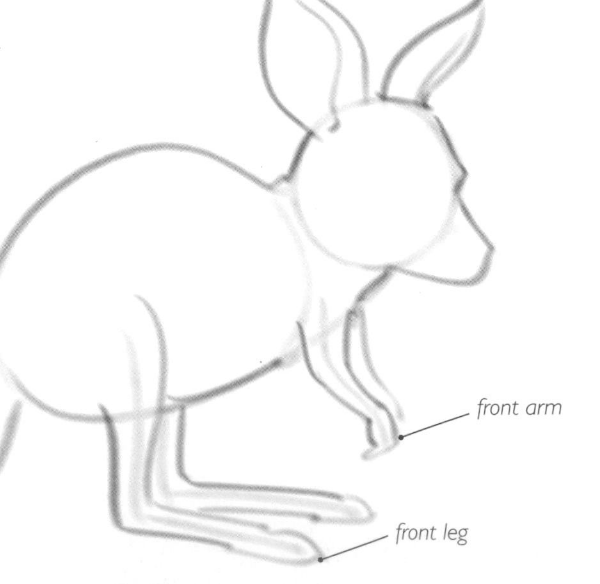

Step 3

Darken the outline of the joey. Add a shape next to the brow for the eye. Draw lines for the nose, mouth and paws.

Step 4

Shade the upward marks underneath the body using a light pressure. Define the neck area and lightly shade the snout and brow. With a mid-grey tone, shade the ears and nose. Add details inside the left ear and eye. Draw a furry line around the bottom. Don't forget the eyelashes and nostril.

Once you draw the joey's habitat, it will be ready to bounce over the rocks!

DRAWING TIP

Don't be afraid to draw your own habitat for your character to live in. If you need to, look up references on the net or in books. Otherwise, trust your imagination and experiment with your own ideas!

INTERESTING FACT

Sick joeys should never be fed cow's milk, as kangaroo milk is very different from the milk humans can drink.

Funky Things to Draw – Baby Animals

HARP SEAL PUP

Harp seals are born on floating ice or isolated beaches. When they are born, they are covered with a thick layer of white fur. After birth, the pups nurse on their mother's rich milk for around two weeks. Because the milk is made up of around fifty per cent fat, it helps create a thick layer of blubber, which keeps the seals warm. After about two weeks, the pup starts to lose its white coat which is replaced by grey fur.

Before you begin

This drawing is mainly constructed with curved line work and a basic oval shape. Note how the line work for the body curves under and behind the pup. The pup's form is larger at the front but becomes smaller as it moves into the background. This is called *foreshortening*. The flippers must also be positioned carefully so you can draw the pup from the correct angle.

curve sweeps wide

oval on slight angle

front paws on angle

face on angle

Step 1

Draw lightly at first. Sketch an oval on a very slight angle for the head. Add line work for the body under the head. Draw a line sweeping wide and curving around to meet the head. First sketch the right flipper and then left flipper on the same angle. Draw a wavy shaped tail.

Step 2

Note the direction that the nose, mouth and eyes are facing. Draw the top of the nose jutting out to the right. Sketch the rest of the mouth on an angle and add nostrils. Add the almond-shaped left eye and then the right eye behind the nose. Add the marks behind the head.

Step 3

Define the outline with fuzzy line work. Using the side of your pencil, softly draw the fur texture around the edges of the body. Shade the eyes and nose area with a mid-grey tone. Add line work for the flippers, tail and whiskers. Draw the chunky edges of the floating ice. Your seal pup is ready for a swim!

INTERESTING FACT → With the onset of spring, around one third of the world's seals gather to give birth on the Magdalen Islands and in Labrador, in Canada.

EMPEROR PENGUIN CHICK

Emperor penguin chicks are born in large colonies. The mother lays an egg in winter and then travels out to sea to feed. The male carries the egg on his feet, protected by a flap of skin. When the female returns in spring, she regurgitates food for the hatched chick and the father leaves to feed. Two months after they hatch, chicks huddle with other chicks in a group called a crèche while the adults look for food.

Before you begin

This drawing is created with a series of simple shapes. The most important element to focus on is the perspective the penguin is seen from. Observe the direction the beak, feet and eye are facing, and the angle of the line work used to draw them.

Step 1

Draw a slightly squashed circle for the head. Add a bottle shape for the large body. Sketch the left wing shape, ensuring it overlaps the body. Draw the right wing in line with the left. Sketch paddle shapes on an angle for the feet.

Step 2

Define and smooth the outline of the form. Draw details for the tail, stomach and claws. Draw a beak halfway down the right side of the head, pointing out to the right. Add a half circle on a slight angle for the eye.

Step 3

Darken the chick's outline. With a clean eraser, rub out any unnecessary line work inside the body. Using a medium pressure with the pencil, shade a mid-grey tone around the head and the right wing. Shade the beak in a lighter tone. Apply soft line work for the texture of the feathers on the rest of the body.

Draw line work to create the chunky edges of the ice. Your penguin chick is now ready for its journey out to sea!

INTERESTING FACT → **If the chick hatches while its mother is at sea, it feeds on a milky liquid produced by its father's oesophagus.**

ELEPHANT CALF

Elephant calves are born with great fanfare, as their mother and the herd trumpet loudly when they are born. Shortly afterwards, the herd will welcome the baby by touching it with their trunks. Herds are such close-knit groups that all the elephants help raise the calves. Baby elephants learn how to use their trunks by watching adult elephants.

Before you begin

You will notice that no construction lines are used to build the form of the baby elephant's body. This is because this drawing is made up of a series of curved and rounded shapes. Once the head and ears are drawn, it is easy to connect the rest of the solid shapes to create the body. Practise drawing the shapes you see on a separate piece of paper, using a loose pencil grip.

Step 1

Using light pencil work, draw a circle for the head. Attach leaf-shaped ears to the sides of the head. Note the width of the ears and how they point upward. Draw a curve for the body, connecting it to the right ear and the middle of the chin. Next, draw two cylinder-shaped front legs and then a back leg. Draw a trunk curving down to the middle of the front leg.

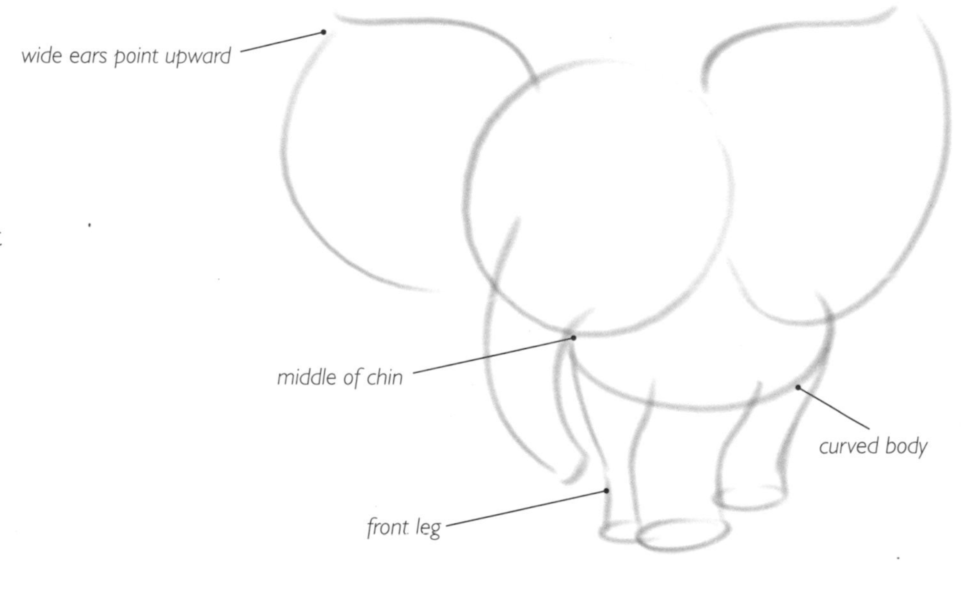

Step 2

Define and smooth the curved outline of the elephant calf. Pay attention to the way the ears dip in at the bottom. Add an opening for the mouth and the trunk. With a clean eraser, rub out any unnecessary line work inside the body.

Step 3

Darken the outline of the elephant and add half circles for the toes. Draw half circle shapes above the corner of the mouth for the right eye. Add the left eye in beside the top of the trunk, making sure it is in line with the right eye and slightly smaller. Also draw in the eyebrows.

Step 4

Sketch wavy line work inside the ears and a pattern across the trunk and knees. Apply a dark tone to the inside of the eyes. With a light pencil grip, shade a light tone across the body where required. Make sure the shading is darker under the belly.

Draw a branch in the foreground of the picture and texture for the grass. Once you've drawn the tree and bush in the background, your elephant calf will be ready to roam with the rest of the herd!

DRAWING TIP

Follow the drawing instructions carefully, as they teach you to create the elements of a sketch in a specific order. This makes it easier to develop a drawing correctly as you progress.

INTERESTING FACT

Young elephant calves are very clumsy with their trunk. A calf will even trip over its trunk until it learns how to use it.

FAWN

When they are born, fawns are licked clean by their mother so that predators can't detect their scent easily. Even though they can stand up minutes after being born, fawns aren't strong enough to walk with their mother. While their mothers feed, fawns lie hidden in dense undergrowth, well camouflaged by their spotted fur coats.

Before you begin

The drawing of the fawn is based around a series of different-sized shapes and construction lines. The baseline supports the fawn's structure and indicates the direction it faces. Study each step to observe the size and shape of all the elements of the fawn's body before you begin.

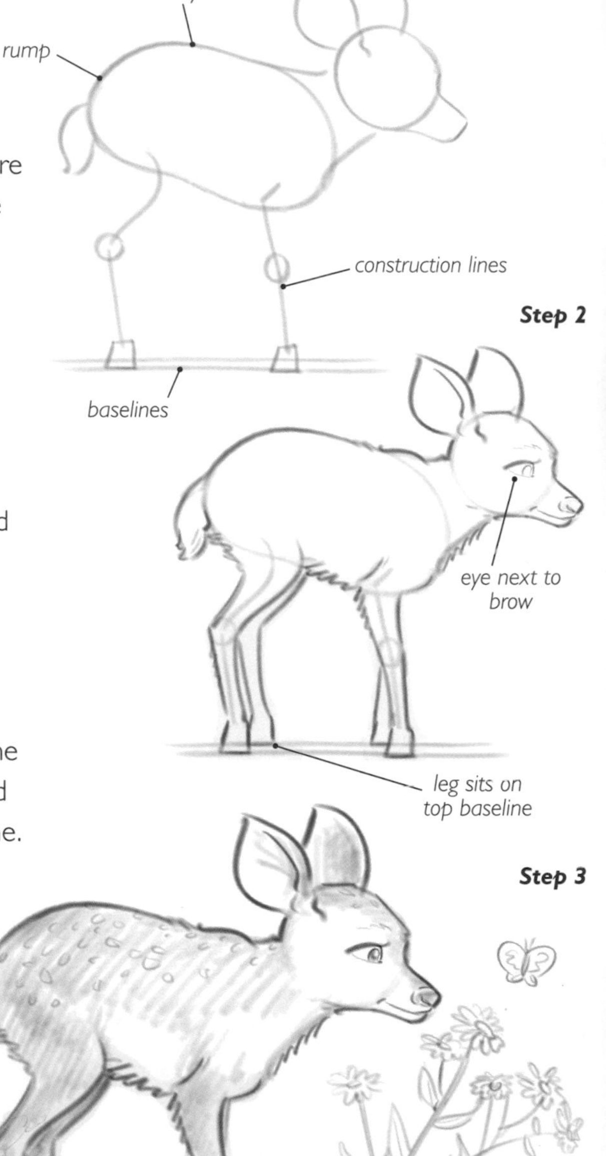

Step 1

Draw a baseline. Sketch a bean-shaped body above the line, allowing enough space for the long legs. Draw a head next to the top right corner of the body. Add necklines and a curved snout shape. Draw a leaf shape pointing upward for the left ear and add the right ear behind it. Draw a tail on the rump. Next, draw construction lines for the legs, making sure the back leg is curved. Add joints and hooves.

Step 2

Create shapes for the front legs around the construction lines. Using the top baseline as a guide, draw the back legs. Add furry line work around the belly, chest, tail and legs. Define and darken the curves of the outline. Sketch line work for the nose, mouth and ear, and add details next to the brow for the eye.

Step 3

Using the side of your pencil, shade a medium tone across the top of the fawn's body and down the legs. Notice that the shading around the rump is darker. Shade the ear, head, chest and tail, and darken the nose and eye area. Once you draw the habitat, your fawn is ready to chase a butterfly!

INTERESTING FACT → Male fawns are born with two tiny bumps on their heads that grow into antlers when they are young bucks.

BEAR CUB

Bears live in many different areas, from grasslands and forests to mountains and snowfields. Bear cubs are usually born in winter in a den after a period of hibernation. They are blind and bald when they are born. Cubs will stay by their mother's side for around two to four years. During this time, the mother is fiercely protective of her young.

Before you begin

This drawing is based around an oval and a series of basic solid shapes. Pay close attention to the direction of the nose and the placement of the legs. This will help you draw the correct pose. Shading is also an important element of this picture. Notice that the shading is darker at the cub's feet and that the rest of the body has lighter and more open shading.

Step 1

Lightly draw an oval on a slight angle for the body. Draw the head above the oval in the top left corner. Add an ear shape, then attach lines for the neck. Connect the curved shape of the snout to the neck and head. Attach a solid curved shape for the front leg to the middle of the body. Attach the back legs, making sure they are in line with each other.

Step 2

With a clean eraser, rub out any unnecessary lines inside the body. Add fuzzy marks around the chest and belly for the fur. Define the cub's outline. Add a smile and a 'v' shape on the same angle for the eye. Draw the details for the ear and nose.

Step 3

Using the side of your pencil, gently shade in a light tone across the cub's body. Apply a mid-grey tone around the legs and inside the ear. Darken the bottom of the nose and add detail to the eye. Draw points for the claws. Sketch a line pattern over the chest and faint fur marks around the neck.

Once you draw the habitat, your bear cub is ready to play!

INTERESTING FACT → When bear cub siblings play together, they use the snow as a slide!

LION CUB

Lions live together in a group called a pride, which is led by up to four territorial males with the rest of the brood consisting of females and their cubs. The mothers care for litters of around three cubs, unless food is scarce. Lion cubs will learn how to hunt and kill by play-fighting with each other.

Before you begin

The most important art elements of this drawing are shape and texture. The lion cub is built around a series of rounded shapes. Note how the body looks like a loaf of bread. The edges of the drawing are defined by a texture formed with a series of lines.

Step 1

Lightly draw a bread-loaf shape for the body, ensuring it is flatter on the bottom. Attach a circle for the head at the top right of the body. Draw a light construction line that curves across the middle of the face. Add half circles for the ears on either side of the head. Draw curves for the tail and hip and add construction lines for the legs with circles for the paws.

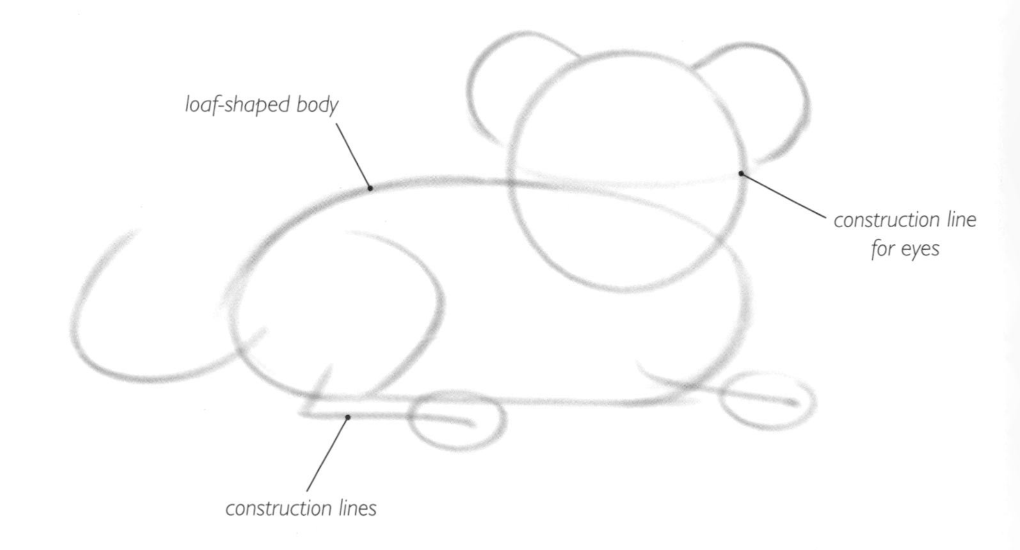

Step 2

Build tail and leg shapes around the construction lines. Add almond-shaped eyes above the construction line. Draw a curve for the nose under the left eye, a mouth over the bottom of the circle and a chin below the circle. Don't forget a line for the back leg.

Step 3

With a clean eraser, rub out any unnecessary line work inside the body. Define and darken the cub's outline, paying attention to the furry marks around the edges of the body and ears. Add curves for the toes and the inside of the ears, and draw double circles for the pupils.

DRAWING TIP

To create a light pencil shading, press lightly with a pencil using a right to left drawing motion. As you continue, press more heavily using the same motion to gradually create darker tones. You can use the side or tip of a pencil.

Step 4

Darken the eyes with different levels of shading. Using the side of your pencil, lightly shade texture marks around the edges of the body. Pay attention to the shading inside the ears and on the tip of the nose. Don't forget faint whiskers!

Once you have created a wilderness in the background, your lion cub is ready to play!

INTERESTING FACT → An adult lion's roar can be heard around 8 km away!

LAMB

Within minutes of a lamb's birth, its mother (called a ewe) licks the lamb clean and nudges it until it can stand. Lambs drink their mother's milk for three or four months before they start eating hay, grass and grain. They don't stray far from their mother and will bleat loudly if they are in trouble.

Before you begin

This drawing is built around a basic oval and circle, which create the rounded body shape. The form of the body is also shaped by a wavy outline, which enhances the fluffy plump coat. The baseline is an important element of the drawing, as it indicates the correct position of the legs.

Step 1

Draw a baseline first. Place an oval for the body above the baseline. Add construction lines for the legs, making sure the feet sit under the baseline. Attach a circle for the head to the top left of the oval. Draw almond-shaped ears and a curved shape for the snout.

Step 2

Draw the lines for the neck and chin and the curved lines for the chest and tail. Build shapes for the front legs around the construction lines. Add shapes for the back legs.

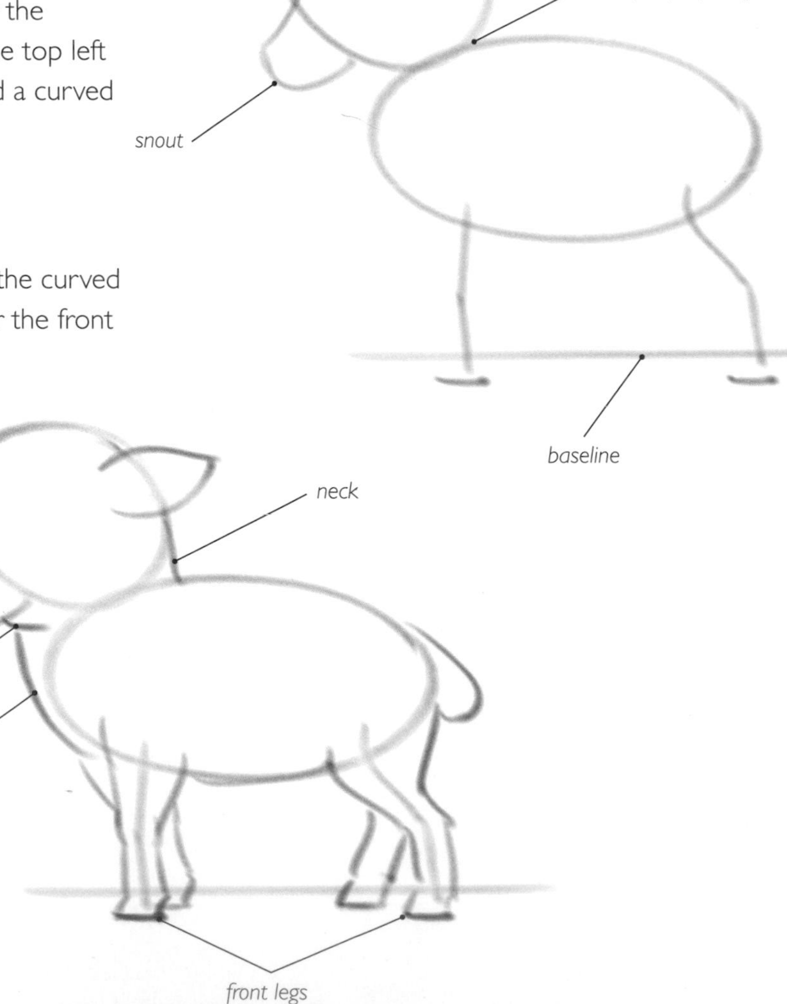

Step 3

Draw a bumpy line around the head and body, defining the form. Add marks around the ears and feet, and draw lines for the nostril and smile. Develop line work around the snout. Add marks on the forehead before sketching the eye.

Step 4

Use the side of a pencil to softly shade the edges of the body. Create the texture of the wool by sketching the darker marks. Shade a mid-grey tone over the back legs and inside the front ear, and add details inside the eye.

To sketch the hay shed in the background, first draw the poles and then the roof on an angle. When drawing the hay bales, start in the front right corner. Add patterns to the ground. Your lamb is now looking for friends to play with!

DRAWING TIP

Remember not to press too hard with the pencil when starting a picture. Draw lightly at first, as you can always add more detail as you go.

INTERESTING FACT → Lambs form their own friendship groups. You'll often see them playing together!

FOAL

Foals are usually born at night so the darkness helps protect them from danger. Foals can stand up soon after birth and are able to gallop with other horses within a few hours. Male foals are called 'colts' and females are called 'fillies'. When they are first born, their legs are almost the length of an adult horse's legs.

Before you begin

Shape is the most important art element in this drawing, as it creates the foal's distinct form. Make sure you draw the rounded shapes of the foal's body at the correct size, otherwise the foal will look out of proportion. Pay attention to the direction and the length of the leg, as these will give the drawing a sense of movement.

Step 1

Draw a bean-shaped body on a slight angle. Sketch a thick shape for the neck in the top right corner and add a circle for the head. Draw a pointy shape for the front ear and then add the back ear. Next, draw a squashed shape for the snout. Sketch construction lines for the legs, beginning with the front straight leg. Add bent lines for the other legs and sketch in all the joints.

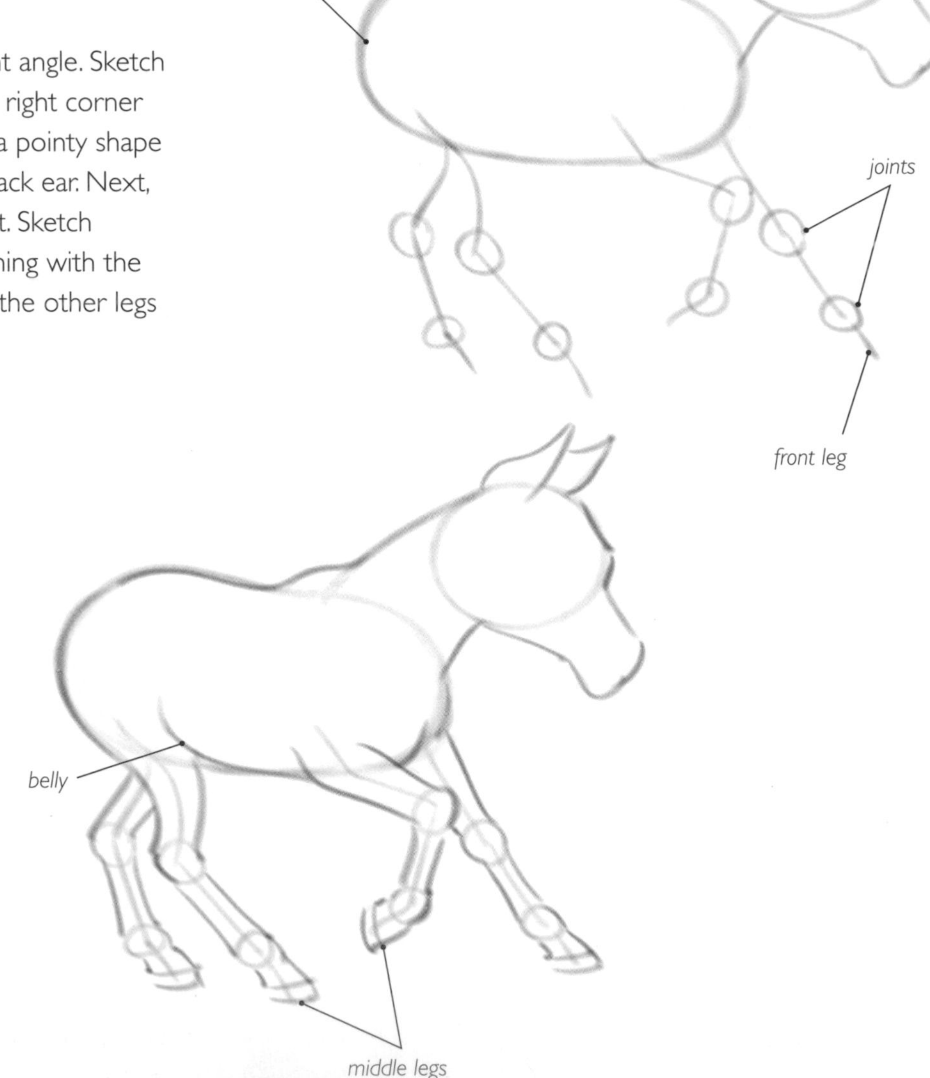

Step 2

Define and smooth the curved outline of the body and head. Add a mark to show the foal's belly. Build leg shapes around the construction lines, beginning with the legs and then the outside leg shapes. Draw lines to show the hooves.

Step 3

With a clean eraser, rub out any unnecessary line work inside the foal's body. Draw a puffy shape trailing out behind for the tail. Draw a flowing wavy mane and line work for the front ear. Sketch details next to the brow for the eye. Add an opening for the mouth and an oval for the nostril.

DRAWING TIP

For something different, try drawing your picture with a black fine-tip marker and then colour it in with a marker. Try not to touch the black line with the marker, as it may smudge.

Step 4

Darken the outline of the foal's form. Add darker tones to the eye, nostril, ear and hooves. Using the side of your pencil, softly shade the edges of the whole body using a right-to-left motion. Pay attention to shaping the area around the joints.

The background is simple to draw. Draw different-sized posts for the fence and then add the wire. Draw in whatever type of grass and clouds you like. Your foal is now ready to gallop through the fields in springtime!

INTERESTING FACT → It is thought that the best time of the year for a foal to be born is in springtime, due to the ideal weather conditions.

KID

Goats are bred for their hair, meat, milk and skin. When a baby goat (called a kid) is born, it stands up within minutes and remains close to its mother for protection. Goats usually give birth to twins. The birthing of a baby goat is called 'kidding'!

Before you begin

The legs are the most important element of this drawing, as they allow the kid to be seen from the correct viewpoint. The baselines are positioned on slightly different angles. All the legs vary in length and sit on the baselines. The joints shape the structure of the legs. Pay attention to how the body is drawn on a slight angle. Remember to draw lightly at first!

Step 1

Begin by drawing a bean-shaped body on a slight angle. Attach a circle for the head in the top right corner and add curved lines for the neck and snout. Draw a front baseline under the chest and nose, and a back baseline under the belly. Add straight front legs and bent back legs. Draw hooves against the baselines and then add the joints.

Step 2

Draw a shape over the back of the head for the left ear, sitting against the body. Draw the right ear sitting behind the left ear, and curving outward. Develop curves for the back, nose, chest and belly. Rub out any unnecessary line work with a clean eraser.

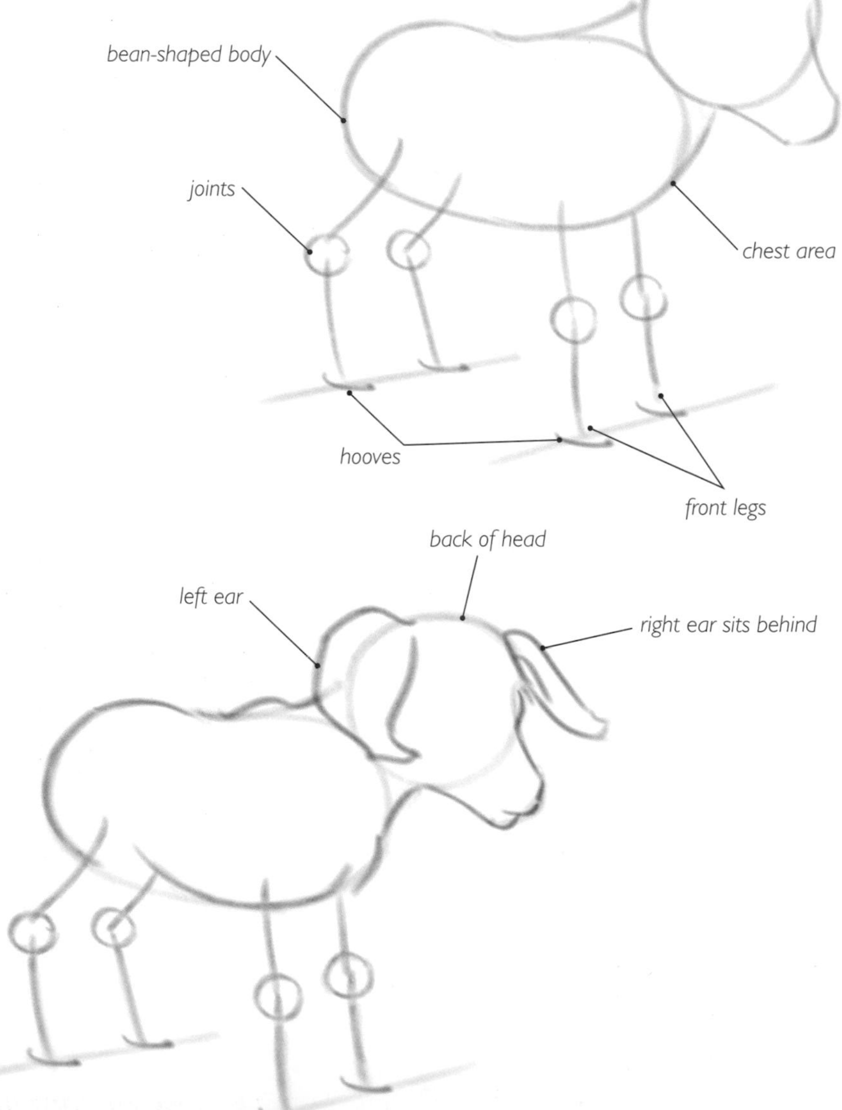

Step 3

Build leg and hoof shapes around the construction lines, paying attention to where they connect to the body. Add furry marks around the edges of the body, including a tail shape. Draw an eye next to the brow. Sketch a mouth and a nostril. Darken and define the outline.

Step 4

Draw a loop for the collar around the neck and attach a bell. Using a light pressure, shade open lines of texture across the body. Darken the shading for the back leg and the chest area. Shade the nose, eye and hooves with a medium grey tone. Remember to leave any white areas clear.

Once you add the background, your kid goat is ready play with its friends!

DRAWING TIP

Baselines are an important guide when constructing a drawing. They help to position the limbs correctly and to give figures in a drawing the correct perspective.

INTERESTING FACT

Centuries ago, goatskins were made into bottles that carried wine or water.

Funky Things to Draw
in the Ocean
in the Ocean
Paul Könye
Kate Ashforth

Funky Things to Draw in the Ocean

INTRODUCTION

There are many different kinds of creatures that live in the sea, but unless you go scuba diving, you will rarely get to see them up close.

When you draw, you can use your imagination to discover these sea creatures. You could be swimming through tropical blue waters or past massive ice bergs! Imagine you are watching a clownfish peeping out of a sea anemone or a starfish on the sea floor. Maybe you are drifting by a dolphin showing off his acrobatic tricks?

THINGS YOU WILL NEED

- An HB or 2B pencil (they are light and won't smudge too easily)
- A pencil sharpener and a small dish for shavings
- A4 cartridge paper or copy paper and some scrap paper for experiments
- A clean eraser
- Confidence: a positive attitude will help improve your skills
- Imagination: don't be afraid to explore your own style or ideas

Drawing guidelines

There's a few things you should be aware of when you draw your sea creatures.

1. Many subjects are constructed using rounded shapes, such as ovals.
2. Most creatures from the sea have their own distinctive shapes, like seahorses or turtles.
3. Line is an important art element that can create a unique pattern or texture on the body of a sea creature.
4. Curved or wavy lines are used to build the form (the whole shape) of a subject.
5. Use light pencil work when you begin a drawing. This means you can erase any pencil lines you don't need. You will darken the line work of your sketch when you are closer to finishing it.

Stages of drawing

Some sea creatures can be easy to draw while some are more complex, with many details that need to be included to build the whole picture. Make sure you read the steps carefully before you begin. The instructions will tell you what should be drawn first. Each lesson also teaches you skills that will help improve your knowledge of drawing.

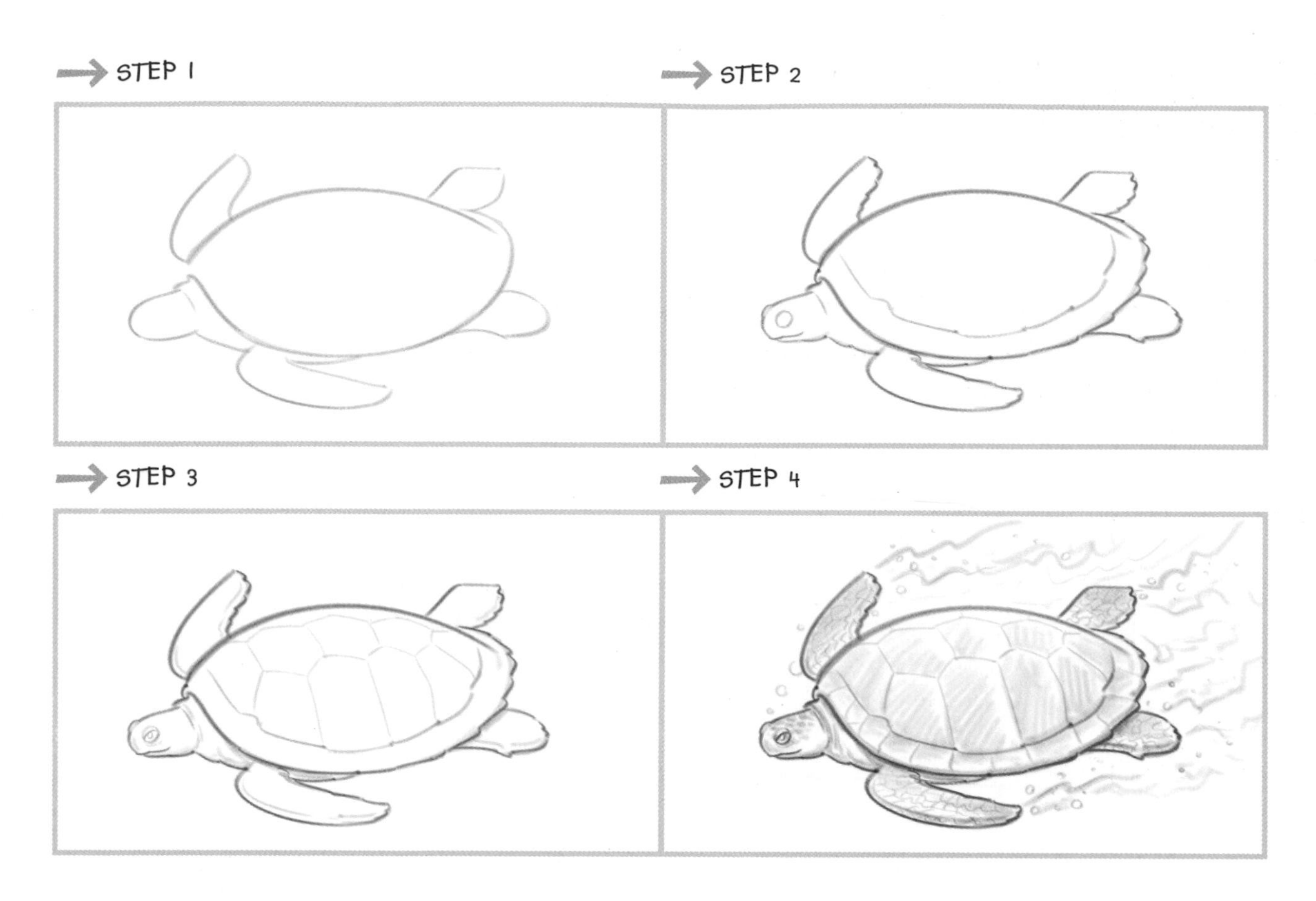

Study each step, observing the different shapes and line work. Look at the unique form of each subject and study the types of lines that have been used. What needs to be drawn first? What changes are there between each step? How dark is the shading? What patterns are used in the drawing?

Skills and techniques

Here are some examples of the different art elements and techniques you will learn about.

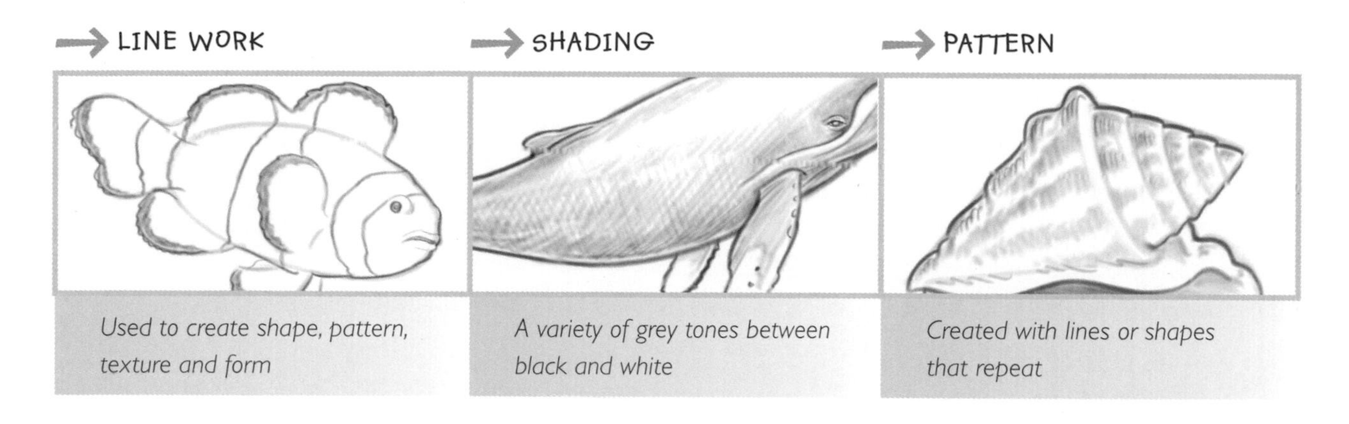

Used to create shape, pattern, texture and form

A variety of grey tones between black and white

Created with lines or shapes that repeat

Be patient when you are drawing your sea creatures. Look closely at all the details in each step and take your time drawing them. Remember, your eyes are your most reliable tools, so use them as your guide!

DOLPHIN

Dolphins are loved for their friendly nature and they will happily swim and socialise with humans. They are one of the planet's most intelligent creatures and have amazing hearing and eyesight. They can be trained and can leap six metres above water to perform acrobatic tricks. Dolphins swim in a group called a pod. They talk with each other through a series of clicks and whistles.

Before you begin

The dolphin has a basic but distinctive shape. The form of the dolphin (the whole, rounded shape) is enhanced by shading. Shading uses grey tones between black and white and is a technique you can explore using a pencil. Create different shades of grey tone depending on how lightly or heavily you press with your pencil. Practise before you begin and study each step carefully.

Step 1

Drawing lightly, sketch an oval for the middle of the dolphin's body. Create the rest of the shape by adding a rounded head and pointy tail. Don't forget the snout.

Step 2

Add a curved fin to the middle of the back and a front fin underneath. Use the oval as a guide to see where the fins should be drawn. Add a curved shape for the front of the tail. Then add the other tail shape behind. Define the outline of the dolphin's form.

Step 3

With a clean eraser, rub out any unnecessary line work inside the dolphin. Lightly sketch the teardrop-shaped eye. Draw a smile for the mouth. Check that you have shaped the curves of the outline correctly, as this will help make it look like the dolphin is jumping out of the water.

Step 4

Shade the edges of the dolphin's form with a medium grey tone. Use a left-to-right drawing motion to achieve this. Draw lightly at first and work over the area until you achieve the correct level of shading. Don't forget to darken the outline.

Now draw the background. Softly sketch wavy line work across the page underneath the dolphin. Add crinkly line work for the water, splashing out from the edges of the tail. Your dolphin is now jumping out of the water to say hello!

DRAWING TIP

Your eyes are your most trusted tools. Once you have drawn each step a few times, try copying the final step by yourself.

INTERESTING FACT → Dolphins enjoy riding waves and can be seen surfing coastal swells together.

HUMPBACK WHALE

Humpback whales are known for breaching (or jumping) into the air and falling back to the water with a huge splash. The male humpback is the most musical of the whales, singing complex and beautiful songs that last up to 30 minutes. Humpbacks dive to a depth of around 200 m and can remain underwater for up to thirty minutes. They grow to around 16 m long and eat about 2,500 kg of marine life a day when feeding.

Before you begin

The most important elements in this drawing are line, shape and texture. Pay attention when drawing the curved outline of the whale. Note the basic oval shape that the whale's form is built around and the angle at which it is floating. The pencil technique for the texture of the whale's skin is called cross-hatching, which is series of lines that run across one another. Practise this on a separate piece of paper before you begin.

Step 1

Lightly draw an oval on an angle for the whale's body. Attach the pointy tail shape and the curved snout.

Step 2

Draw a shape for the front flipper and then the one behind. Add a small dorsel fin on the top of the body. Draw a wavy line for the mouth, making sure it sits above the front flipper. Draw the thinner part of the tail on the inside, making sure it is drawn on an angle. Attach the second curved piece of tail to the end of the body. Smooth and define the shape of the whale's outline.

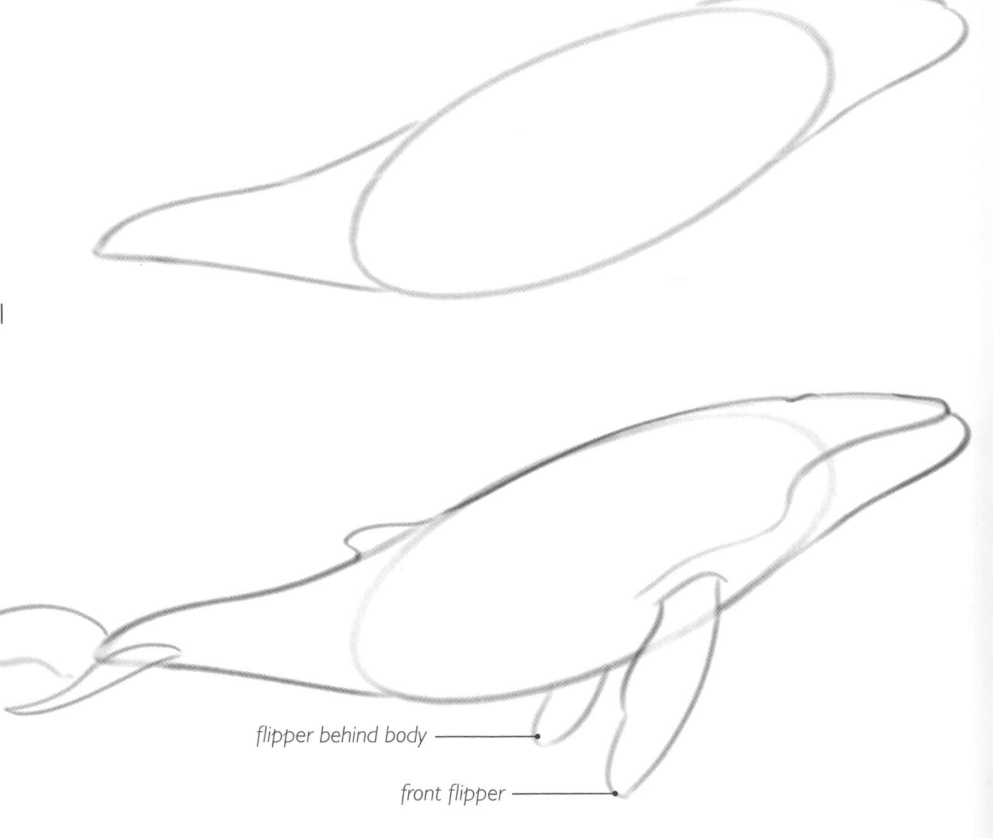

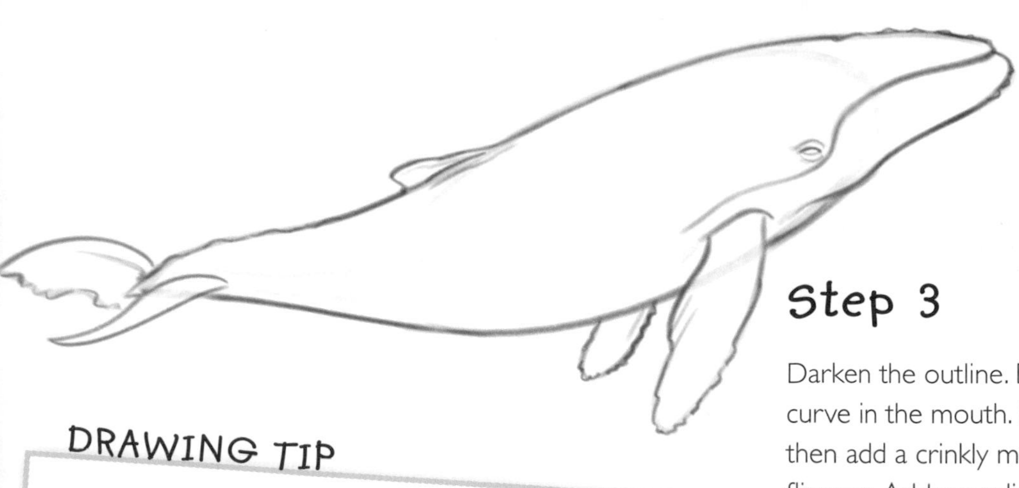

Step 3

Darken the outline. Draw a tiny eye next to the curve in the mouth. Define the shape of the chin, then add a crinkly marks to the head, mouth and flippers. Add wavy line work around the tail, and any other necessary marks. Rub out the inside line work of the oval with a clean eraser.

DRAWING TIP

When sharpening your pencil, always have a dish next to you to empty pencil shavings into. That way you won't have to keep getting out of your chair to use the bin or stray shavings smudging on your drawing.

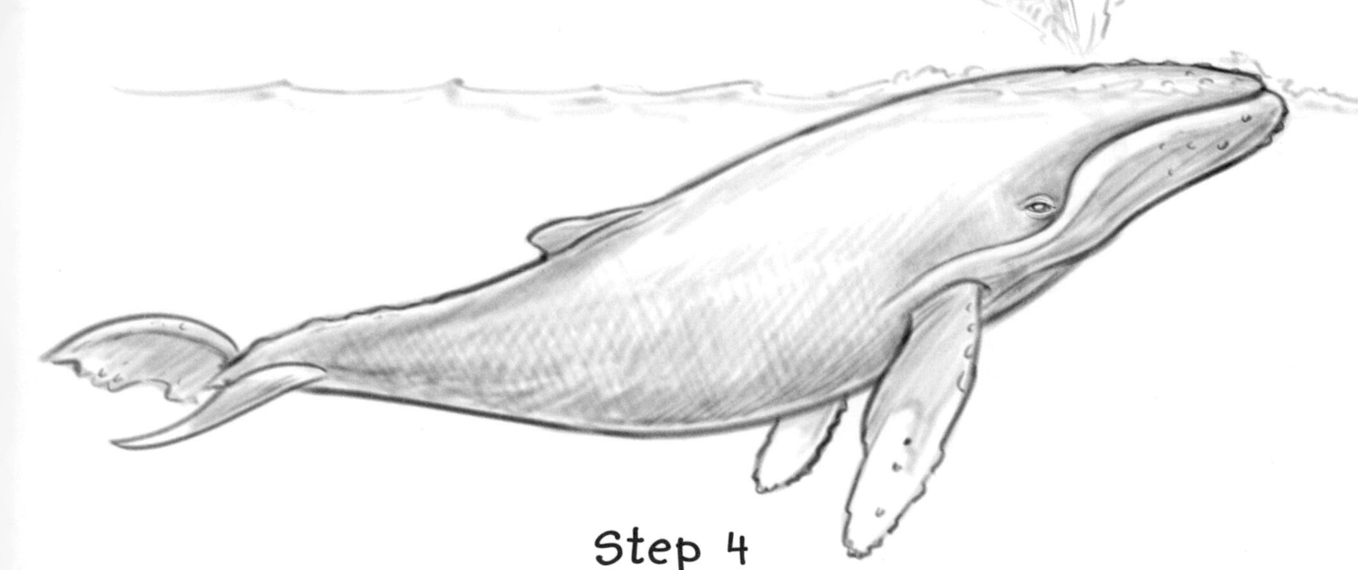

Step 4

Draw a bumpy pattern around the mouth, flipper and tail and lines for the ridges of the chin. Notice that the shading and texture of the skin is darkest around the edges. As you shade and draw the cross hatching, make sure it gets lighter toward the middle of the body.

Draw a faint puff of water above the blowhole and waves in the background, using light pressure with your pencil. Your whale is now ready to surface for the next acrobatic show!

INTERESTING FACTS

- Groups of humpback whales blow bubbles to herd small fish, making feeding easier.
- Humpbacks are named because of the way they arch their back into a 'hump' before they dive.

PELICAN

Pelicans are found all over the world except in Antarctica. The seven species of pelican are similar in shape and are mainly white. A pelican's most noticeable feature is its long bill and massive throat pouch. It uses its bill like a fishing net, skimming across the water to scoop up its catch. Humans enjoy feeding pelicans, as the birds will happily socialise with them and accept food.

Before you begin

The pelican's form is easy to draw because it is made up of very distinctive shapes. Pay attention to the oval shape for the body, the circle for the head, the knife-shaped bill and the paddle shapes for the feet. A series of lines makes up the texture of the feathers.

Step 1

Draw an oval on a slight angle for the body and construction lines for the legs. Notice that the front leg is longer than the back. Draw a baseline across the bottom of the legs so you can position the feet. Sketch paddle shapes for the feet over the baseline. Draw a curved shape for the neck at the top left of the body and attach a circle for the head. Draw a knife shape over the edge of the circle for the bill.

Step 2

Smooth and define the pelican's shape. Starting with the bill, draw curved lines for the mouth. Don't forget a bump on the back of the head. Sketch a wavy line inside the body for the wing and connect a pointy shape for the tail. Draw the outside line work to thicken the legs and a curve for the hip.

Step 3

Darken the outline of the form. Draw circles for the eye and a fuzzy line on the back of the head. Draw a sharp hook on the end of the beak and define the beak's shape. Sketch in the lines for the webbed feet.

DRAWING TIP

It takes practice to draw rounded shapes correctly. Improve your skills by creating a page of experiments. Try sketching different-sized ovals and circles. First draw them quickly and then more slowly.

Step 4

To create the texture for the feathered wing, draw a series of lines close together. Use a medium pressure with your pencil. When you finish, draw darker lines over the top. Draw spiky marks on the bottom for tail feathers. Add in shading around the edges of the body, beak and feet.

For the stump the pelican is standing on, sketch a flat circle under the feet. Connect the lines for the edges and draw a pattern on the stump using a series of soft lines. Add in any other necessary details. Your pelican is now sunning itself, waiting for its next catch!

INTERESTING FACT → You may sometimes see a seagull sitting on a pelican's head, waiting for any leftovers to spill out from its bill.

SEAL

Seals can be found in all of the world's oceans. Seals move very awkwardly on land but are very nimble in the sea. Their torpedo shape helps them propel themselves through the water with their back flippers, while they use their front flippers for steering. Seals are often hunted by animals such as polar bears and the great white shark.

Before you begin

The drawing of the seal is based around the backbone. The backbone indicates the direction in which the seal is sitting. Be aware of the smooth curve of the backbone, the sausage shape of the body around the backbone and the direction of the lines for the flippers.

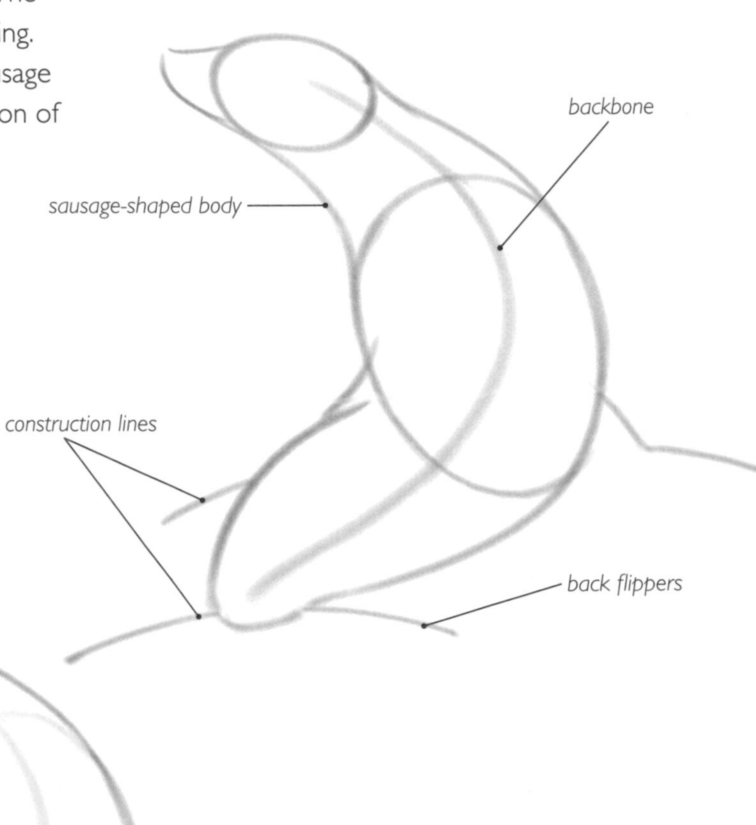

Step 1

Draw lightly to start. Sketch the smooth curve of the backbone. Connect an oval to the middle of the backbone. Build a sausage shape around it by drawing the tail and neck shapes. Attach an oval for the head and a tip for the nose. Draw a line for the back flippers and then one for the front ones.

Step 2

Define and darken the outline of the seal. With a clean eraser, rub out any unnecessary lines inside the body. Create the shapes for the flippers around the construction lines. Add a mark for the nostril and a circle for the eye.

Step 3

Draw an almond-shaped eye inside the circle. Shade it in a dark tone, leaving a white dot. Add a bump for the ear opening and a soft shadow where the whiskers will go. Add a pattern for the edges of the flippers, using a series of lines.

Step 4

Using the side of your pencil, gently shade the edges of the body. Start at the tail and work your way up to the head. Add a light tone to the flippers and soft whiskers to the face. Create a shadow under the belly by gently moving your pencil from left to right.

Add in wavy line work to the background for the ground and waves. Your seal is now lazily resting on the rocks in the sunshine!

DRAWING TIP

Remember not to press too hard with the pencil when beginning a drawing. Draw lightly and add more detail at the end.

INTERESTING FACT → Some seals can dive for over an hour and have been known to reach depths of over 100 metres!

POLAR BEAR

Polar bears may look cute and cuddly, but they are actually very dangerous. These large creatures can be curious and aggressive by nature. Polar bears are excellent swimmers and have been found miles from land looking for dinner. Their white fur allows them to camouflage themselves against the ice from unsuspecting prey. They can capture big animals like seals or even small whales!

Before you begin

Line work is the most important element to focus on with this drawing, as it gives the polar bear its curvy rounded shape. Before you begin, observe the curved rounded shapes that the polar bear is built around, how the outline is developed around the shapes and how the light texture of the fur helps define its form.

Step 1

Using light pencil work, draw an egg shape for the body. Sketch the baseline underneath the belly. Next, draw two curved shapes for the front legs. Notice that the feet drop under the baseline. Attach the shapes for the two rear legs and sit the feet on the line. Draw a thick neck shape on the right side of the body and an egg-shaped head. Don't forget a point for the nose.

Step 2

Focus on the outline of the form. Smooth and define the outline using curved line work. With a clean eraser, rub out any unnecessary line work inside the body.

Step 3

Sketch a shape for the nose and curved lines for the mouth and eye. Add an ear shape behind the eye. Draw line work to show the toes. If you haven't already, erase the baseline.

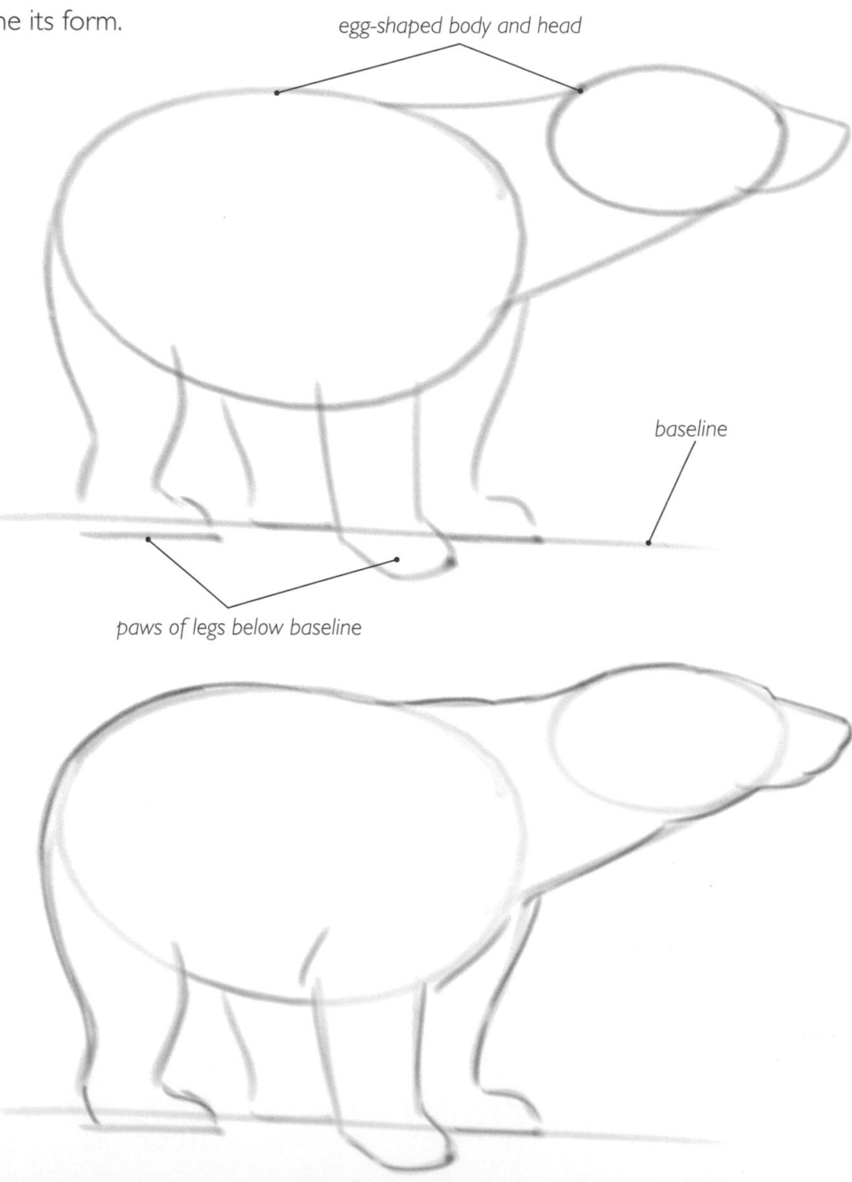

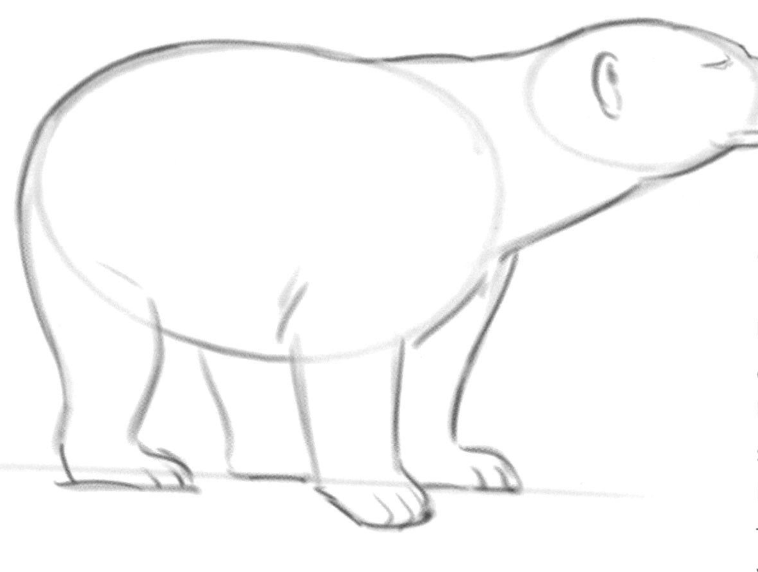

Step 4

Use darker line work at this stage. Before you draw over the outline, study how it has been drawn. Using the side edge of your pencil, lightly draw a series of lines to make the texture of the fur. Darken the line work underneath the belly and feet to create a shadow. Pay attention to the fine line work around the face. Colour in the nose.

Softly sketch in the line work for the ice and the water. Your polar bear is now waiting to catch an unsuspecting seal!

DRAWING TIP

You explore line work all the time in drawing. Make a page of line work experiments to help improve your skills. Practise your pencil technique by changing the pressure you exert on your pencil. Draw many little lines together and sketch different types of line. Use the point of your pencil or the side.

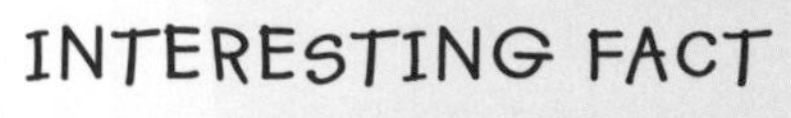

Each hair of a polar bear's fur is a clear hollow tube that channels the heat of the sun to keep them warm.

TREASURE CHEST

Treasure is a favourite subject in pirate stories! Throughout history, ships have sunk during wild storms carrying treasure, which is lost to the seas. Chests would be filled with gold, silver, ivory and expensive jewels. Who knows how many treasure chests are still sitting at the bottom of the ocean, waiting to be discovered by treasure hunters?

Before you begin

The treasure chest is a three-dimensional form, which means that the sides of the chest can be seen from different viewpoints as a whole. To draw the chest correctly, study each step carefully before you begin. Observe the line work, shapes and details used to construct the treasure chest.

Step 1

Begin by drawing a three-dimensional box for the bottom of the chest. Draw the front rectangle of the box first, then the sides, paying attention to the angle they sit at. Add a flat rectangle shape leaning to the right for the inside of the box. Draw a squashed rectangle leaning to the left for the inside of the lid and the edge that runs across the lid. Sketch the curved sides of the lid and draw a line for the top of the chest.

Step 2

Draw a smaller rectangle inside the front of the chest. Add three squares inside the rectangle with gaps between them. Notice that they don't fit perfectly at the bottom. Draw a rectangle inside the chest, just in from the edges. Draw the line work inside the lid and two shapes on the side of the chest. Add the curved shapes that run over the back of the lid and a square in the middle of the edge for the latch.

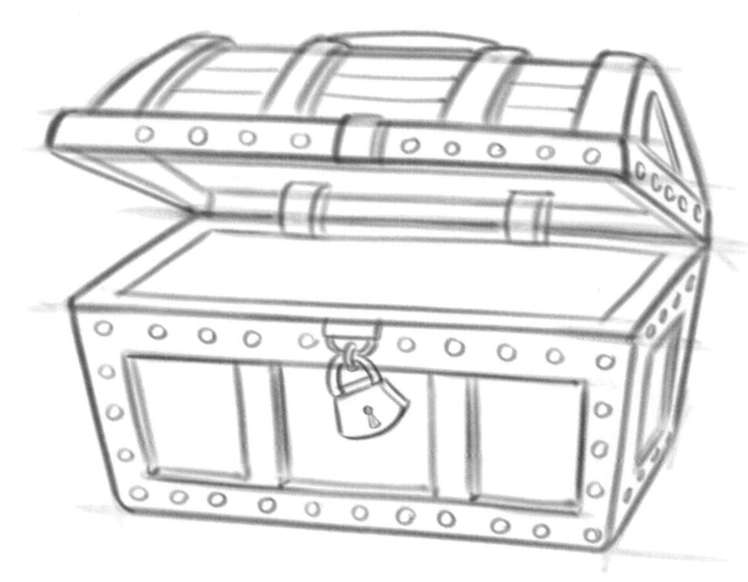

Step 3

Draw the padlock. Add the handle on the lid and line work for the wood pattern. Draw hinges inside the chest and add a pattern for the studs on the outside edges.

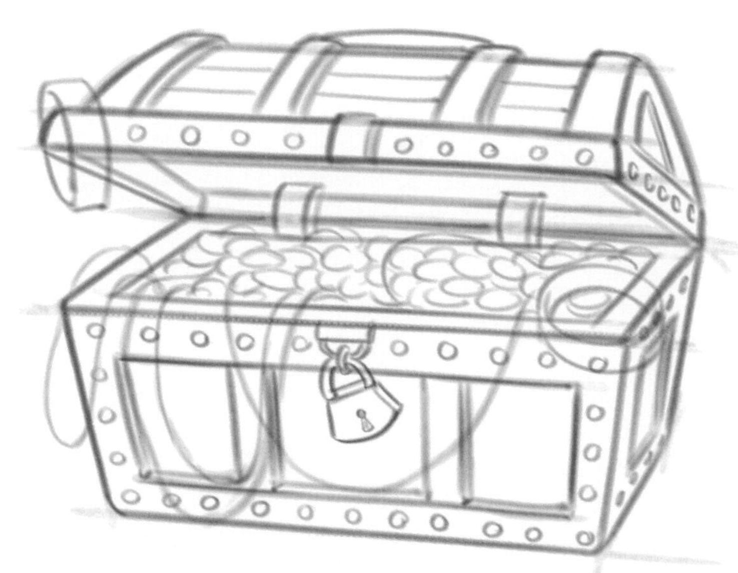

Step 4

Draw line work for the loops of pearls and shapes for the bracelets over the corners of the box. Sketch oval shapes for the gold coins, ensuring they are connected to each another.

Be confident and patient when drawing detailed pictures. Don't worry if your picture isn't perfect first go. Your skills will improve with practice.

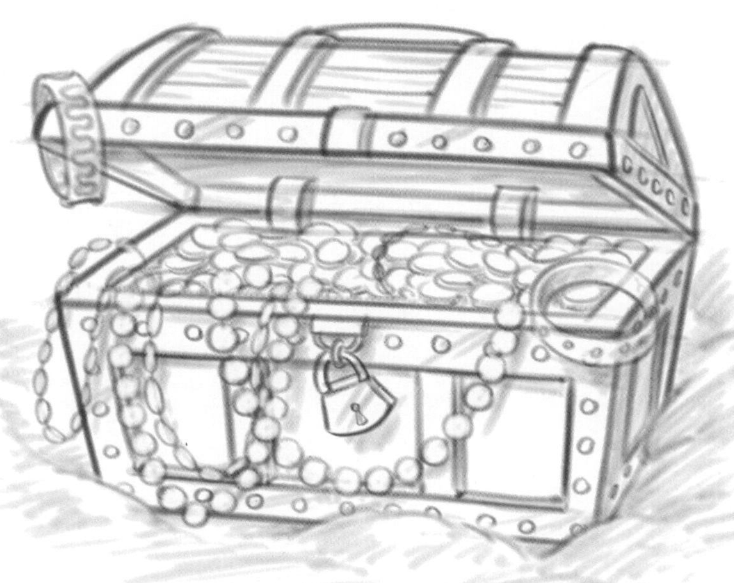

Step 5

Draw circles and squashed oval shapes for the loops of pearls. Add details to the edges of the coins and decorate the bracelets. Sketch in any other necessary details or shading.

Lightly draw sand overlapping the edges of the treasure chest. Your pirate treasure is ready, waiting to be discovered!

INTERESTING FACT → It is thought that over two thousand ships sank off the coast of Florida (in the USA) between 1600 and 1900. Only a small number of these shipwrecks have been found.

TURTLE

Turtles are one of the oldest reptile groups living today, having existed for around 200 million years. The biggest of all turtles is the leatherback sea turtle. It can weigh over 900 kilograms and reach 2 metres in length. Turtles mainly live in water, although the female turtle comes ashore to lay her eggs.

Before you begin

In this drawing, you will explore the art elements of shape and pattern. Shape helps to construct the turtle's form (its whole shape) and pattern creates its distinctive markings. Pay attention to the peanut-shaped shell, the curved flippers that make the turtle look like it is swimming and the line work that creates the patterns on the shell and body.

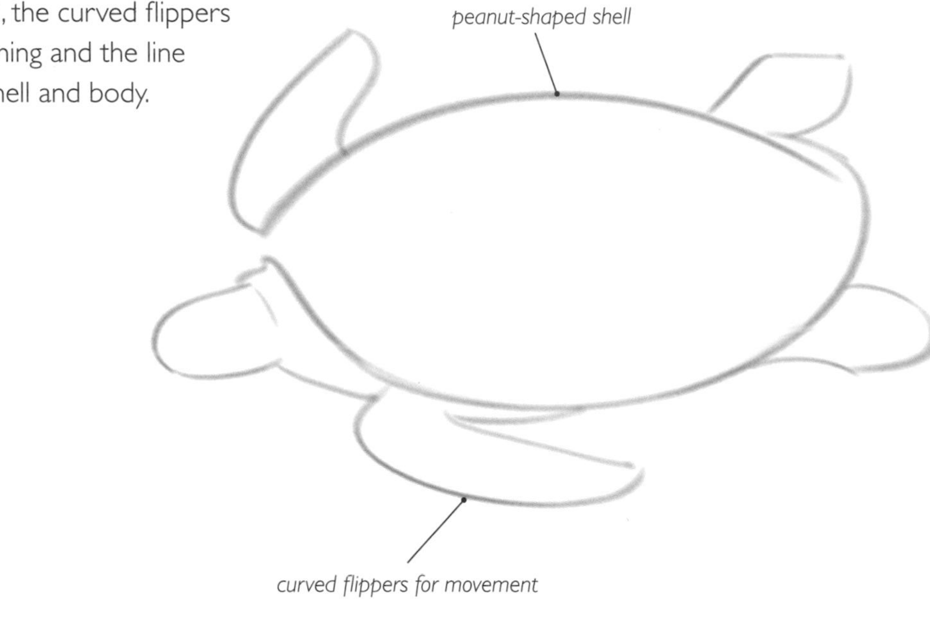

Step 1

Draw a peanut-shaped shell. Add rounded line work to create the shape of the head and the curved flipper shapes just below the head, paying attention to the direction they point in. Draw paddle shapes for the back flippers.

Step 2

Define the shape, using darker line work. Draw crinkly edges for the back of the shell and the bottom of the flippers. Include wavy details on the inside of the shell and circular shapes for the eye. Add curved lines for the neck and mouth.

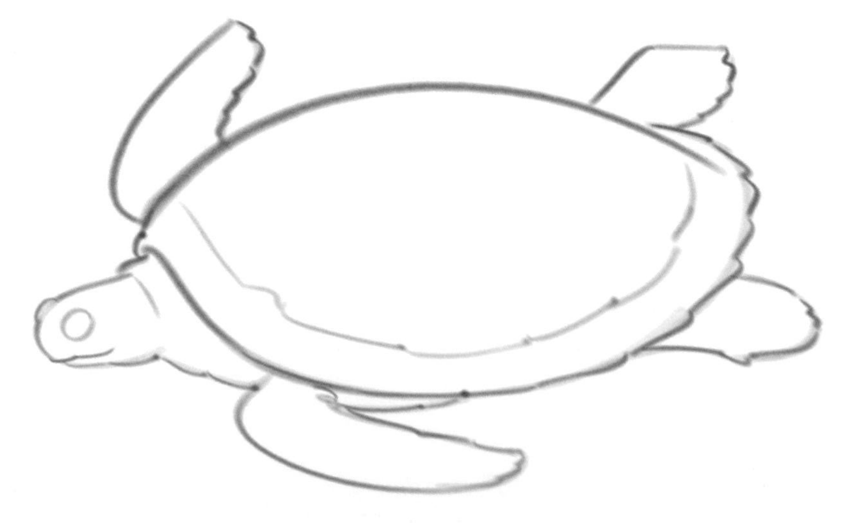

Step 3

Take care when drawing the pattern on the shell, as the shapes in the pattern are small at the top and larger towards the bottom. Draw vertical lines at the bottom of the shell first and then connect the rest of the pattern. Add details to the eye and any other necessary marks.

Step 4

Lightly draw a wrinkly line pattern on the flippers. In a circular motion, shade in spots on the head. Add a medium grey tone to the flippers and under and around the face and neck. Add a light tone around the edges of the shell and soft line patterns running across the surface of the shell.

Using the side of your pencil, create soft wavy lines for the water details and sketch in the bubbles. Your turtle is now gliding through a slipstream, having an awesome time!

DRAWING TIP

Find a place to sit and draw with a good amount of natural light. This will help you see the details of your artwork more clearly.

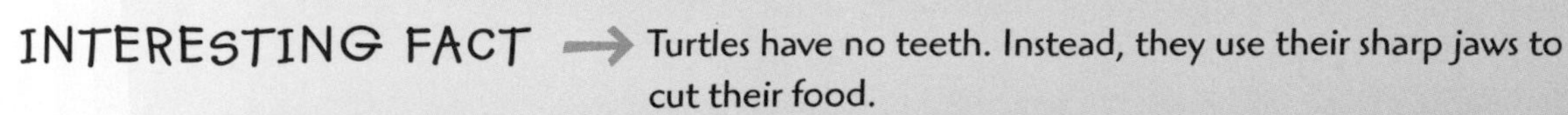

INTERESTING FACT → Turtles have no teeth. Instead, they use their sharp jaws to cut their food.

SEAHORSE

Seahorses' attractive curly tail and horse-like snout make them popular among marine lovers. Seahorses use their tails to anchor themselves to seaweed. The male and female court each other to secure their bond as a pair. The female lays her eggs in the male's pouch, who carries them until they hatch.

Before you begin

To draw the seahorse's unusual form, you will use art elements such as line, shape and pattern. The line work you use will give a sense of movement to your seahorse. Be aware of the circular shapes that make up the head and tail and the sweeping curved line work used for the body, fins and tail. Note the pointy shapes running down the backbone and the decorative line work used for the pattern on the body.

DRAWING TIP

You can see lots of different patterns in a marine environment. Exploring different types of line and shape, create a page of patterns that you imagine you would see underwater.

Step 1

Draw lightly at first. Sketch a circle for the head and draw a wavy line for the backbone and another for the chest. Attach a circle to the body for the end of the tail. Add the shapes for the fins and the snout.

Step 2

Define the outside shape of the body using darker pencil work. Focus on the curly line work for the tail, using the circle shape to guide you. Add a flame shape for the mane and points for the beard. Draw a curved line through the middle of the body and a circle for the eye.

Step 3

Create the pattern that decorates the body, tail and fins and add a wavy line to the back fin. Define the face by adding another circle inside the eye and extra line work for the face.

Step 4

Add shading to your seahorse. Draw extra line work to enhance the pattern on the body and shade the visible parts of the body using a mid-grey pencil tone. Pay attention to the detail of the eye and the pointy shapes running down the back and tail.

When drawing the background, notice that the plant is larger than the seahorse. Start by drawing the outside shape of the plant. Sketch the branches, making them darker. Add furry marks to the outside shape of the plant and line work to decorate the leaves. Your seahorse is now gliding gently through the ocean, looking for a mate!

INTERESTING FACT → Seahorses have been used as a form of medicine in some Asian cultures for over 500 years!

CLOWNFISH

Clownfish were named because of their bright black, white and brilliant red colour. They live in harmony with sea anemones and are the only fish that can swim among their tentacles without being stung. The clownfish attracts other fish for the sea anemone to eat by using its bright colours. Clownfish usually live in pairs among the safety of a sea anemone.

Before you begin

Shape is an art element that helps to construct a picture. To create the form of the clownfish, pay close attention to the shapes that are used. Notice that the body of the fish is a basic oval. Most of the fins are bumpy, rounded shapes and there are two fan-shaped fins underneath him.

Step 1

Using light pencil work, draw an oval-shaped body on an angle. Next, add an ear shape for the fin in the middle of the oval. Draw bumpy-top fins and tail. Add two fan-shaped fins underneath, drawing the front one first.

Step 2

Define the fish's outline using jagged line work. Draw a curved line for the mouth and a circle for the eye. Don't forget the bumps for the eyelids.

Step 3

Darken the clownfish's outline. Draw curved stripes that wrap around the body. Add a dark tone to the eye and an outline for the lips. Add a stripey pattern to the fins.

Step 4

Add shading for the form. Start by adding a dark tone around the tips of the fins. Notice that the stripes are crinkly on the edges. Shade a soft grey tone to the underside of the tail and belly and to the front of the face. Add faint grey tones to the pattern inside the fins and darken the outline of the whole body.

Now you can draw the sea anemone. Softly sketch the furry curved base. Draw the bottom tentacles and work your way up to the top ones. Add in the shading and erase any part of the clownfish that shouldn't be visible. Your clownfish is looking for a mate, so maybe you can draw another fish in the background!

DRAWING TIP

Pencil can smudge easily. Watch where your hand is on the page and make sure that it is not rubbing across your drawing.

INTERESTING FACT → Clownfish are known for living in pairs. If the female dies, the male clownfish can change into a female!

CONCH SHELL

Conches are shelled animals that live on the sea bed in warm climates. Their shells have many uses. They can be made into jewellery or used for decoration and can also be used as an ingredient in porcelain. In the Pacific islands and Asia, they are made into instruments by removing the end to create a mouthpiece. They are said to be the musical instrument of mermaids!

Before you begin

The most important element of this drawing is the unusual shape. Carefully observe the pattern and shading, as this gives the shell its form and definition. Be aware of the ice cream cone and ear shapes that start the drawing, the wavy outline of the shell and the pattern and graduated shading on the shell's surface.

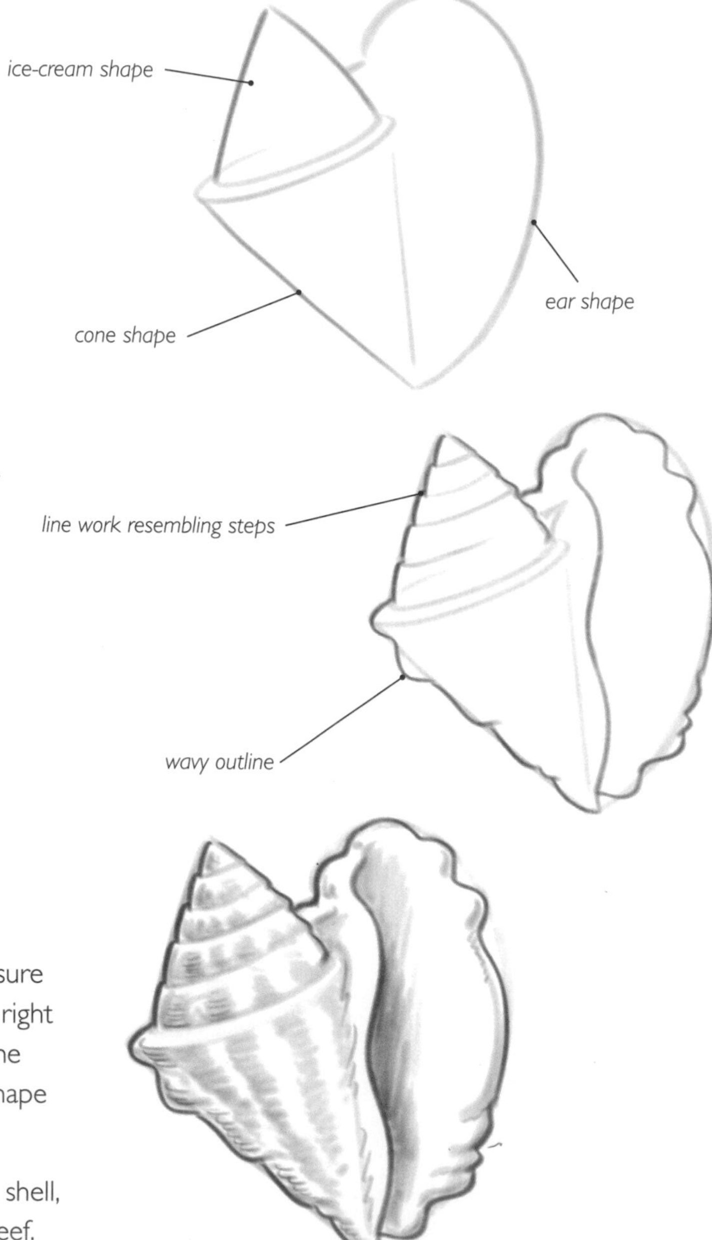

Step 1

Draw a cone shape for the bottom of the shell. Add an ice cream-shaped triangle to the cone. Attach an ear shape to the right side.

Step 2

Define and darken the conch shell's outline. Begin with the top point of the shell (the ice cream shape). Notice that the line work on this part looks like steps. Create a wavy outline around the cone and ear shapes.

Step 3

The pattern on the shell is made up of a series of lines. Ensure they are darker on the left side and get lighter around the right side of the ice cream shape. The pattern also goes down the cone shape in stripes. Add a darker shade inside the ear shape and a lighter shade to the edges.

Now you have completed both the starfish and the conch shell, you will be able to sketch them in a drawing of the coral reef.

INTERESTING FACT → In some cultures, the animal that lives inside a conch shell is eaten raw, or cooked and made into salads or burgers.

STARFISH

Starfish (also known as sea stars) can be found in a wide array of colours, ranging from red through to violet. They are covered in decorative patterns made up of stripes and spots. Starfish move at a very slow pace. Their eyespots are found at the end of each arm and their mouth is underneath the centre of their body. Starfish eat oysters, mussels and clams and digest their food in two stomachs.

Before you begin

The following drawing of a starfish will focus on shape and pattern. Your starfish is built around a series of basic shapes and construction lines. Notice that the centre circle of the starfish is a little squashed and that the starfish is on a slight angle. The construction lines form the direction of the starfish's pattern.

Step 1

Draw a circle to help construct the starfish's shape and a rounded triangle for the top arm. Follow with the top left and right arms, ensuring they are in line with each other. Add the bottom two arms.

Step 2

Lightly sketch the construction lines, starting with a large circle in the centre. Add a smaller circle inside it. Draw the lines that travel out through the middle of the arms. Darken and define the outline.

Step 3

Add the bumps that run around the outside shape of the starfish. Then add circles of bumps in the middle and any other details over the rest of the construction lines. Draw any other necessary bumps and the soft shading.

INTERESTING FACT → When some starfish lose an arm, they are able to grow it back!

Costumes & fashions

Funky Things to Draw

Costumes & Fashions

INTRODUCTION

Fashion, with its ever-changing face, has played an important role in culture for centuries. Fashion has been influenced by art, music, technology, movies, war and the social attitudes of the time. Many eras or cultures have a specific look that is instantly recognisable.

Throughout the ages, fashionable outfits, haircuts and shoes have inspired people to dress differently. To get into the drawing mood, imagine yourself wearing these looks. Visualise yourself with an afro hairdo, flares and platform shoes. Picture yourself as a Hollywood starlet wearing a glamorous gown, walking down the red carpet. Imagine you're wearing an Indian sari and dancing to Hindi music.

THINGS YOU WILL NEED

- An HB or 2B pencil (they are light and won't smudge too easily)
- A pencil sharpener and a small dish for shavings
- A4 cartridge paper or copy paper and some scrap paper for experiments
- A clean eraser
- Confidence: a positive attitude will help improve your skills
- Imagination: don't be afraid to explore your own style or ideas

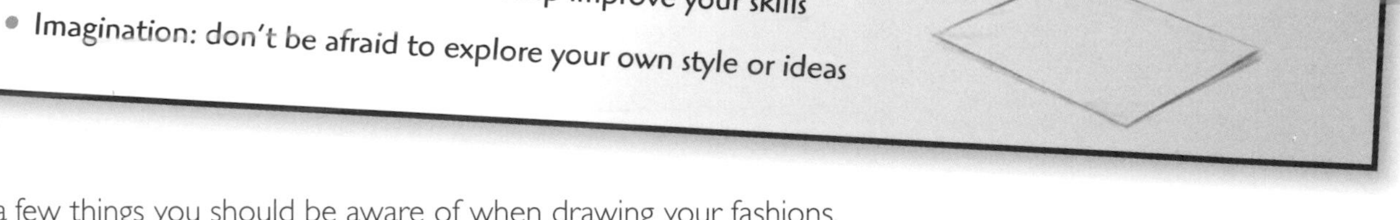

There are a few things you should be aware of when drawing your fashions.

1 All characters are built around a skeleton, which is made up of a series of lines, shapes and joints and a backbone. Draw the form of the body around the skeleton.
2 Begin by lightly drawing the structure of the subject, otherwise it will be obvious in the final drawing. Where possible, rub out any unnecessary line work with a clean eraser as you go.
3 When sketching the human form of each character, ensure you draw the skeleton to the right size and length, so the body is in the correct proportions.
4 Pay close attention to the angle and positioning of the body parts and where the cross that indicates the position of the face is on the head. This will ensure the drawing is in the correct pose.
5 Different types of line are used to create the curved outline of a subject, the folds of clothing, the patterns of fabric and the texture of hair.

Stages of drawing

People can be difficult to draw. However, it becomes easier if you build the shape of the human form around an initial structure. This structure is called a skeleton. Read the steps carefully before you begin so you understand what is needed to create the right body shape and the correct pose of a character.

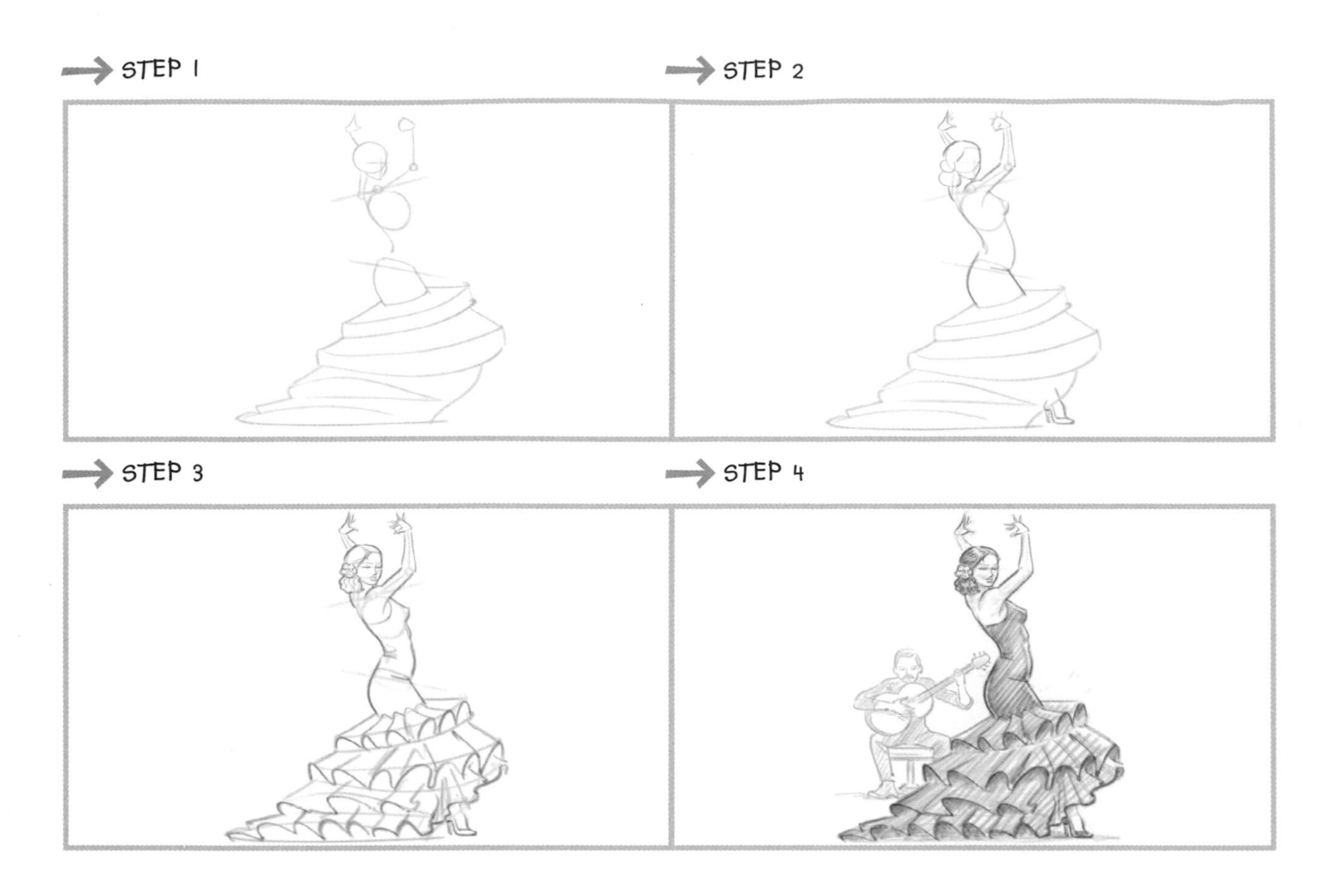

When drawing the human form or clothing, you will notice that they are made up of different types of line. What kinds of curved, wavy or straight lines are used to create the body of a subject? How is line used to decorate or add definition to clothing? Shading technique highlights a character's form and clothing. What level of shading (such as a light, medium or dark tone) is applied and where?

Skills and techniques

Here are some examples of the different techniques and art elements you will learn about.

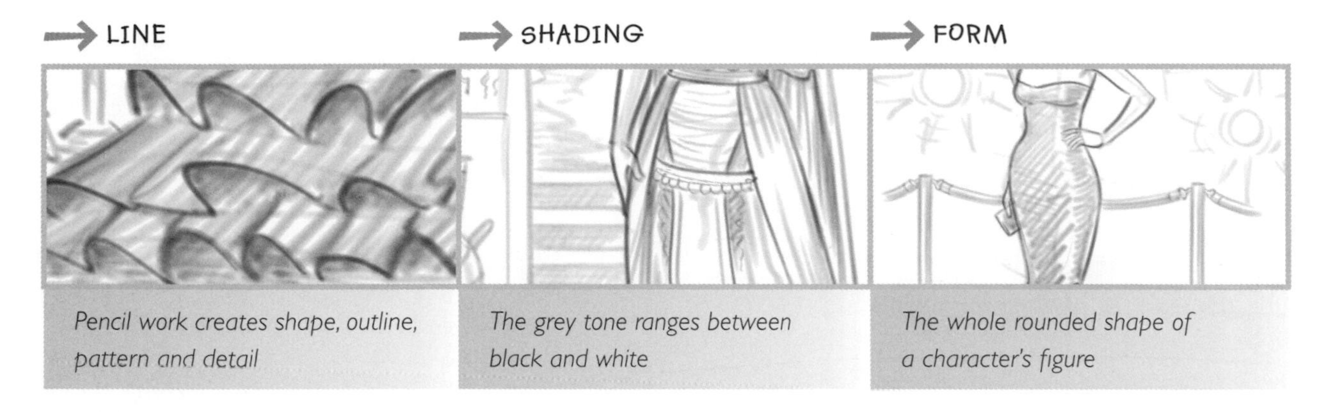

Pencil work creates shape, outline, pattern and detail

The grey tone ranges between black and white

The whole rounded shape of a character's figure

Fashion designers sketch images of people wearing their clothing designs before they have them sewn. They develop their design style over time by drawing with different pencil techniques and flourishes. Be confident about experimenting so you develop your own style!

ANCIENT EGYPTIAN

In Ancient Egyptian times, fashion was as important as it is today. Egyptians developed their own unique style. Sheep wool wigs were worn to parties and women dressed in linen ankle-length dresses with straps that tied at the neck. Jewellery was made from silver or gold. Rich women wore heavily bejewelled collars called wesekh. Women tinted their lips and cheeks with red ochre and lined their eyes and brows with black kohl using a fine reed.

Before you begin

This drawing is created around a skirt shape for the bottom half of the body and a skeleton for the top half. Large and small ovals are used to create the form of the skirt. Carefully observe the way line work, shape and pattern decorate the figure and the background.

Step 1

Lightly draw a large, slightly angled oval that tapers in at one end. Draw a small oval a leg length above it, adding the sides of the skirt. Add a backbone, a circle for the head, a chin pointing down and a cross facing left. Draw a circle for the chest with shoulders running across. Sketch the left arm hanging down and the right arm across the backbone. Add the joints and hand shapes.

Step 2

Build the shape of the body around the skeleton. Define the face and neck and create the shape of the hair around the head. Working down the body, draw the outline of the shoulders, create the shape of the chest and arms, and sketch a waistband.

Step 3

Define, smooth and darken the outline. Starting at the head, draw a headband and medallion, earring shapes and a lock of hair. Draw eyes looking down on either side of the cross, a nose and mouth. Add a curved choker, a pendant and the curves of the wesekh collar and armholes. Create an open hand with a stone in it. Add two vertical folds from the waistband. Draw the wavy hem and the folds around the bottom oval.

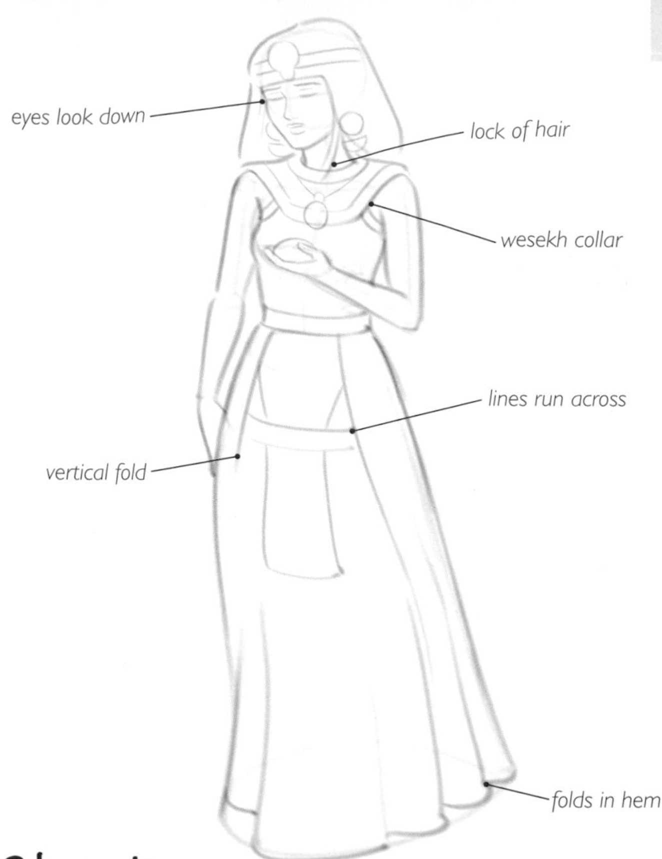

Step 4

Study the levels of shading over the whole figure. Add fine details to the medallion, earrings, choker and pendant. Draw a snake armband and add patterns to the skirt. Sketch a cloak over the shoulders. Using soft line work, create the texture of the hair and add folds to chest, skirt and cloak. Shade a medium grey tone over the hair, collar and waistband, and inside the cloak, using light pencil pressure. Apply lighter shading over the body and folds of the skirt. Darken the facial features and the stone.

Draw the outline of the arch around the woman and then the stairs. Once you add the hieroglyphs to the arch, the pyramids and the urn, your Egyptian will be ready for her party!

DRAWING TIP

If you want to add colour to your artwork, use coloured pencil, as markers will cause a shaded pencil drawing to smudge.

INTERESTING FACT

Ancient Egyptian women applied perfumed oil made from wood, flowers and oil or fat. The perfume was used to prevent the skin from drying out.

GEISHA

Geisha are traditional Japanese hostesses who dance, play music and perform the traditional tea ceremony. Geisha wear an elaborate kimono with an obi sash around the waist. They apply white make-up to their face and red lipstick to their lower lip so it looks like a flower bud. Geisha put great effort into maintaining their silky hair, even sleeping on a special pillow to keep it in good condition. Geisha must show charm, beauty, grace and artistic talent.

Before you begin

The geisha is constructed using a series of shapes. The triangular shape of the kimono is angled at the bottom. Start at the shoulders and draw the whole outline first. There are many folds and details added to the kimono, so carefully study the changes between each step and observe how the patterns and shading are applied.

Step 1

Lightly draw an oval for the face with a rounded shape around the head for the hair. Add a cross on the face and a neck. Draw the outline of the shoulders, chest and arms. Sketch a collar crossing over to the left and hands meeting at the front. Add the outside triangular skirt of the kimono, the triangular opening and the angled outline of the bottom, with a fabric train trailing behind.

Step 2

Define and smooth the outline. Create the curved details for the hair. Draw the obi around the waist, with fabric folds over the collar and a piece of fabric hanging down the back. Add a rectangular line of fabric under the hand, define the folds hanging inside the opening of the kimono.

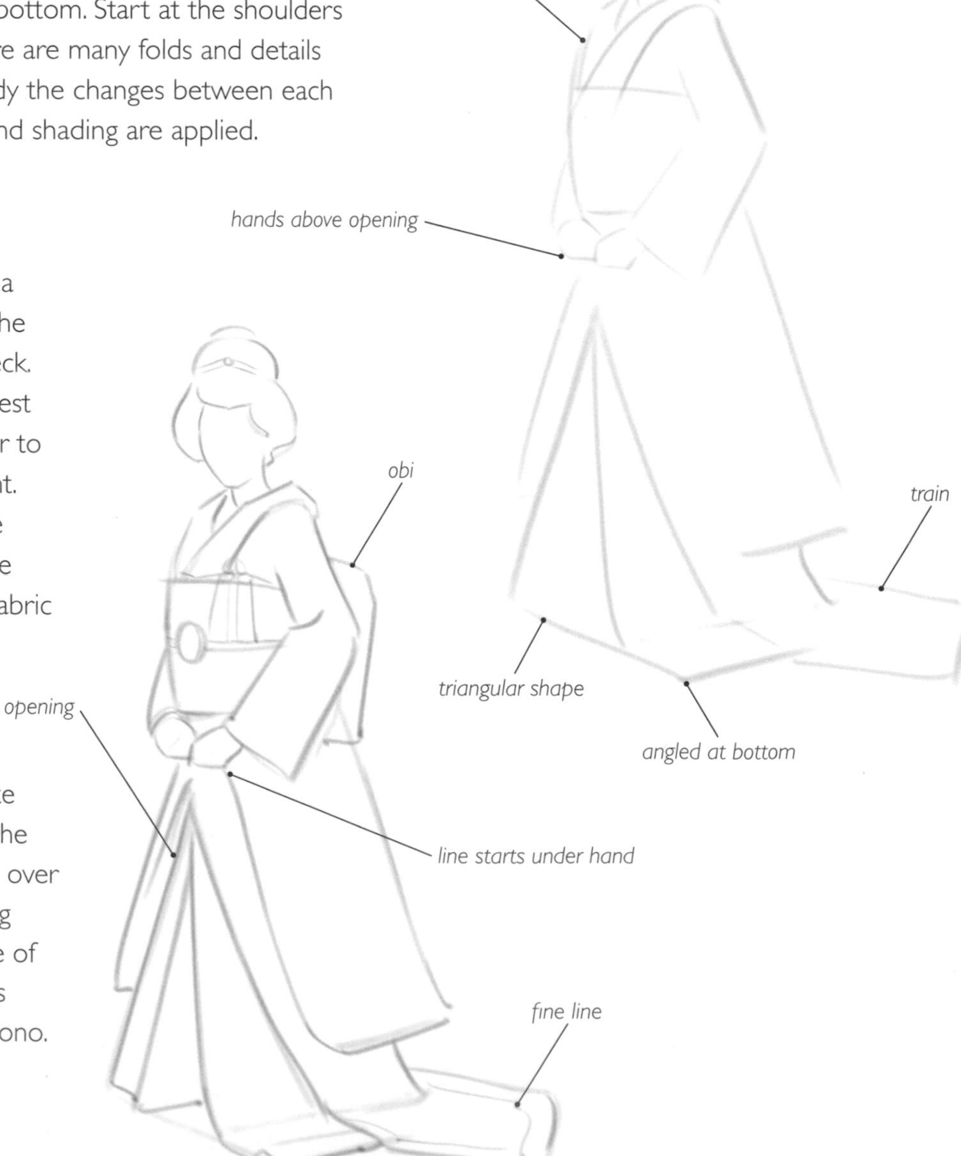

Step 3

Draw eyes on either side of the cross, a nose and a mouth. Add circular details for the headpiece, decorative elements over the chest and lines for fingers. Define the folds of the sleeve and skirt.

DRAWING TIP

Practice makes perfect. Some subjects will be harder to draw than others, but be confident and know that your skills will improve with time.

Step 4

Add a soft cherry blossom pattern to the kimono and lines for the texture of the hair. Create the fine details of the headpiece and brooch and develop the facial features. Study the level of shading over the figure. Apply an open mid-grey tone over the kimono and darken the shading of the hair and the folds of the fabric. Apply soft, lighter shading to the obi and the underskirt.

Faintly draw the horizontal lines of the mat above the train. Once you draw the vertical lines of the screen and add checked panels, your geisha will be ready to perform!

INTERESTING FACT

Because a kimono is difficult to put on, geisha have their own dressers to fold and wrap the layers of fabric around them.

INDIAN SARI

The Indian sari is thousands of years old and is still worn today by many Indian women. The sari is made without a single stitch. It consists of several metres of fabric loosely wrapped, tied, folded and pleated around the body with great skill. Saris are often made from colourful and luxurious fabrics embellished with fine embroidered details and metallic thread. There are several different ways to wear a sari, with many regional variations.

Before you begin

This drawing uses an hourglass shape and a skeleton for the top half of the body. The hourglass-shaped skirt curves in at the bottom. Observe the way the skeleton sits on top of the hourglass. Also, line and pattern are important art elements explored in this drawing. Carefully study the types of line and pattern used to decorate the sari.

Step 1

Lightly draw a baseline with an oval a leg length above it. Add the curves of the hourglass shape, dipping it below the baseline. Draw a backbone on top of the oval, adding a square chin and a circle for the head. Sketch a circle under the chin for the chest, with shoulders running across. Add a bent left arm leaning on the hips and a right arm bending outward.

Step 2

Build the curvy figure around the skeleton. Define the face and neck, and draw the shape of the hair around the head. Sketch the shoulders, the left side of the body and the arm. Develop the outside line of the right arm and add a line to create the triangular piece of sari. Lightly define the right side of the body. With a clean eraser, remove any unnecessary line work.

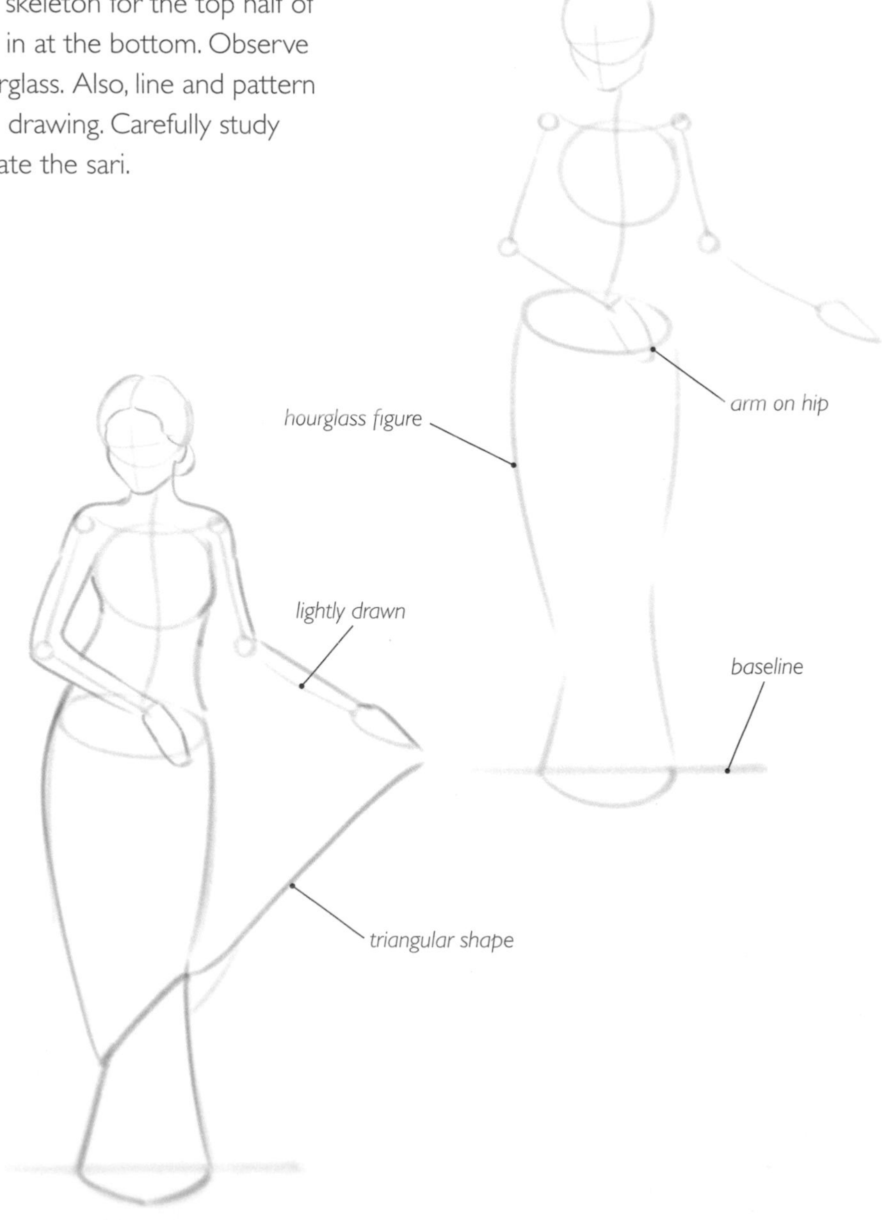

Try designing your own Indian sari fabric. Look up some images on the internet for ideas. Remember that most fabrics have different patterns that repeat.

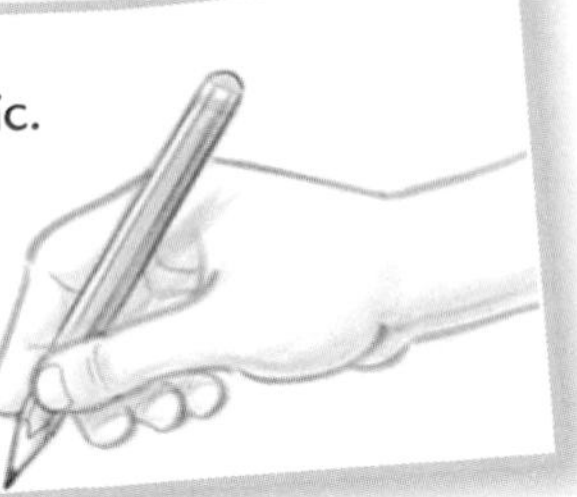

bangles

fabric behind

pleats

Step 3

Define, smooth and darken the line work. Define the outline of the hair, the top and the neckline of the sari and choker. Draw eyes on either side of the cross, a nose, a mouth and leaf-shaped earrings. Add line work to create the band across the neckline and the bottom of the sari. Draw irregular folds over the fabric and open pleats in the underskirt. Add lines for bangles, fingers and the fabric behind.

Step 4

Study the pattern and levels of shading. Draw fine circular patterns over the sari and boxes on the left side. Add a zigzag along the edge of the fabric, tassels and a pattern next to the pleats. Draw the earrings, choker, bangles and fingers. With a light pencil pressure, apply a mid-grey tone over the hair, the top, the boxes on the fabric and the underskirt. Darken and define the facial features and use a soft, lighter tone across the folds of the sari, body and underskirt.

Faintly draw a wavy archway around a straight doorway. Once you add the building at the back, an elephant and the water's edge, the scene will be complete!

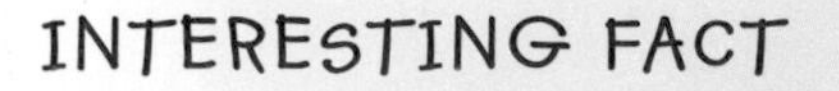

Many women still wear the sari, even when they are working in the fields. They just tie it differently so they can move their arms and legs freely.

1920s FLAPPER

The Roaring Twenties saw a new era of change for women and the birth of the 'flapper'. After the hardship of the First World War, young women sought to be more liberal and outrageous. The trend of the flapper introduced short, bobbed hair and make-up. Flappers attended parties and jazz clubs. They wore straight, open-armed dresses that fell around the knee so it was easier to move when doing dances like the Charleston.

Before you begin

To draw the flapper in the correct pose, position the arms, hands, legs and feet correctly. Using the construction lines as a guide, study how the left leg angles sharply over the right leg. The right thigh is hidden behind the left leg and the top of the right arm sits against the body. Pay attention to how the left hand faces down while the right hand is open. Both shoes are drawn side-on.

Step 1

Lightly draw a baseline and add an oval a leg length above it. Sketch the right leg with a shoe shape on the baseline. Draw the left leg sharply angled over the right knee with a shoe shape facing left. Sketch a backbone through the oval, adding a circle for the head, a chin and a cross looking left. Draw a chest circle under the neck with shoulders across the top. Add a bent right arm with an outstretched hand shape and a bent left arm with a hand shape facing down. Draw the joints.

Step 2

Build the shape of the body around the skeleton. Starting at the head, define the face and neck and add the shape of the hair and hat around the head. Draw the shoulders, arms, dress, front leg and back leg. With a clean eraser, remove any unnecessary line work.

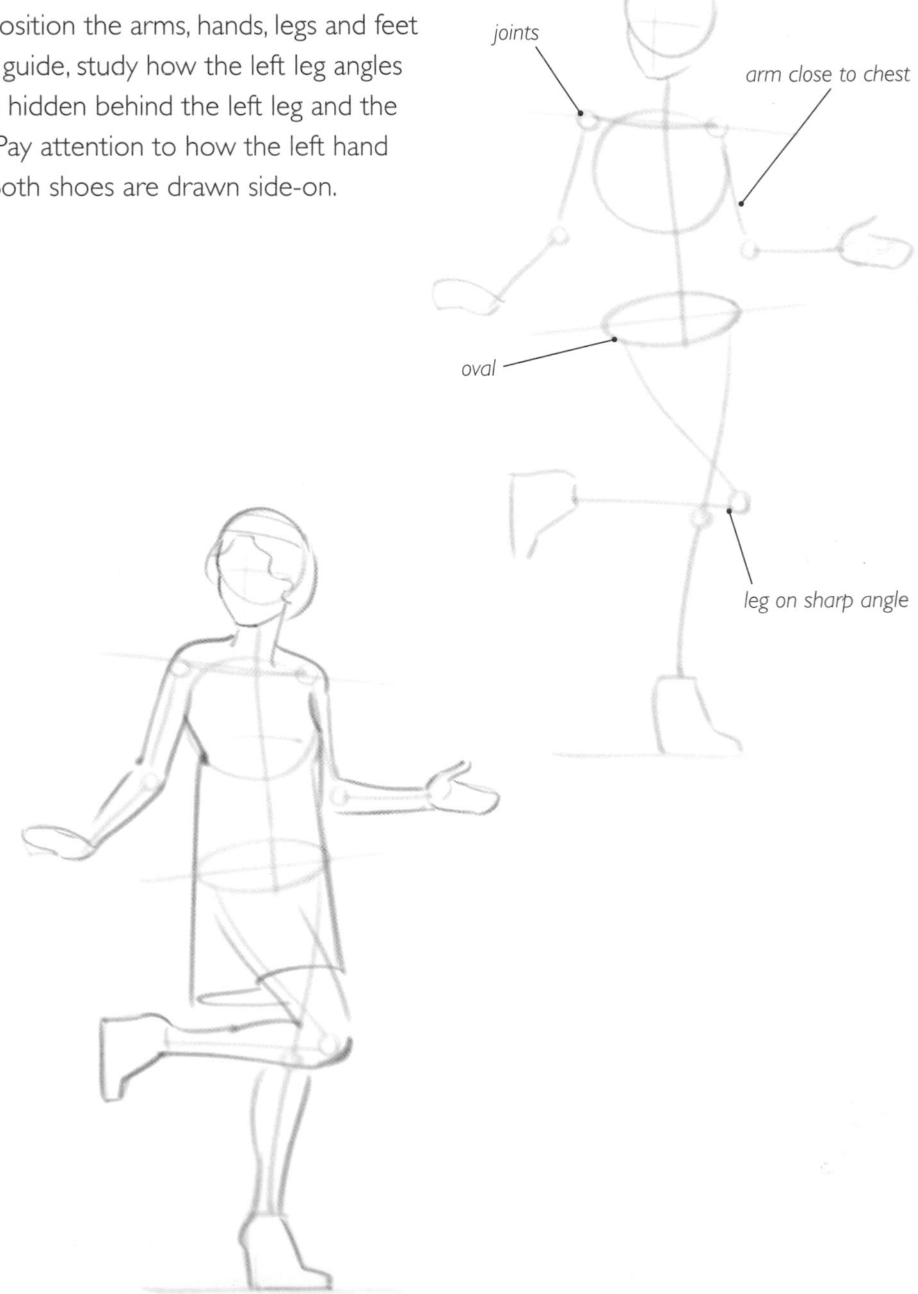

Step 3

Define, smooth and darken the outline. Draw eyes on either side of the cross and add a nose and mouth. Create the curls of the hair, the opening for the neckline and the armholes of the dress. Lightly draw curved lines for the shawl around the shoulders and arms, and add a band around the hem. Develop the shape of the shoes.

DRAWING TIP

Observation is an important tool when following instructions. Carefully study all elements of a drawing before you begin, so you are confident through the process.

Step 4

With a light pencil pressure, apply a mid-grey tone to the wavy texture of the hair, the shoes and the inside the hem. Shade open line work across the dress and gently shade the back leg. Using soft, fine lines, create the shawl's furry texture. Add a criss-cross pattern for the hat and tassels. Develop the facial features and the details around the neckline.

Draw the base of the table in line with the right heel. Add a stand and an oval shape for the tabletop. Once you draw the glassware and shadows on the floor, your flapper will be ready to dance the Charleston!

INTERESTING FACT

It is not known where the word 'flapper' comes from, but the term was known in parts of Britain from as early as 1912, where it meant 'teenage girl'.

1960s MOD

The mod culture developed in the early 1960s in London, but its influence soon spread around the world. Mods wore black outfits or clothes with bold geometric patterns. Fashion was heavily influenced by pop art and areas with boutique designer shops such as Carnaby Street in the London Soho district became popular. The mini skirt was all the rage and haircuts were straight, cropped and severe.

Before you begin

To draw this character in the right pose, pay attention to the angle of the shoulders, hips and knees. Use the construction lines as a guide and observe the length and direction of the body parts. The left side of the body is slightly bent, while the right side is straight. Observe how the right hand leans on the hip and the right leg points out slightly.

Step 1

Lightly draw a baseline, with an angled oval a leg length above it. Add the legs to the oval and add shoe shapes sitting on the baseline. Sketch angled knee joints and a backbone, adding a circle above the backbone for the head, a chin and a cross facing right. Draw a chest circle in the middle of the back with shoulders running across. Add a left arm hanging down and a bent right arm with the hand shape on the hip. Sketch the joints and the left hand.

Step 2

Build the shape of the body around the skeleton. Define the face and neck and add a bobbed hairstyle around the head. Working down the body, sketch the shoulder, neckline and dress. Create the shape of the arms and legs. With a clean eraser, remove any unnecessary line work.

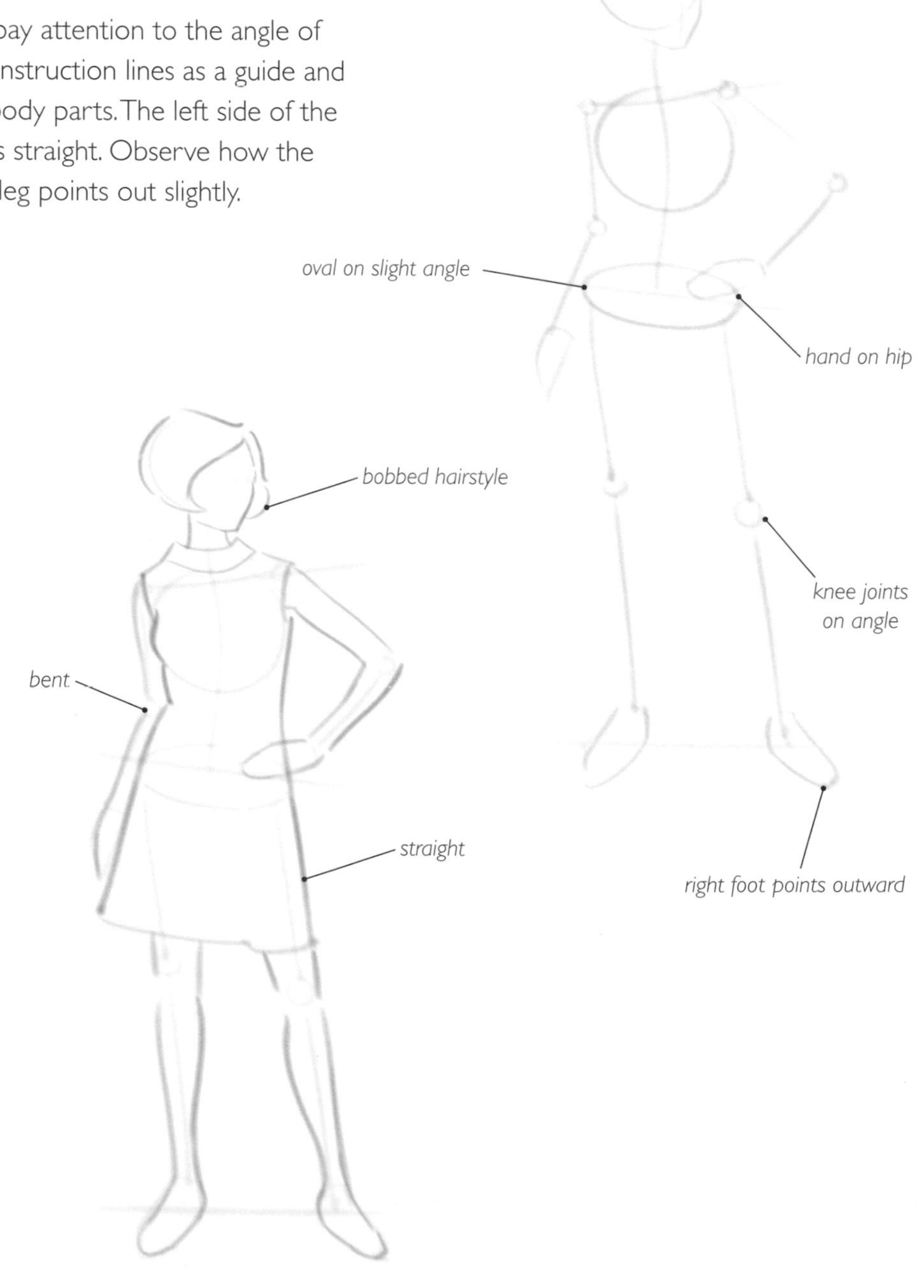

Step 3

Define, smooth and darken the outline. Draw eyes on either side of the cross and a nose and mouth. Add the line work for the fingers, the creases in the clothing and the shoes.

DRAWING TIP

An easy way to remember what 'horizontal' means is to think of the horizon line. A vertical line resembles the mast of a boat.

Step 4

Study the levels of shading over the body. Using a light pressure with your pencil, shade a mid-grey tone over the top and apply soft line work for the hair's texture. Add darker shading to the rectangles on the top and the shoes. Develop the facial features and apply soft, lighter shading to parts of the body, such as the arms and legs.

Draw a faint oval for the base of the chair and add the stand. Add an oval for the seat, the arms and the back of the chair. Draw the base of the wall in the background and then the vertical panel. Once you add horizontal lines to the wall, your mod will be ready to strut her stuff!

INTERESTING FACT

The term 'mod' comes from the word 'modernism'. Mods were known for riding scooters. They often came into conflict with another group: the rockers, who rode motorcycles and wore leather jackets.

1970s DISCO

Following the birth of the hippie era, the 1970s saw major changes in fashion. It became more expressive and carefree, with fashions such as bell-bottom jeans, wide lapelled shirts, platform shoes and, of course, the famous afro hairdo. The disco scene was also developing, which saw dance wear become tighter and more revealing. Clothes were often made of synthetic fabrics such as gold lamé, lycra and spandex.

Before you begin

This drawing is seen from a side-on view. Use the baseline and construction lines as a guide. Pay attention to the positioning and angle of the body parts, especially the curve of the backbone. Note that one arm is hidden behind the body and that the rear leg and foot behind sit higher than the front leg.

Step 1

Lightly draw two parallel baselines a few millimetres apart and an oval a leg length above them. Sketch two shoe shapes on the baselines, making the front one larger. Draw the legs between the shoes and hips, adding knee joints. Add a backbone with the neck curving forward. Sketch a short collarbone below the neck and a circle for the chest. Bend the arm with the hand shape on the hip and add the joints. Draw a circle for the head, a chin pointing down and a cross facing down on the left side of the head.

Step 2

Build the shape of the body around the skeleton. Starting at the head, define the face, neck and the hair's outline. Draw a collar shape, making it smaller behind the neck. Sketch the chest, hips and bottom, followed by the arm and hand. To create the flared jeans, draw the front leg first and then the one behind. Define the shoes.

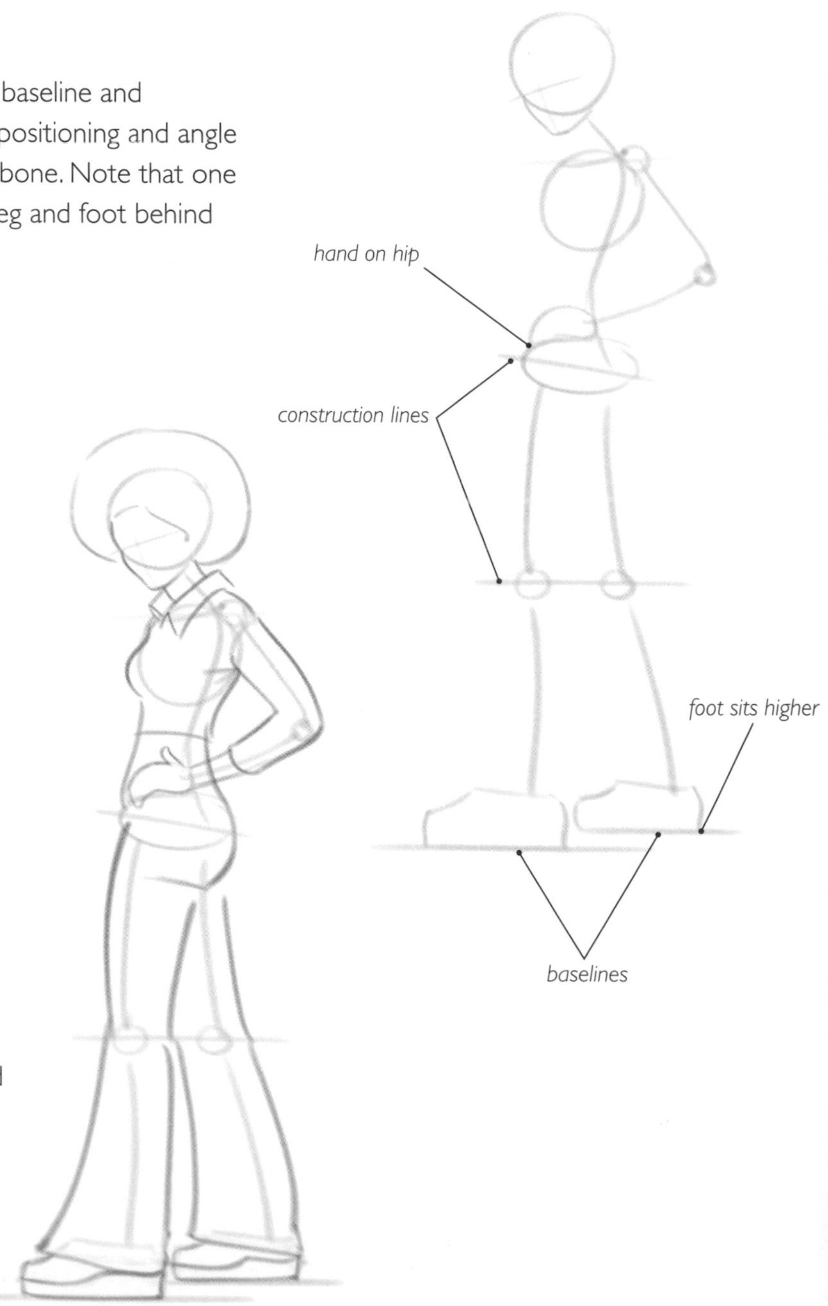

DRAWING TIP

Always begin your picture by drawing lightly so you are able to erase any marks you are unhappy with.

Step 3

Define, darken and smooth the outline. Draw eyes on either side of the cross, making the eye on the far side smaller. Add a nose and mouth, and draw hoop earrings under the afro hairstyle. Define the collar and the folds of the top and draw a knot around the waist. Add fingers, details for the jeans and shoes. With a clean eraser, remove any unnecessary line work.

Step 4

Create the fuzzy outline of the afro. Using a light pressure with your pencil, apply a mid-grey open shading across the hair and shoes. Use soft line work to add a swirly pattern over the shirt and details inside the earrings. Apply a light, open shading to the back of the jeans and highlights to the shirt.

For the background, draw the faint outside shape of the swirly pattern first and then add the details inside. Once you create soft shadows, your 70s girl will be ready to boogie!

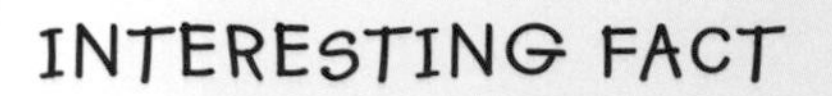

INTERESTING FACT

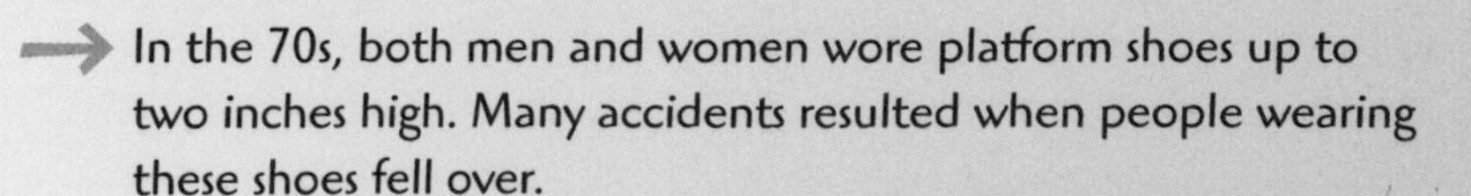

In the 70s, both men and women wore platform shoes up to two inches high. Many accidents resulted when people wearing these shoes fell over.

1980s GIRL

1980s fashion included trends such as large shoulder pads, tight, acid wash jeans, baggy shirts and tops and fluorescent clothing. Other clothing items of the period included lingerie worn as outerwear, leather, spiky hair, pointy heels and fingerless gloves. Pop music made its mark with Madonna and Michael Jackson influencing fashion.

Before you begin

To draw this character in the correct pose, pay attention to the angle of the shoulders, hips, knees and feet. Use the baseline and construction lines as a guide. Observe the placement of the limbs, the direction the head is facing and the positioning of the feet.

Step 1

Lightly draw an angled baseline, a parallel construction line above it and another construction on the opposite angle. Draw a small oval on the oppositely angled construction line. Add the legs, standing apart, and flat-bottomed foot shapes. Sketch knee joints on the same angle as the baseline. Add a backbone, a circle for the chest and shoulders running across on the same angle as the hips. Sketch a circle for the head, a cross for the face and a chin pointing down. Add the right arm reaching up, the left arm bending around to the hips, the joints and the hand shapes.

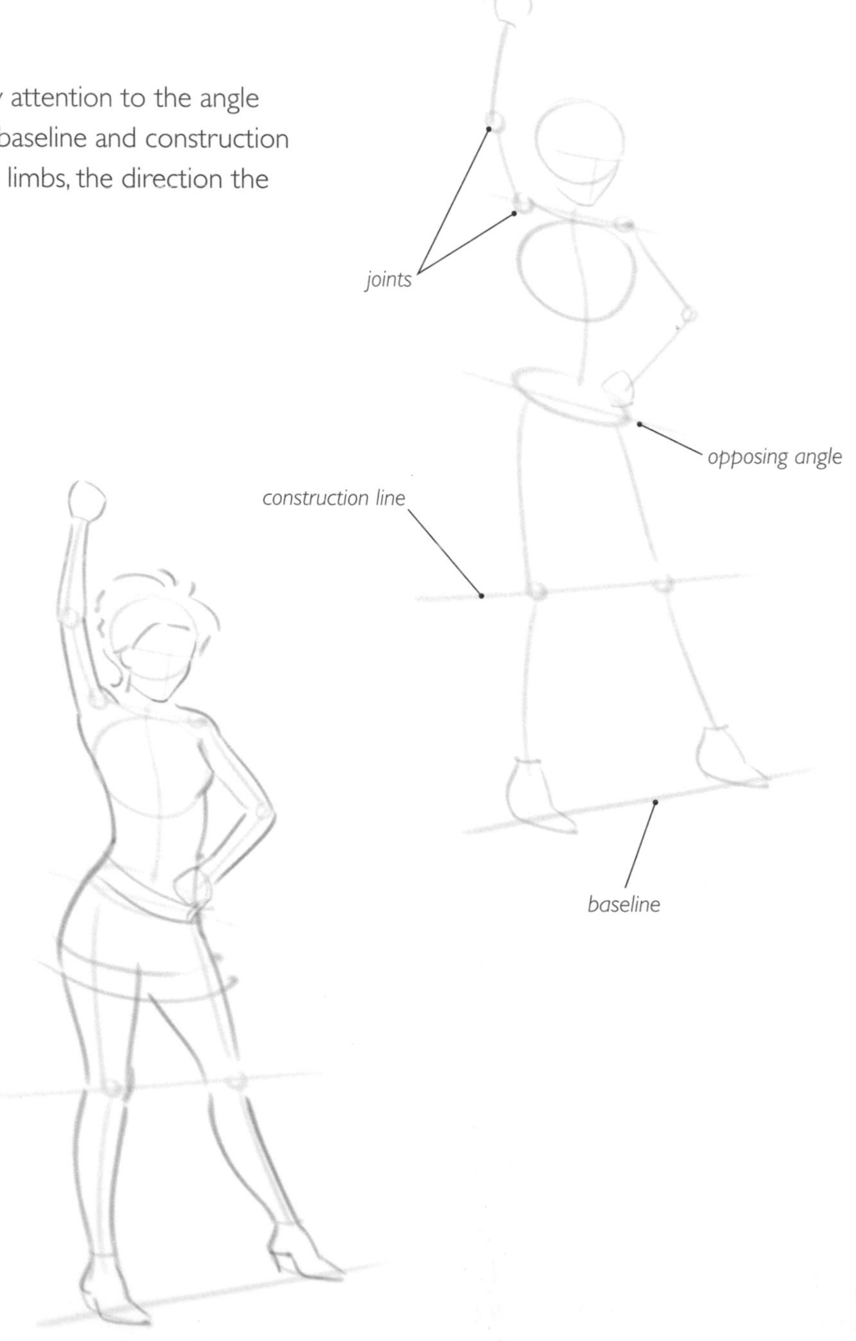

Step 2

Build the shape of the body around the skeleton. Starting at the head, define the face, ear and neck. Add spiky hair around the head. Build the arm, torso and the lines of the miniskirt. Develop the shape of the legs and the shoes.

Step 3

Define, darken and smooth the outline of the body. Draw eyes on either side of the cross, a nose and a mouth. Add line work for the hair, fingers, choker and bangles. Sketch a tank top and add the skirt, stockings, shoes and glove. Define the underarm, elbow and knees. With a clean eraser, remove any unnecessary line work.

DRAWING TIP

Pattern is an art element that adds detail to artwork. It can be drawn using shape and line. Try creating your own page of pattern experiments using coloured markers or pencils.

Step 4

Study the different shading and the patterns over the body. Using a light pressure with your pencil, shade a mid-grey tone across the hair, clothing, jewellery and shoes. Add a belt, a criss-cross pattern over the stockings and a zigzag detail to the skirt. Add a series of lines across the chest area.

For the checked floor, draw the line work in the same direction as the shoes. Once you draw a disco ball, your 80s girl will be ready to dance!

INTERESTING FACT → A popular music and fashion movement in the 80s was called, 'New Romantic', which saw men wearing make-up and frilly shirts, inspired by bands such as Duran Duran, Spandau Ballet and Roxy Music.

PUNK

Punk was a music and fashion movement that emerged during the mid-1970s. It was a result of people rebelling against mainstream culture. Clothing styles made anti-fashion statements, as outfits were bought from charity shops and were often ripped and decorated with pins. Colourful mohawk hairstyles were popular, along with Doc Marten boots, piercings and tattoos. Music was loud and confronting, often making statements about social and political issues.

Before you begin

The punk is drawn in a front-on pose. To draw it correctly, observe the positioning of the square chin, the cross for the face and the way the arms sit alongside the body. Pay attention to how the left leg is slightly angled, with the foot side-on and how the right foot faces the front. Study the shadings and patterns that complete the picture.

Step 1

Lightly draw a baseline and add an oval a leg length above. Sketch boot shapes underneath and over the baseline, with the left pointing out and the right front-on.

Add legs and knee joints. Draw a backbone to the top left of the oval, with a circle for the head, a square chin and a cross facing forward. Sketch a circle in the middle of the back for the chest, with shoulders running across. Draw slightly bent arms leaning on the hips and the arm joints.

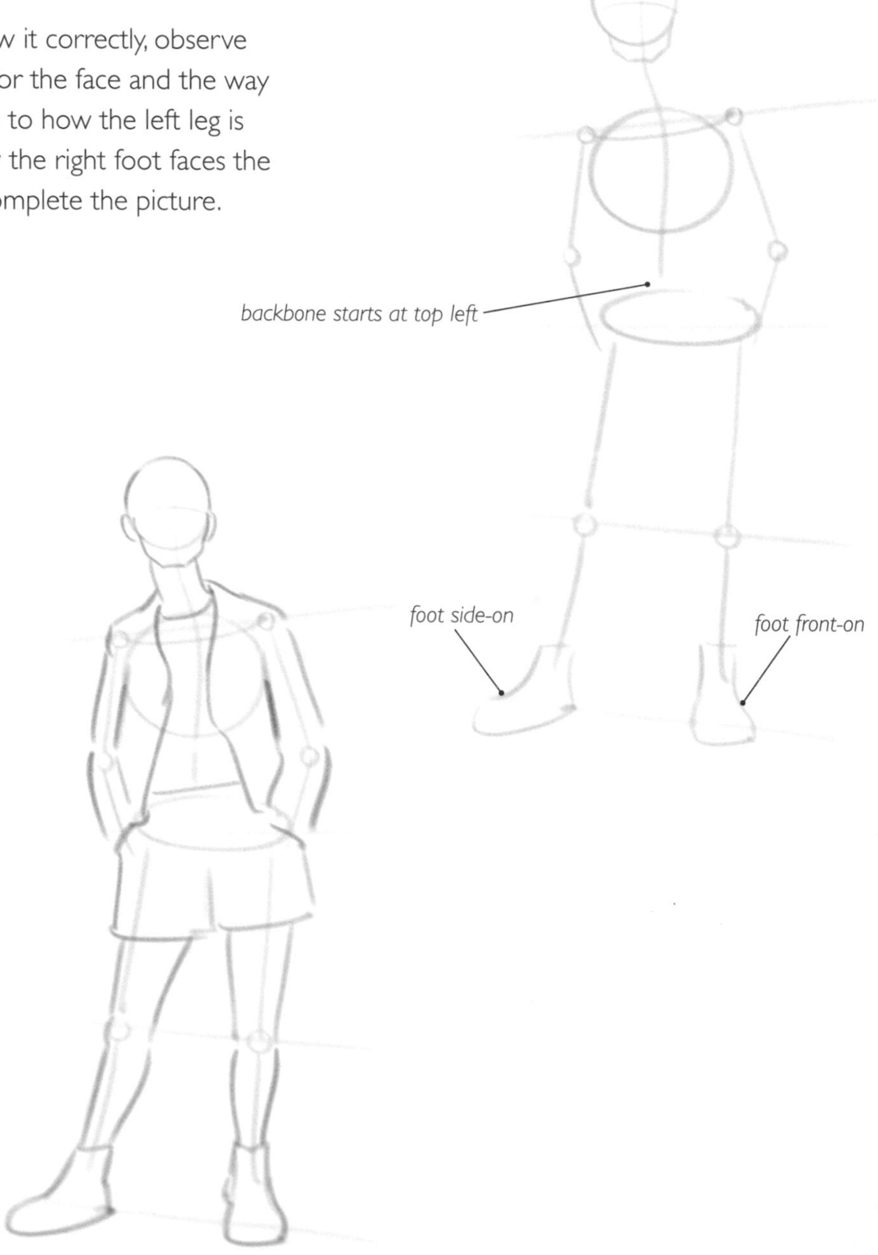

Step 2

Build the shape of the body around the skeleton. Working down from the top, create the shapes of the head, ears and neck. Create the arms, the jacket and lines for the t-shirt. Build the shape of the shorts, the legs and the boots. Remove any unnecessary line work with a clean eraser.

Step 3

Define, smooth and darken the outline. Draw a shape for the mohawk, eyes on either side of the cross, a nose and a mouth. Create the shape of the lapels and develop the curves and folds of the clothing. Add the details for the Doc Marten boots.

DRAWING TIP

Pencil can smudge, so watch where your hand is on the page and check that it is not rubbing across your drawing.

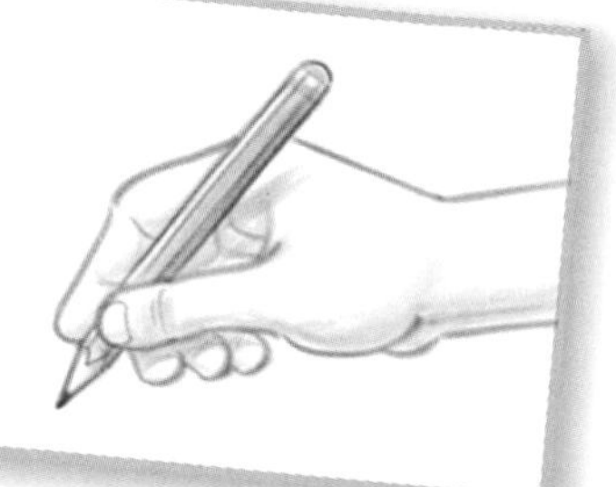

Step 4

Study the shading and the pattern over the picture. Draw an earring, buttons on the jacket, patterns on the t-shirt and fish-net stockings. Develop the facial features and add fine line work for the hair's texture and the laces on the boots. Using a light pencil pressure, apply mid-grey, irregular shading over the jacket and boots. Add soft shading over the rest of the body and clothing.

For the faint background, draw an angled base of a wall and add the bricks. Once you add the spray painting and details on the ground, your punk will be ready to rock!

INTERESTING FACT → The punk motto was 'DIY', which stands for 'do it yourself'.

FLAMENCO

Flamenco dancing and singing is a traditional art form that originated in Andalusia in Southern Spain. Flamenco developed in the 19th century, where it became popular entertainment in cafés. The core element of flamenco is the cante, which is a tragic and profound song with a strong sense of emotion. The dancer accompanies the music with rhythmic finger snapping, hand clapping and shouting; the flamboyant gown helps to emphasise the intensity of the movement.

Before you begin

The most important elements of this drawing are the layered skirt of the gown and the position of the arms. Study the irregular shape of the skirt: it resembles a set of stairs. Observe the curved backbone and how the arms are elevated from the shoulders, with the left arm behind the head. Pay attention to the levels of wavy fabric layered on top of one another like a cake.

Step 1

Lightly draw a baseline. Above it, sketch the hip area of the skirt, shaping it like a sun hat. Add the left side of the skirt, making sure it looks like stairs. Draw the curvy right side of the skirt. Sketch irregular line work to create the layers of the skirt. Draw a backbone curving up from the hips, adding a circle for the head, a chin pointing down and a cross facing right. Add an oval under the chin for the chest. Draw the right arm bending sharply upward, the left arm behind the neck, the joints and the hands.

hip area

shaped like sunhat

looks like stairs

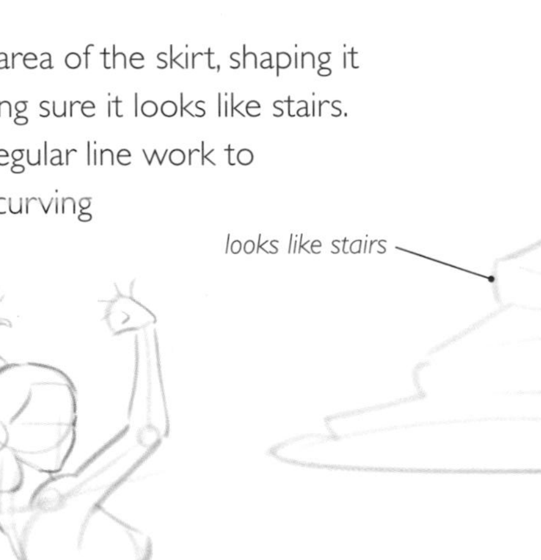

Step 2

Build the shape of the body around the skeleton and skirt. Define the face and create the rounded shapes of the hair. Develop the curve of the back and the shape of the shoulder, arms and hands. Define the chest, torso and hips, and add a shoe pointing right.

curved back

first layer

second layer

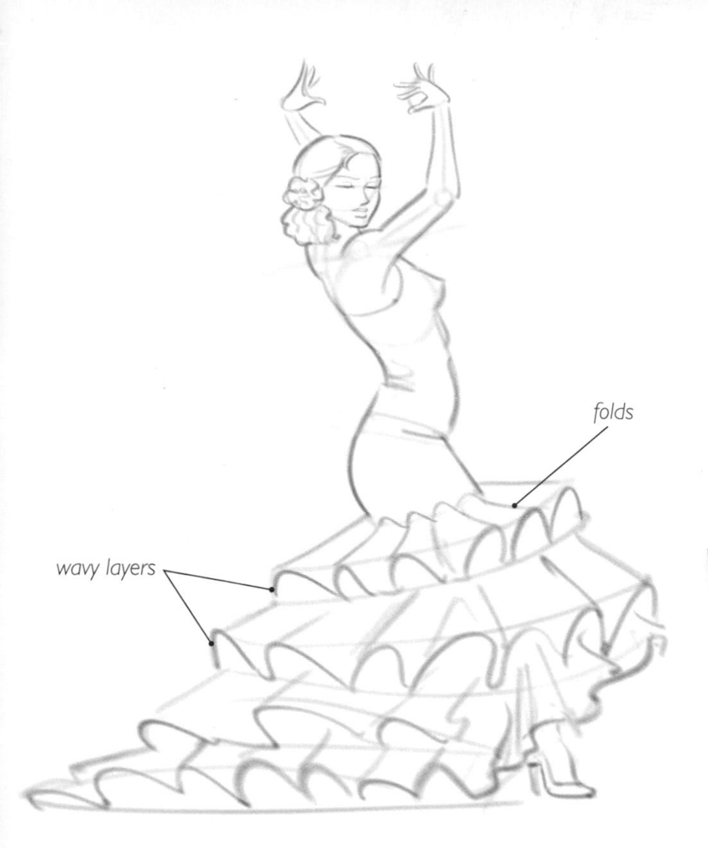

Step 3

Define, smooth and darken the outline. Draw the wavy lines of fabric inside every second layer of the skirt, then create the folds in between. Define the wavy hair, flower, the fingers and details for the dress. Draw eyes on either side of the cross, a nose and a mouth.

DRAWING TIP

Shading creates a light to dark tone. It can help to enhance a three-dimensional form or shape. Press lightly with your pencil to create a lighter tone, using a left-to-right drawing motion. Press more heavily as you go, using the same motion to gradually create darker tones.

Step 4

Study the level of shading over the figure. Add soft line work for the flower and the texture of the hair. With a medium pencil pressure, shade a dark, open grey tone across the dress, hair and under the folds of fabric. Apply a lighter open tone to define the folds of fabric and add soft shading around the face and shoulder. Darken the shoe and the facial features.

Once you draw the faint details for the musician in the background, your flamenco dancer will be ready to perform.

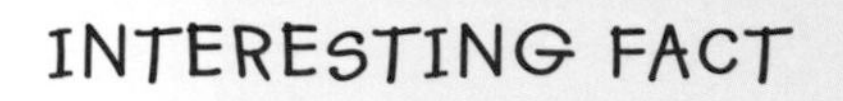

INTERESTING FACT → The origins of flamenco are believed to stretch as far back as the 8th century, when the Moors invaded and occupied parts of Spain.

HOLLYWOOD STARLET

Female movie stars have been setting fashion trends since the early 20th century. Each decade, certain Hollywood starlets become style icons, being photographed for their dazzling gowns as they walk the red carpet at the Oscars or at film premieres. They dress in outfits made especially for them by top fashion designers, which then appear in magazines and on television.

Before you begin

The drawing of the Hollywood starlet is built around a skirt shape and a skeleton. Observe how the shape of the skirt resembles a mermaid's tail. To draw the starlet's figure correctly, observe the size and length of the body parts and where they are positioned. Use the construction lines as a guide. Study the curved outline that creates the body's form.

Step 1

Draw lightly at first. Sketch a mermaid-shaped skirt with a curved hem and add a slightly angled oval for the waist. Draw a backbone, a circle for the head, a chin pointing down and a cross facing left. Add a circle in the middle for the chest, with shoulders running across. Add the left arm hanging against the body and the right bent with the hand on the waist. Sketch the joints and hand shapes.

Step 2

Build the shape of the body around the skeleton. Starting at the head, define the shape of the face, ear and neck. Draw the shape of the hair around the face. Create the shoulders, the shape of the arms and the dress. Define the fingers and the bag. With a clean eraser, remove any unnecessary line work.

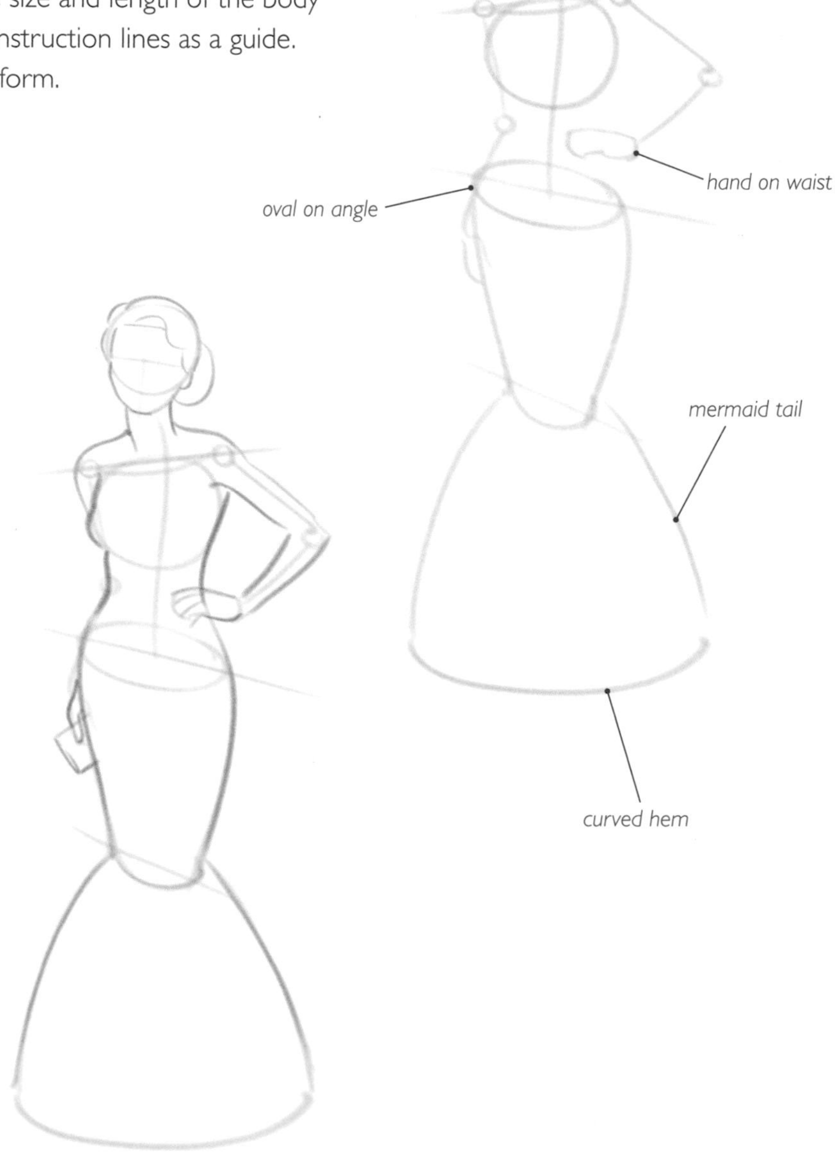

Step 3

Define, smooth and darken the curves of the outline. Draw eyes on either side of the cross, a nose and a mouth. Add wavy line work to the hair and create the lines of the bust. Add a crumpled piece of fabric trailing out behind the gown, folds to the skirt and a wavy outline around the hem.

Step 4

Develop the facial features and add a necklace and faint lines for the hair's texture. With light pencil pressure, shade an open mid-grey tone across the dress, leaving some areas white.

Sketch the red carpet above the skirt and the barrier behind the figure. Once you draw faint camera flashes, your Hollywood starlet will be ready to pose for the paparazzi!

DRAWING TIP

Once you have drawn your Hollywood starlet, pretend that you are a top fashion designer and try sketching your own outfits for her to wear.

INTERESTING FACT

Movie stars wear gowns by fashion houses such as Versace and Chanel. Gianni Versace opened his fashion house in Milan in 1978. Coco Chanel was a pioneering fashion designer who began her fashion house in Paris in 1910.

ANGRY!

Funky Things to Draw
fantasy
Paul Könye
Kate Ashforth
fantasy

Funky Things to Draw

Fantasy

INTRODUCTION

There are many legends, myths and fables from different cultures that have been passed down through the generations. These colourful tales inspire the imagination and take us on journeys to faraway places.

Tales of fantasy are a great way to develop creative thoughts, skills and ideas. Let your imagination run free into the world of fantasy creatures. Picture a magical unicorn galloping through a sparkling river or an enormous giant as tall as a castle. Imagine a genie appearing before you, ready to grant you three wishes!

THINGS YOU WILL NEED

- An HB or 2B pencil (they are light and won't smudge too easily)
- A pencil sharpener and a small dish for shavings
- A4 cartridge paper or copy paper and some scrap paper for experiments
- A clean eraser
- Confidence: a positive attitude will help improve your skills
- Imagination: don't be afraid to explore your own style or ideas

Drawing guidelines

There are a few things you should be aware of when drawing your fantasy creatures:

1. Some of these creatures are built around a skeleton, which is made up of a series of lines, shapes, joints and a backbone.
2. Begin by lightly drawing the structure of your subject, otherwise it will be obvious in the final drawing. Where possible, rub out unnecessary line work with a clean eraser as you go.
3. Pay close attention to where each creature's limbs are placed and where the cross indicating the position of the face is drawn on the head. This will help to draw the creature in the correct pose.
4. To draw each subject with the correct proportions, pay close attention to the type and the size of the shapes used to create the initial structure. Also, see in some drawings that a three-dimensional element is required.
5. Carefully observe the angle at which each creature is positioned in the first step. Make sure you focus on the length and the direction of all the body parts. This will allow your subject to be seen from the correct perspective.

Stages of drawing

Some of the fantasy creatures in this book are easier to draw than others. All of them are built around basic structures; either a skeleton or a series of shapes. You will notice certain drawings are particularly detailed and show different

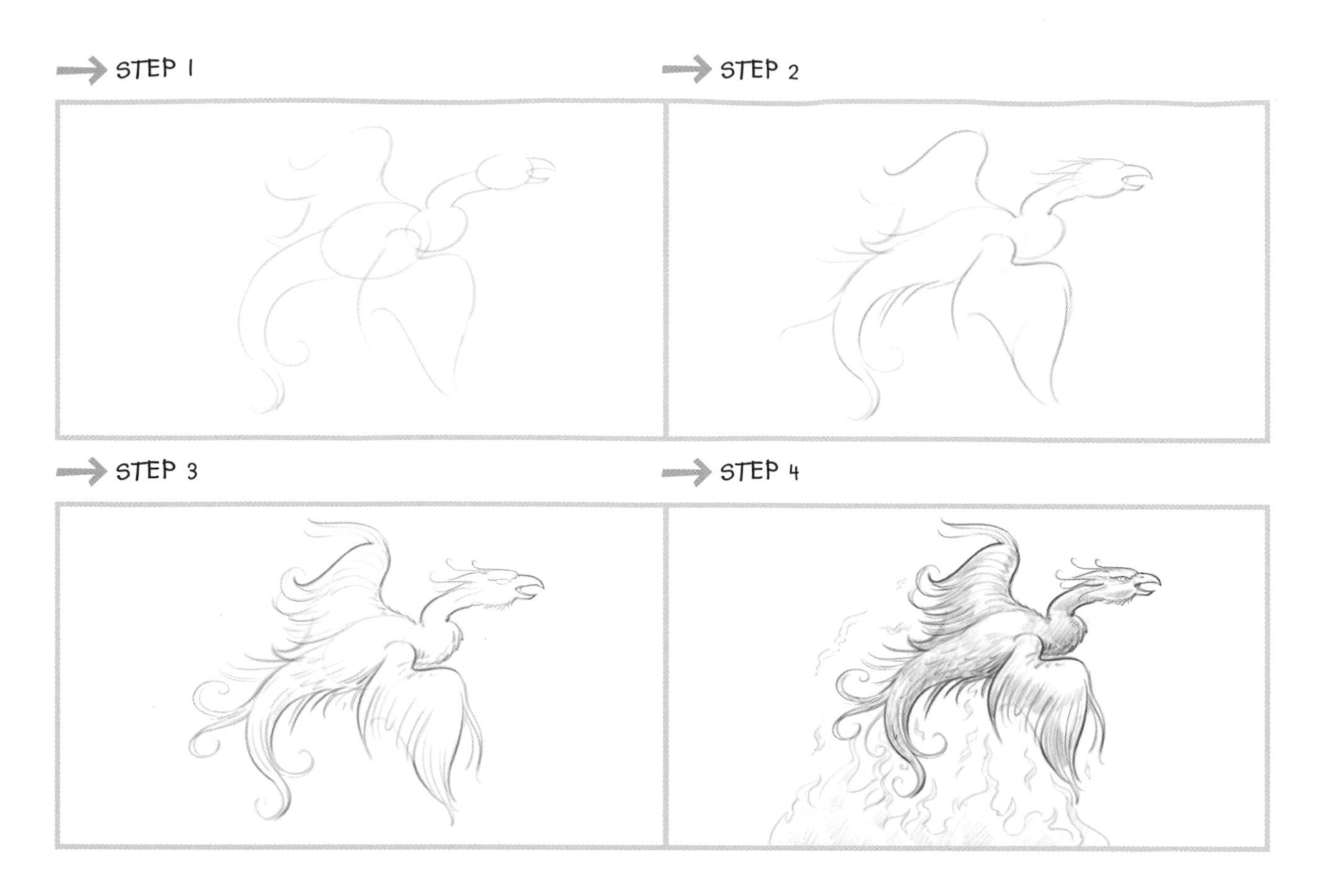

levels of shading and technique. Observe the pencil work used before you begin and read all of the instructions so that you have a clear understanding of the drawing process.

Study the initial structure of your subject and the types of lines and shapes used to create it. Notice how the form of your creature is built around this structure. Observe the pencil technique used for each step. What kinds of texture, pattern and shading do you see? What types of lines and shapes have been used to create these textures and patterns? How light or dark is the grey tone created with the shading?

Skills and techniques

Here are some examples of the different techniques and art elements you will learn about.

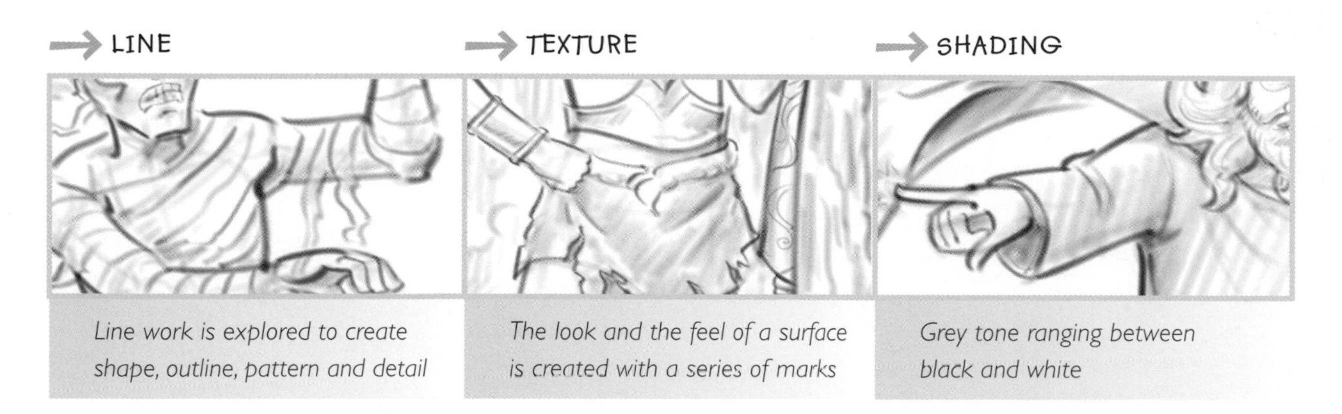

Line work is explored to create shape, outline, pattern and detail

The look and the feel of a surface is created with a series of marks

Grey tone ranging between black and white

When a picture appears to be very detailed and different pencil techniques are explored, it is a good idea to practise your pencil technique. Experiment with the shading, pattern, line, shape and texture you see for each picture. Remember that challenging pictures can be rewarding to draw when you apply yourself!

GENIE

Genies are supernatural beings from Arabian mythology. It was believed that they could change shape or make themselves invisible. Genies could be both good and evil. In traditional stories about genies, a person can free a genie from a lamp by polishing it. On being released, the genie will grant the person three wishes.

Before you begin

The genie is built around a series of simple shapes and lines. Observe the size of shapes and the direction and length of the lines. Notice that the lamp is three-dimensional and is viewed from above. Study the type of shapes used to draw the lamp and where they connect.

Step 1

Lightly sketch a head shape, with a cross for the face. Add a backbone curving down and an oval at the base for the hips. Draw a circle in the middle of the backbone for the chest and add shoulders. Sketch the arms crossed over the chest and add joints and hand shapes. Draw a curved shape on a slight angle for the skirt. To the left of the genie, lightly draw an oval for the top of the lamp and a shape for the lid. Sketch a handle curving upward, the base of the lamp and an opening for the spout.

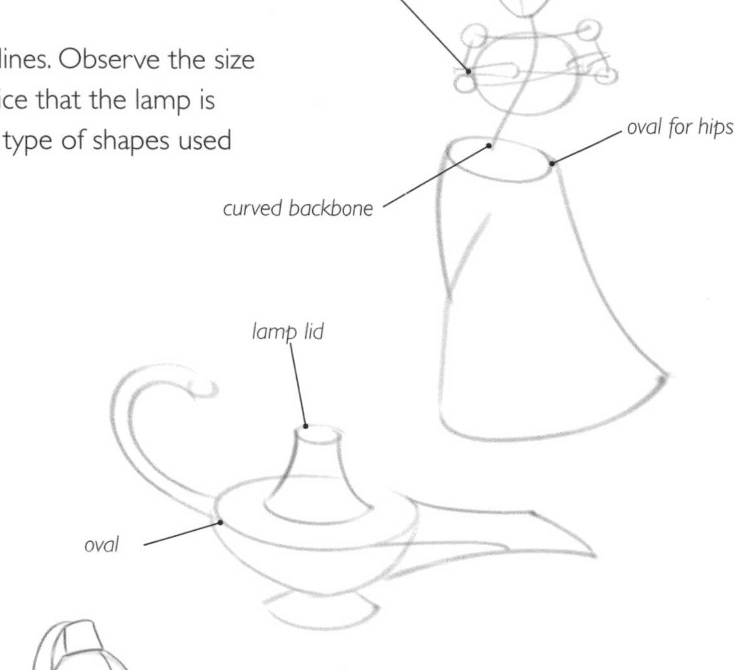

Step 2

Define and smooth the outline for the genie and the lamp. Build the shape of the genie around the construction lines. Draw hair and a hat, and then a ponytail and a veil. Develop the facial features. Sketch the shape of the front and rear arms and add a vest and the stomach.

Step 3

Darken the outline. Using soft pencil work, draw a wavy outline running from the lid around to the spout for a puff of smoke. Draw almond-shaped eyes on either side of the cross, a nose and a mouth. Add decorative details to the hat, clothing and lamp. Don't forget the marks in the hair.

DRAWING TIP

Pencil can smudge. Watch where your hand is on the page and make sure it is not rubbing across your drawing.

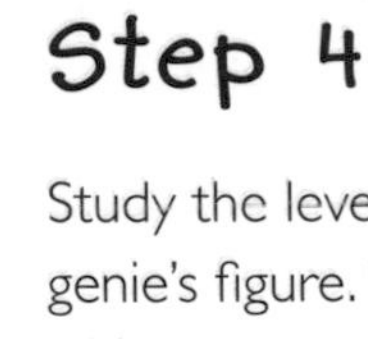

Step 4

Study the level of shading over the genie's figure. Using a light pressure with your pencil, softly shade parts of the clothing and the veil. Darken the facial features and draw beads under the arms.

Add a medium grey tone across the lamp. Remember to leave some areas white over the whole drawing. Draw a wavy pattern on the top of the lamp with the tip of a pencil. Once you add soft shading around the smoke, your genie is ready to grant three wishes!

INTERESTING FACT → The English word *genie* originated from the Arabic word *jinn*, an invisible spirit created from smokeless fire.

MUMMY

A mummy is the preserved body of a person who has died. In Ancient Egypt, people believed that a person would need their body in the afterlife. The most famous mummy discovered in recent times was of a pharaoh called Tutankhamen. His tomb was thought to be cursed due to the early or unusual deaths of people involved in the discovery of the tomb. Reanimated mummies have been popular subjects of horror films.

Before you begin

The form of the mummy is built around a skeleton. Observe the sizes and types of shapes used to construct the mummy's figure. Look at the positioning of the limbs and the length and types of lines used to draw them. Use curvy line work for the bandages, as this gives the mummy a sense of dimension. Drawing curvy line work around the body will make it look more muscular.

Step 1

Lightly draw a circle for the head on an angle. Add a chin and a cross on the right side of the face. Draw a curved backbone under the chin with an oval at its base. Sketch construction lines on slight angles for legs and flat-bottomed shapes bent inward for the feet. Sketch a circle under the chin for the chest and add shoulders running across. Draw a bent construction line for the right arm and a hand pointing up. Bend the left arm over the chest with a hand facing down.

Step 2

Study the outline of the mummy's muscular form. Beginning at the head, build the curved shape of the body around the skeleton.

Step 3

Observe how the curved and wavy line work wraps around the body. Draw eye sockets on either side of the cross. Sketch a nose and a fierce mouth with bared teeth. Working down the body, use a medium pressure with your pencil to draw the bandages. Draw the wavy scraps flowing out and add fingers to the hands.

DRAWING TIP

There are many different types of line that can be used in a drawing. For example, there are bent, straight, curly, spiral, wavy, loopy and curvy lines. Experiment with drawing lines and observe the effects!

Step 4

Darken the outline and the facial features. Using a light pressure with your pencil, add soft shading around the edges of the body.

For the background, add faint line work for the moon and clouds behind the mummy's torso. Add a small and a large pyramid in line with the hips. Once you sketch details on the ground, your mummy is ready to frighten someone!

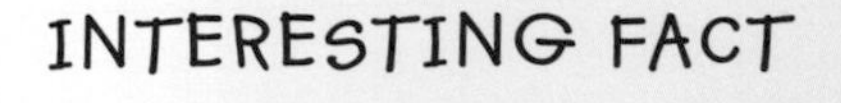

INTERESTING FACT → Today, around the ancient pyramids of Cairo, tombs and mummies of the pharaohs continue to be unearthed.

MERMAID

Mermaids are mythical, aquatic creatures who have the torso of a woman and the tail of a fish. Legend has it that they can be found sunning themselves on rocks at sea, gazing into a mirror and combing their hair. Sailors believed that mermaids would try and take them to their kingdom at the bottom of the ocean, drowning them in the process.

Before you begin

The rock is the most important element in this drawing, as it supports the mermaid's form. To position the mermaid correctly, pay attention to where the hips and left arm are placed. Observe the angle of the head and backbone. Also, notice the positioning of the tail over the rock and the size of the fin.

Step 1

Lightly draw a curved rock shape. Sketch an oval on an angle on top of the rock for the hips and a backbone curving upwards. Add circles for the head and chest, a chin and a cross for the face. Draw shoulders above the chest and construction lines for the arms, the left arm leaning on the rock and the right arm on the tail. Add shapes for the joints and hands.

Step 2

Draw the shape of the hair flowing down the back of the head and around the face. Add curves inside the hair to make it look wavy. Build the shapes of the arms, hands and torso around the construction lines and define the curves of the tail and fin.

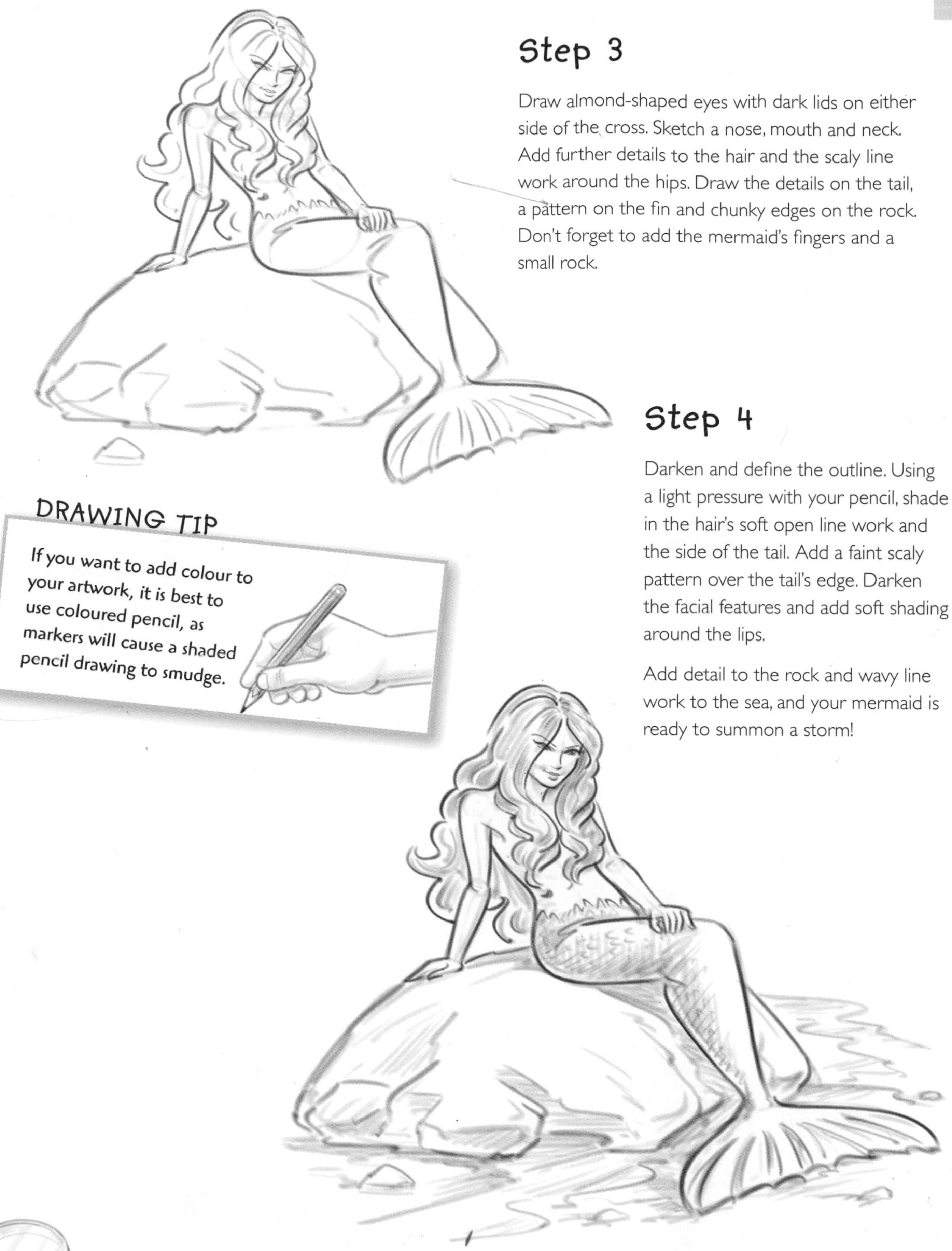

Step 3

Draw almond-shaped eyes with dark lids on either side of the cross. Sketch a nose, mouth and neck. Add further details to the hair and the scaly line work around the hips. Draw the details on the tail, a pattern on the fin and chunky edges on the rock. Don't forget to add the mermaid's fingers and a small rock.

DRAWING TIP

If you want to add colour to your artwork, it is best to use coloured pencil, as markers will cause a shaded pencil drawing to smudge.

Step 4

Darken and define the outline. Using a light pressure with your pencil, shade in the hair's soft open line work and the side of the tail. Add a faint scaly pattern over the tail's edge. Darken the facial features and add soft shading around the lips.

Add detail to the rock and wavy line work to the sea, and your mermaid is ready to summon a storm!

INTERESTING FACT

It is thought that the mermaid legend originated from sailors spotting dugongs or manatees out at sea and mistaking them for mermaids.

WHITE WITCH

White witches are good witches who perform white magic to help improve the lives of others. A white witch will heal people, remove curses and protect people from evil witchcraft. Some claim that white magic practitioners use the forces of nature and balance to achieve their aims, while black magic practitioners use evil spirits and forces of chaos.

Before you begin

The witch's figure is built around her coat. Study the curved line work that creates the shape of the coat and how it sits on the rock-face. Observe the structure used for the head and how it faces to the right. Study the fine line work used to create the texture of the coat, hair and dress.

Step 1

Draw curves for the rock slope on an angle. Sketch a triangular shape for the opening of the coat and then, starting at the shoulders, add a curved outline for the coat around the opening. Add a circle above the shoulders for the head, with a chin pointing down. Add construction lines and shapes for arms and hands. Draw the curved neck, an ear and a cross facing right for the face.

Step 2

Build the shape of the body. Define the edges of the face and add shapes for the hair. Sketch the shape of the arms around the construction lines. Add a neckline to the dress and add folds to the coat. Draw a staff running through the left hand and pointing over the right shoulder.

Step 3

Define and darken the line work. Draw a nose in the middle of the cross and eyes on either side, facing right. Sketch an open mouth and add texture to the hair hanging over the shoulder using curly line work. Develop the furry edges of the coat and add fingers to the hands.

DRAWING TIP

Texture is a series of marks that create the look and feel of a surface. Using different types of pressure with your pencil, practise drawing texture on a separate page. Experiment with size, length and thickness.

Step 4

Darken the outline. Add pupils to the eyes and define the facial details. Draw lines that cross one another to pattern the dress. Sketch diamonds around the neckline and details on the staff. Using a light pressure with your pencil, create the soft, furry texture of the coat. Apply a light grey tone across the dress and the staff, and shade a mid-grey tone over the hair. Add line work and shading for the hair's texture.

Once you add a shard of light in the hand and the bumpy details of the rock, your white witch will be ready to wield her good magic!

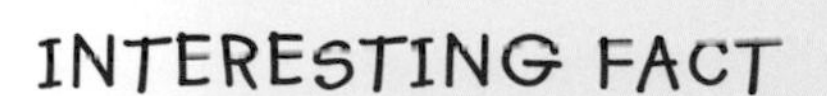

INTERESTING FACT → In medieval England, some white witches were called 'toad doctors'. They would claim they could cure people of skin disease by hanging live toads or toad body parts around people's necks!

WIZARD

Wizards are magical people who use their craft to master the elements of nature. They appear throughout the ages in legends and myths and are popular figures in literature. Wizards seek the truth and often act as advisors or guardians. Wizards are often depicted as scholars in search of magic knowledge, and will often entrust their secrets to a chosen apprentice.

Before you begin

To draw the wizard from the correct perspective, pay attention to the angle of the skeleton. The skeleton is created with shapes, construction lines and joints. Observe how the body is positioned along the angle of the baseline. The left foot is drawn front-on, while the right foot is side-on.

Step 1

Lightly draw an angled baseline with foot shapes positioned over the top. Draw a straight left leg and a bent right leg. Add an oval for the waist and a backbone on a slight angle. Sketch a circle for the head with a cross and a beard. Add a circle for the chest with shoulders sitting above. Draw a brim and a hat, with the top folded over. Sketch the left arm pointing outward and the right bending up. Add hand shapes and draw a crooked staff in the right hand, running alongside the hat.

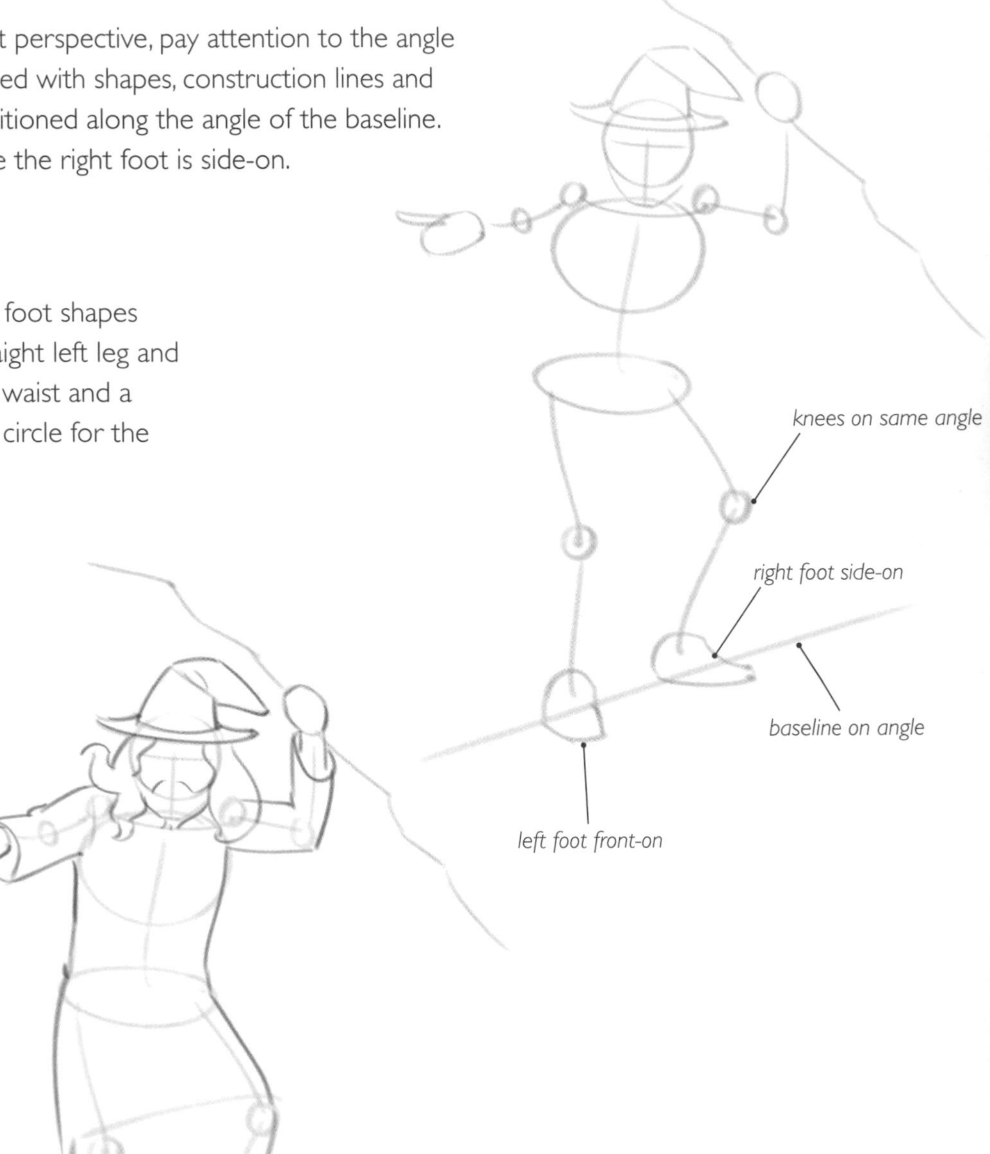

Step 2

Build the shape of the body around the skeleton. Draw the hair around the head and develop the beard. Create the shape of the tunic, paying attention to the opening of the sleeves. Develop the hand shapes and the boots.

Step 3

Define and smooth the outline. Add a belt around the waist and thicken the crooked staff. Define the clothing and add the neckline and the folds of the tunic. Draw eyes on either side of the cross and add a nose and a mouth. Add fingers to the hands and details to the boots. Sketch the outline and underside of the cape.

DRAWING TIP

With a right to left drawing motion, practise your shading technique. Create light to dark grey tones using different pressures with your pencil. Create a loose, open style of shading and more solid shade of grey.

Step 4

Darken the outline. Using a light pressure with your pencil, use soft line work to create a burst of light shooting out from the hand. Loosely shade the open line work of the clothing. Darken the shading on the hat, belt, boots and some parts of the clothing. Define the facial features and add texture to the hair and staff using fine line work.

Once you add a shadow beneath the boots, your wizard will be ready to transform you!

INTERESTING FACT

Famous wizards in myth and literature include King Arthur's advisor Merlin, Gandalf from *The Lord of the Rings* and, more recently, the wizards featured in the *Harry Potter* series.

EVIL WITCH

Evil witches practise black magic and use their supernatural powers to cause harm and destruction. References to witches can be found in many cultures through the ages. In the Middle Ages, it was thought that witches gained their power by making a pact with evil spirits or the devil. To carry out their plans, witches would cast powerful spells that could last a lifetime or tricked people into drinking dangerous potions.

Before you begin

The most important art elements of this drawing are shape and line, as they construct the witch's form. Observe the shapes and construction lines used to create the witch's skeleton. Pay attention to the shape and the angle of the hands and the dress. Study the flowing line work creating the curves and folds of the witch's outfit.

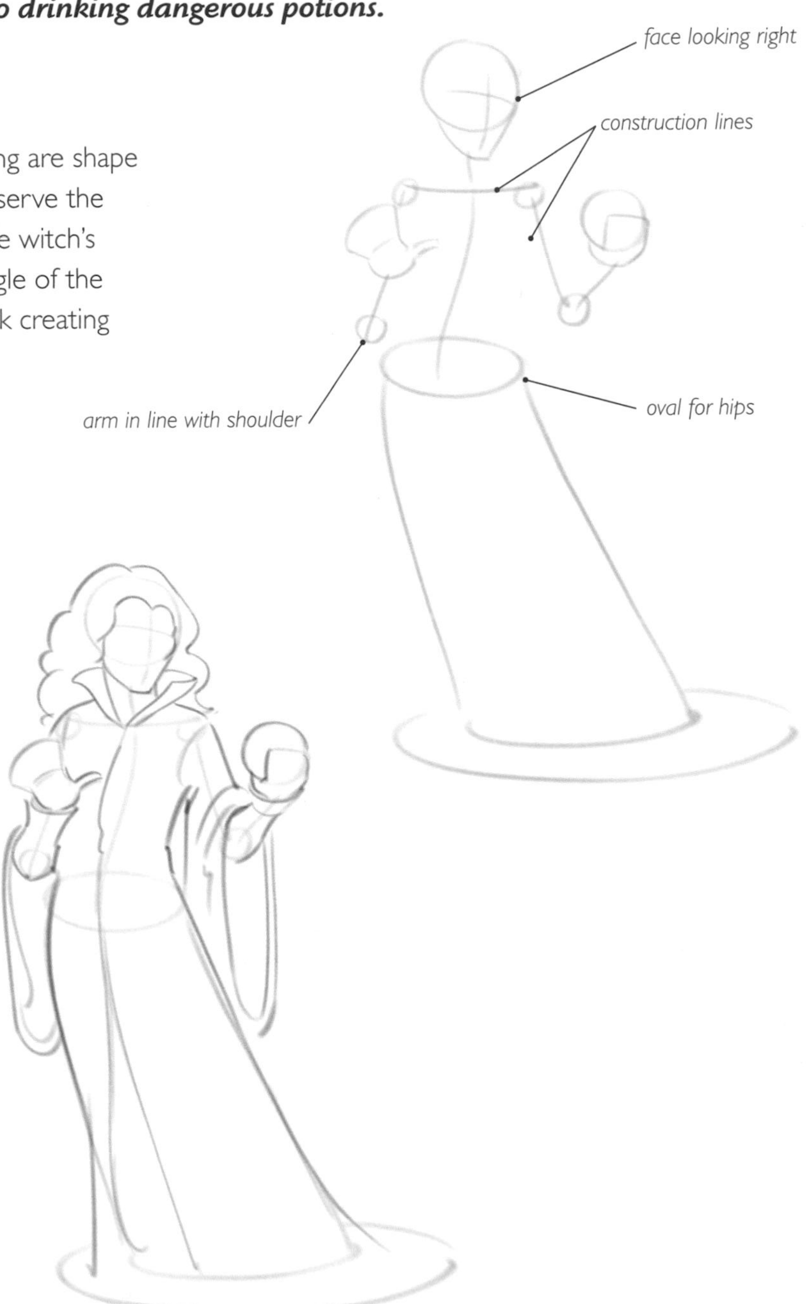

Step 1

Lightly draw a circle for the head and add a sharp chin. Draw a cross looking to the right for the face. Sketch a backbone on a slight angle with an oval at the base. Add shoulders and the bent right arm with a hand shape cupping a crystal ball. Draw the left hand under the shoulder, add a line for the left arm and draw the joints. Sketch a skirt shape on an angle, with a curve around the base.

Step 2

Build the shape of the body around the skeleton. Draw the neck, shoulders and collar. Sketch the face and the wavy hair. Define the dress and draw the folds of the right sleeve. Build the shape of the arms and add folds for the left sleeve.

Step 3

Define and smooth the outline of the body. Add a headband and eyelids on either side of the cross. Draw a nose and an open mouth. Starting at the left, draw a wispy bottom on the dress, trailing out to the right. Add decorative bands around the neck and waist of the dress and add more folds to the dress. Don't forget to define the fingers.

DRAWING TIP

Try adding other art elements to the picture, such as pattern, line or texture. You could add pattern to the dress or use line work to draw curtains. Maybe you could use a series of marks to add texture to the floor.

Step 4

Darken the outline and define the facial features. Using a light pressure with your pencil, shade a soft grey tone around the folds of the dress, arms and crystal ball. Add decoration to the belt and shade a mid grey tone across the hair.

Draw the faint, vertical edges of the windows and the curves at the top. Sketch the chequered floor, drawing the line work on different angles. Once you add the wall and tree, your evil witch is ready to unleash her power!

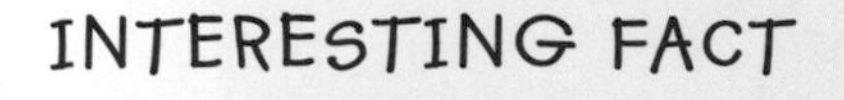

Some witches have a 'familiar', which is a helper in the form of an animal. Common familiars are cats, toads, ravens or bats.

DRAGON

Dragons are ancient, mythical creatures who appear in many culture's legends. A dragon resembles a giant flying reptile or serpent and can be benevolent or evil. Asian cultures regard the dragon as a symbol of wisdom, health and good luck. In European medieval stories, dragons are usually depicted as angry, fire-breathing creatures who battle knights in fierce encounters.

Before you begin

Line is the main art element in this drawing, as it creates the dragon's curved form. Observe the length and direction of the curved and wavy line work. Study the different types and sizes of shapes used to create the body and see where the construction lines are positioned for the legs, wings and tail.

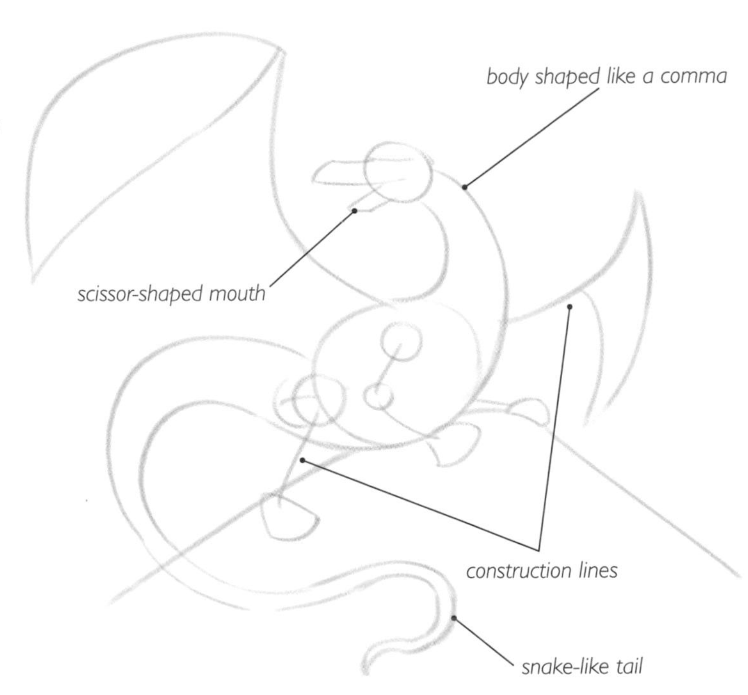

Step 1

Draw a curved line for the mountain and an upside-down comma shape sitting on the peak. Add a circle for the head and a mouth facing left, shaped like open scissors. Draw a construction line for the middle leg, adding legs on either side, joints and feet. Draw a thick, snake-like tail behind the rear leg joint, curving in front of the mountain. Add construction lines for the curved wings, adding pointy shapes to the ends. Notice the left wing is longer and larger.

Step 2

Define and smooth the outline of the body. Starting at the left wing, add wavy line work under both wings. Develop the inside of the mouth and build the shapes of the legs around the construction lines.

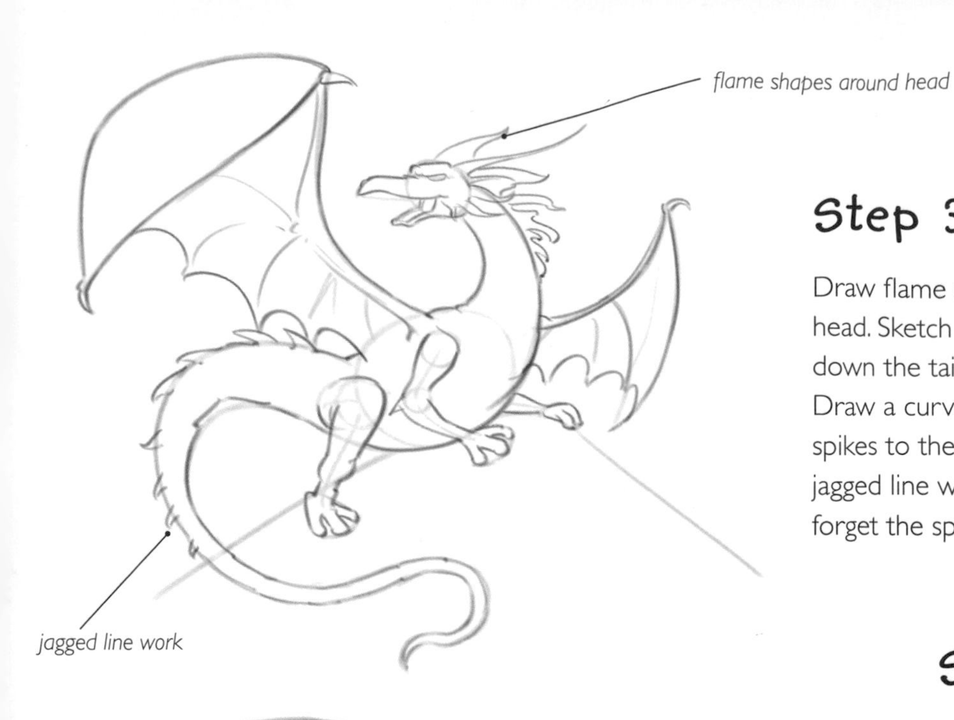

Step 3

Draw flame shapes over the neck and around the head. Sketch an eye next to the mouth and spikes down the tail, getting smaller as you move down. Draw a curved pattern inside the wings and add spikes to the corners. Develop the clawed feet and jagged line work around the tail's outline. Don't forget the spike on the middle leg.

Step 4

Darken the outline. Study the scaly texture of the skin and the different levels of shading over the body. Using a light pressure with your pencil, add a rough, bumpy texture to the neck, body and tail. Draw small spikes for the claws, teeth and wings. Add soft shading over the whole body, leaving some areas white. Notice the body is darker in some areas than others.

Once you add faint details to the mountain, your dragon is ready for battle!

DRAWING TIP

Don't be afraid to experiment by adding your own touches to a drawing. Maybe you could draw a flame coming out of the the dragon's mouth or a castle in the background.

INTERESTING FACT

→ Generally, dragons in the West are depicted with wings, while Eastern dragons can magically fly without wings.

PHOENIX

The phoenix is a mythological and sacred bird that featured in the legends of many ancient cultures. It was depicted as a beautiful bird with bright red and gold feathers. The phoenix was thought to live for centuries. At the end of its life, the phoenix would make a nest out of cinnamon twigs, sit in it and set itself on fire. A new phoenix would then be reborn from the ashes.

Before you begin

The form of the phoenix is made up of a series of curved, flowing shapes. Study the types of shapes and how they connect together. Texture and line are also a focus of this drawing. Observe the feathered and curly line work added in each step. The texture of the phoenix's feathers is made up of fine lines and is shaded in a medium grey pencil tone.

Step 1

Lightly draw an oval on a slight angle for the body. Overlap a smaller oval for the chest and add the neck extending upward. Draw an oval for the head and add an open claw-like beak. Draw a thick shape curving down from the back of the body for the tail. Sketch a wing shape behind the body and draw a front wing shape overlapping the body. Ensure the wings are on the same angle as the body.

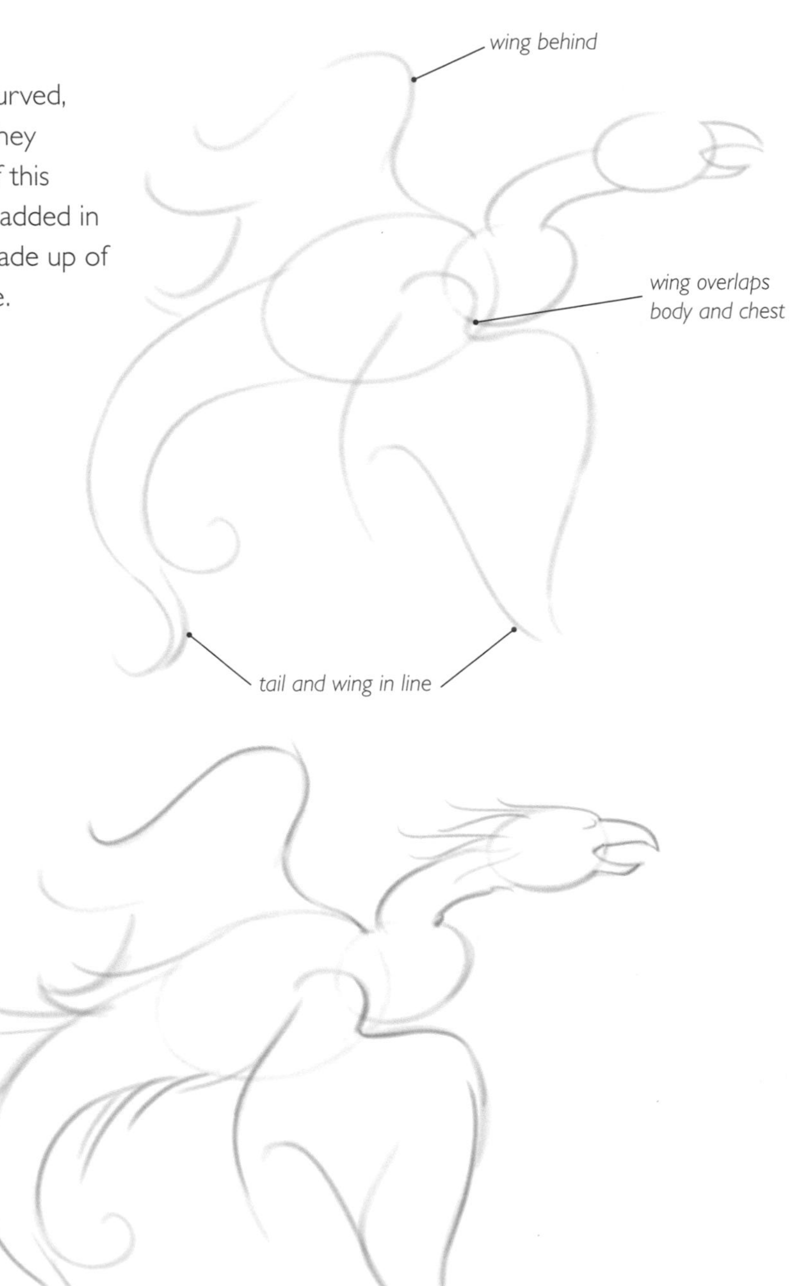

Step 2

Define the shapes, adding spiky shapes around the back of the head and feathered line work to the body and tail.

Step 3

Gently sketch the texture of the feathers with fine line work from head to tail. Add an eye next to the beak and define the tail, wings and head feathers with curly line work.

DRAWING TIP

Remember to use a right to left drawing motion when you are shading. You can use the tip or the side of your pencil, depending on the effect you are trying to achieve. When you shade, begin with a lighter tone and build up to the level of shading you require.

Step 4

Darken the outline. Using a light pressure with your pencil, add soft shading over the body, working in the direction of the feathers. Ensure that the shading is lighter in some areas than others. Add a pupil to the eye and an extra shaded curl to the tail.

Once you have added faint fiery shapes to the background, your phoenix is ready to rise from the ashes!

INTERESTING FACT

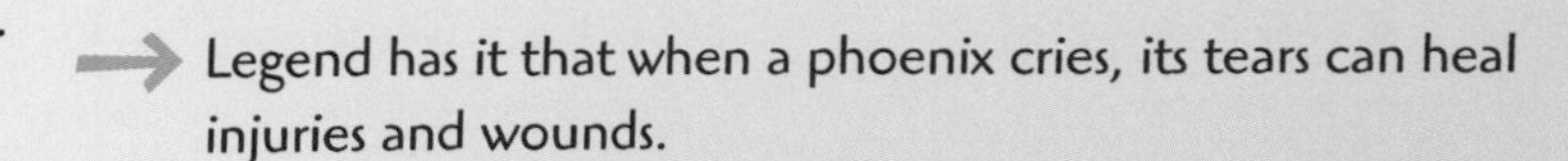

Legend has it that when a phoenix cries, its tears can heal injuries and wounds.

AMAZON WARRIOR

The Amazons were a race of warrior women who ruled their own nation. Legend has it that the Amazons lived near the Black Sea during the Bronze Age, and formed their own kingdom with a queen at the helm. It is said the women were fierce in battle. Most scholars believe the story of the Amazons to be a myth, however there is some evidence of their possible existence.

Before you begin

The drawing of the Amazon warrior is built around a skeleton structure. Pay attention to the size and length of all body parts and how they connect together. There are many details drawn for the warrior's costume. Observe where the shapes for the clothing have been placed on the body. Study the line, pattern and shading applied for decoration. Read each step carefully before you start to draw.

Step 1

Draw a circle for the head and add the chin and a cross for the face. Draw a baseline a body length below. Sketch a backbone with an oval at the base for hips. Draw a slightly squashed circle for the chest, adding shoulders across the top. Add bent lines for the arms. Sketch a rock over the baseline. Draw lines for the legs, adding the left foot against the rock and the right foot on the baseline. Add a bow alongside the body and hand shapes and joints.

Step 2

Build the shape of the body around the skeleton. Define the face and draw the shape of the hair and headpiece. Draw the outline of the body and add shapes for the clothing.

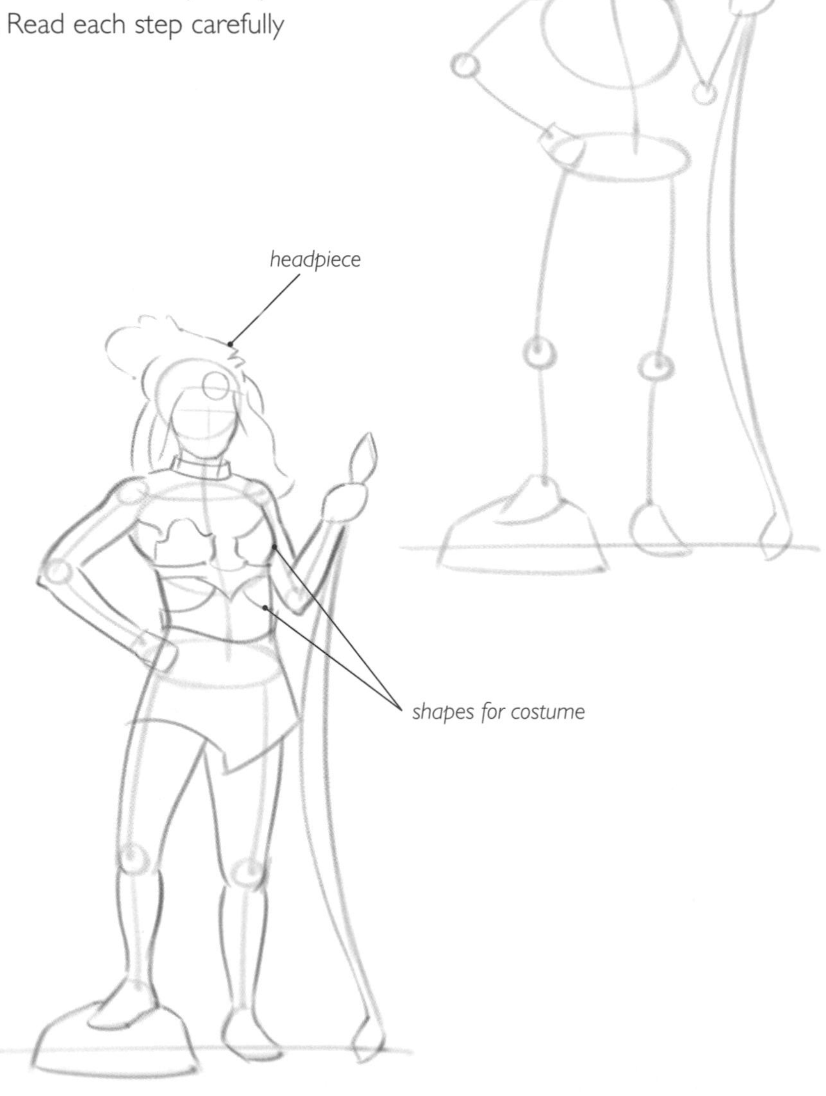

Step 3

Draw eyes on either side of the cross. Add a nose and mouth and develop the details of the headpiece and hair. Draw wristbands, a leg band and boots. Add detail to the rest of the costume, paying attention to the crinkly edges of the neckline and skirt. Don't forget the belt and carvings on the bow.

DRAWING TIP

When using an eraser, make sure you keep it clean. Clean it by rubbing the grey residue off on a separate piece of paper.

Step 4

Study the details of the drawing carefully before shading. Beginning at the head, add texture using a series of fine lines. Darken the facial features and draw wavy patterns on the bow. Add patterns to the leg band and boots. Using a light pressure with your pencil, add soft shading around the edges of the clothing, boots and bow.

Once you faintly draw a twisted, gnarly tree in the background and apply shading to the ground, your Amazon warrior will be ready for battle!

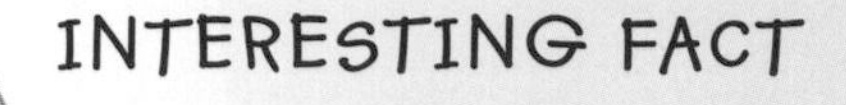

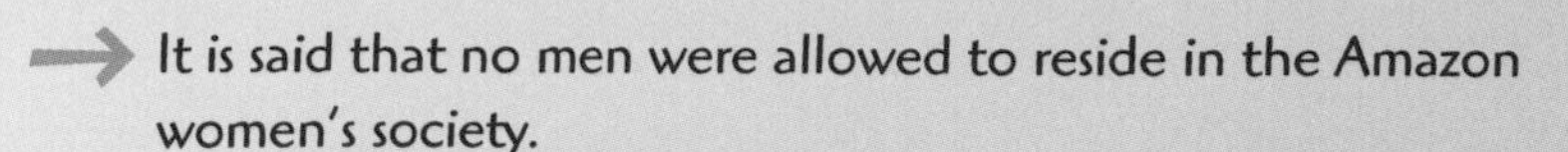

It is said that no men were allowed to reside in the Amazon women's society.

UNICORN

Unicorns are admired for their beauty and their magical spiral horn (called an alicorn). It was thought a unicorn's horn could cure any poison and in the Middle Ages, there was a great demand for cups made from the horn. It is said that the only way it can be captured is by a pure maiden, as a unicorn will lay its head in her lap and fall asleep.

Before you begin

The most important elements in this drawing are the backbone, tail and baseline. These elements create a skeleton around which the unicorn's shape can be built. Observe the flowing, curved line work for the backbone and tail. This will give your unicorn a sense of movement. Draw the baseline on a slight angle, as this will ensure the unicorn is drawn from the correct perspective.

Step 1

Lightly draw a baseline on an angle and add a circle for the hips. For the chest, sketch a slightly larger circle on an angle. Draw a smaller circle above the chest for the head. Add a flat muzzle and a line for the horn. Draw a backbone curving between the hips, chest and head. Sketch a curved line for the tail and construction lines on the baseline for the back legs. Add an extended front leg and the other front leg crossing over. Don't forget to add the joints.

Step 2

Build the curved form of the unicorn around the skeleton. Construct the shape of the head, paying attention to the brow, muzzle and ears. Create the shape of the horn and add an eye to the head. Develop the flowing curves of the body and build the shape of the legs, leaving the back legs until last.

Step 3

With a clean eraser, remove any unnecessary line work. Define and smooth the curves of the body. Draw a flame-shaped mane and the tail flowing out behind. Using line work, add texture to the mane. Develop the mouth and add a nostril and the hoofs.

DRAWING TIP

Notice that the moon is shining from above and behind the unicorn. This means that its coat will be lighter on its back and darker underneath. Always remember where your light source is coming from when you add shading.

Step 4

Darken the outline. Using a light pressure with your pencil, define the body, adding soft shading to the edges. Use fine line work to enhance the texture of the mane and tail. Add a medium tone to the back legs. Darken the eye, nostril and hoofs and add the pattern to the horn.

Once you draw the faint line work for the moon, the clouds and the ground, your unicorn will be ready use its magical powers!

INTERESTING FACT → Unicorn horns, used to make items such as cups and thrones, have actually come from the narwhal, a species of horned whale.

Funky Things to Draw in the garden

in the garden

Paul Könye ★ Kate Ashforth

Funky Things to Draw in the garden

INTRODUCTION

There are some truly fascinating creatures that can be discovered in gardens all around the world. The following pages will teach you to draw a variety of insects and animals using step-by-step instructions.

Before you begin, try venturing out into a garden to see what creatures you can find. Maybe you'll discover a praying mantis hiding in a bush? Or you might see a beautiful butterfly resting on some flowers. Or perhaps you'll hear a robin singing in a tree?

THINGS YOU WILL NEED

- An HB or 2B pencil (they are light and won't smudge too easily)
- A pencil sharpener and a small dish for shavings
- A4 cartridge paper or copy paper and some scrap paper for experiments
- A clean eraser
- Confidence: a positive attitude will help improve your skills
- Imagination: don't be afraid to explore your own style or ideas

Drawing guidelines

When drawing your creatures from the garden, pay attention to the following:

1. Each subject is built around a series of shapes (some being organic shapes that are found in nature).
2. Construction lines are used to help build the initial structure of your subject.
3. Line is an important art element that is used to represent movement, form, pattern and texture.
4. Different pencil techniques are explored to add detail and definition to each subject.
5. Light pencil work is used when you begin drawing a subject. This allows you to erase any pencil lines you don't need. The line work of your sketch is darkened when you are closer to finishing the final steps.

Stages of drawing

Each subject has a number of steps to follow. Ensure that you study all lessons and steps carefully before you begin. They provide information on techniques and art principles that are relevant to drawing creatures from the garden. It will also teach you important skills that will improve your knowledge of drawing animals and insects.

Observe the different shapes you see in the first step. Look for any construction lines that help to build your subject. Pay attention to the different sized shapes and lines that are explored. Study the changes you see between all the steps. What types of line have been added? Is there any shading? What pattern or texture has been drawn?

Skills and techniques

You will explore different techniques and art elements over the following pages.

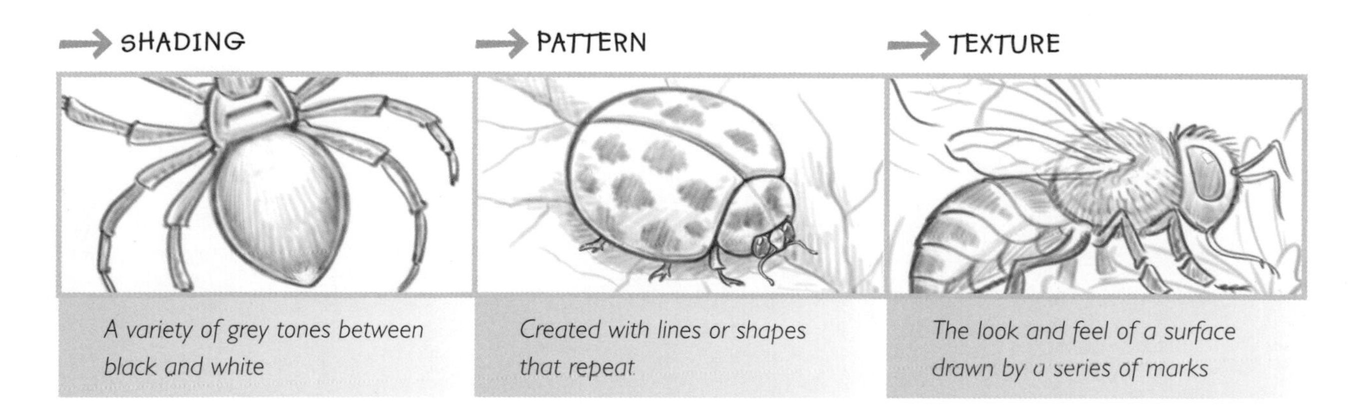

A variety of grey tones between black and white

Created with lines or shapes that repeat

The look and feel of a surface drawn by a series of marks

Be aware that drawing is a skill that is learnt with much practice. Some subjects can be harder to draw than others, so be patient and remember that your skills will develop in time!

BUTTERFLY

Butterflies are admired because of their colourful and decorative wings. They use their bright colours to scare off predators or to attract potential mates. You will often find them sunning themselves in the garden. This is because a butterfly's body needs to stay warm for them to fly. Butterflies feed off the sweet nectar of flowers.

Before you begin

Like all insects, the butterfly has three body parts: the head, the thorax and the abdomen. It also has six legs, which attach to the thorax, and four wings. A butterfly is symmetrical. This means that if you draw a line down the middle of its body, it looks the same on both sides of the line. Keep this in mind when you draw your butterfly.

Step 1

Begin by drawing an upside-down raindrop shape for the butterfly's body. Next, draw a circle for the head and use curved lines to create the shapes for the tops of the wings. Draw the bottom wings, connecting them to the butterfly's body. Remember to use light pencil work at this stage.

Step 2

Add the line work to the body to represent the butterfly's abdomen. Draw fine lines close to the top of the wings. Add antennae with little droplets on the ends, ovals for the eyes, points for the mouth and a stripe for the neck. You will notice that you don't see the butterfly's legs from the viewpoint you are drawing.

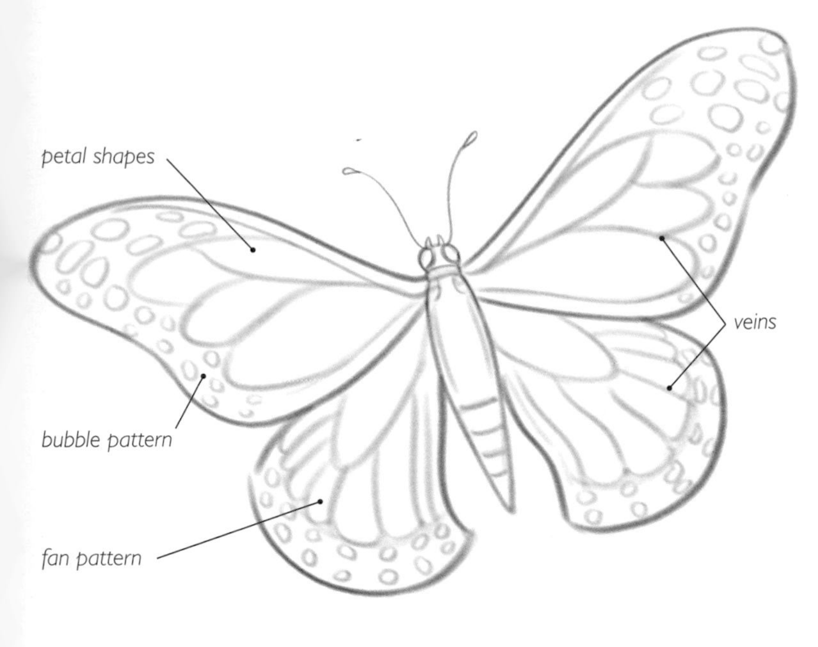

Step 3

Sketch the pattern on the butterfly's wings. Begin by drawing petal shapes inside the top wings to represent the veins. For the bottom wings, draw the single petal shapes on both sides and add the lines to make a fan pattern.

Next, sketch the bubble pattern on the outside of all the wings. Don't forget the fine details on the inside of the body.

Step 4

Start by observing how the shading is done. Beginning with the butterfly's body, shade from the edges into the middle. Make sure that you leave space for any white areas. Use darker pencil work on the eyes and neck. Next, shade the wings and add faint movement lines around the outside.

Now you can draw the butterfly's habitat. Notice that the line work is quite wavy. Start by drawing shapes for the flowers, and then work from there to sketch the leaves. Try sketching your own flowers for the butterfly's habitat!

DRAWING TIP

A pattern is an art element that is nearly always used in drawing. A pattern is made up of repeated shapes and lines. You'll find patterns everywhere in nature.

INTERESTING FACTS

- Depending on its species, a butterfly can live from only 1 week up to a year.
- As a butterfly ages, the colour of its wings fade.

DRAGONFLY

Dragonflies are one of the most spectacular and ancient insects that live today, having existed for millions of years. Dragonflies can be found in vibrant scarlet, green and blue. They often live around water, because their larvae are aquatic. Dragonflies help our environment by eating annoying insects such as mosquitoes and midges. Dragonflies are powerful fliers and can reach speeds of up to 97kph.

Before you begin

Line work is the most important art skill with this drawing. The different types of lines (curved, bent, zigzag) add a decorative element to the picture and a sense of movement. Using a construction line in the middle of the dragonfly will give the drawing direction.

DRAWING TIP

Create a page of different types of line work using a grey lead pencil. Explore vertical and horizontal lines. Experiment by drawing squiggly, curly or pointy lines. Try drawing a large and then a small spiral. Use different pressures with your pencil.

Step 1

Begin by drawing a central construction line. Next, draw a circle for the dragonfly's head. Add ovals for the thorax and abdomen.

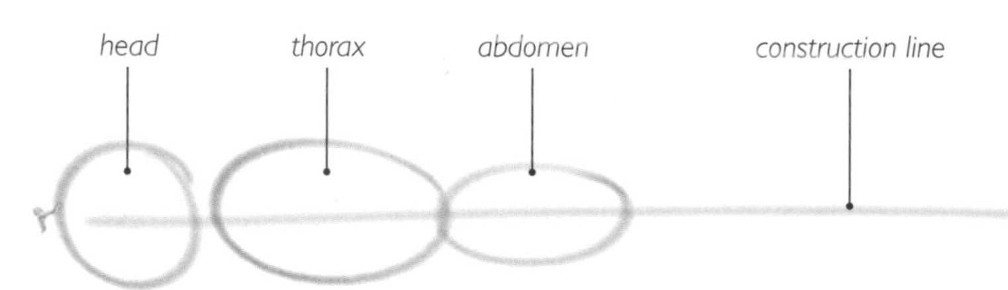

Step 2

Sketch a half-moon shape for the compound eye, then add curved lines around the tail. Note the angle of the wings. Add a construction line for the left wing, followed by a line for the right. Lastly, add bent lines for the legs, beginning with the middle one.

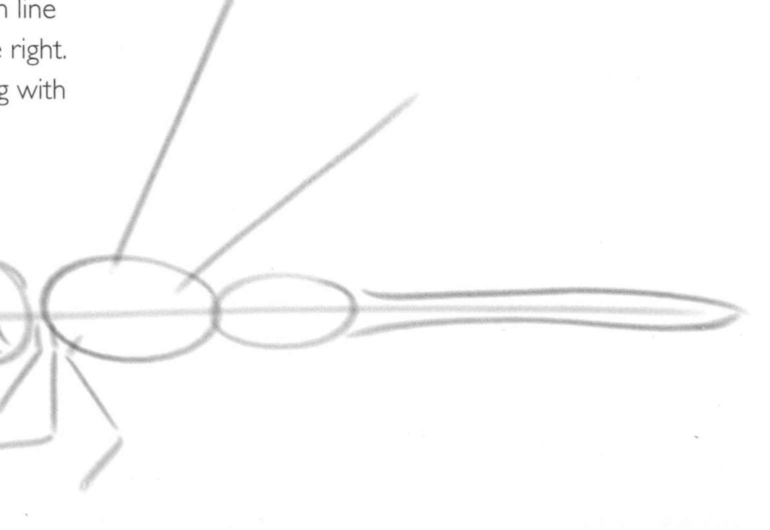

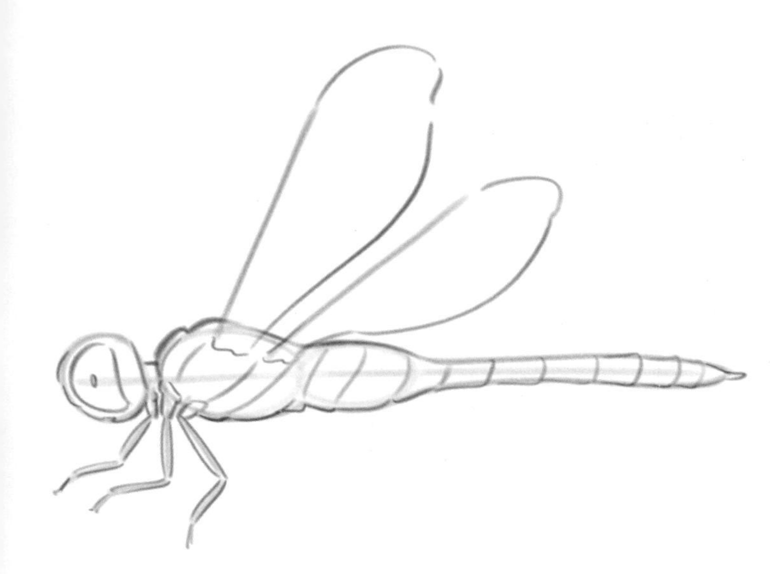

Step 3

Create the outside form of the dragonfly. Define the curved outline, starting with a wavy outline that forms the top and bottom of the wings. Next, draw curved lines to help build the shape of the legs. Draw a tiny oval in the centre of the eye. Add a corkscrew pattern on the body and wavy marks beneath the wings.

Step 4

Darken the line work. Lightly sketch the outside shape of the third wing behind the dragonfly. Softly sketch the extra three legs. Shade the underside of the dragonfly, and then lightly draw the patterns inside the wings.

Finally, be confident when you sketch the background. Begin by softly shading in marks for the water, then draw the curved reeds. Imagine that your dragonfly is now zipping around its natural habitat, looking for dinner!

INTERESTING FACTS

- Dragonflies are efficient hunters that devour their prey mid-flight.
- A dragonfly has 360-degree vision.

GRASSHOPPER

Grasshoppers are interesting insects to watch because of the way they jump and walk. Farmers fear large swarms of grasshoppers because they can cause serious damage to crops, devouring up to 100,000 tonnes of food a day. The male grasshopper sings to attract females, creating a high-pitched sound by rubbing its hind legs together.

Before you begin

It is important to draw the initial line work for the legs of the grasshopper in the right position, as this will make sure it is at the correct angle. Focus on the direction that the lines run in and how long the lines are. Observe the development of the grasshopper in each step before you start to draw.

Step 1

Create a baseline on a slight angle, as this will help you position the grasshopper correctly. Draw a circle for the head and add a point on the underside for the mouth. Draw a squarish shape with the bottom left corner missing and add a long leaf-like shape for the abdomen. Sketch the front legs, drawing the top one on the line and the other just above. Draw the middle leg, paying attention to the angle. Finally, draw the back legs with the joints. Start with the front leg and then add the rear one.

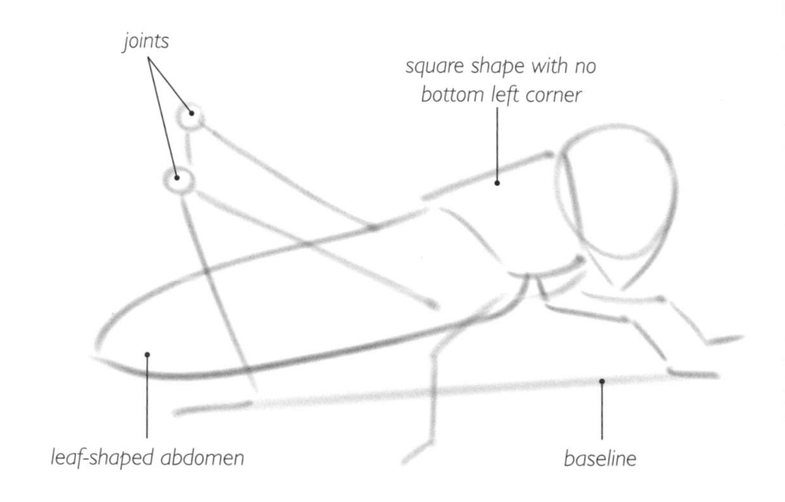

Step 2

Create the grasshopper's form. Focus on making all line work smooth so you begin to define the shape of the whole body. Add the eye and then create the outside line work for the legs. Draw the soft line work for the wing.

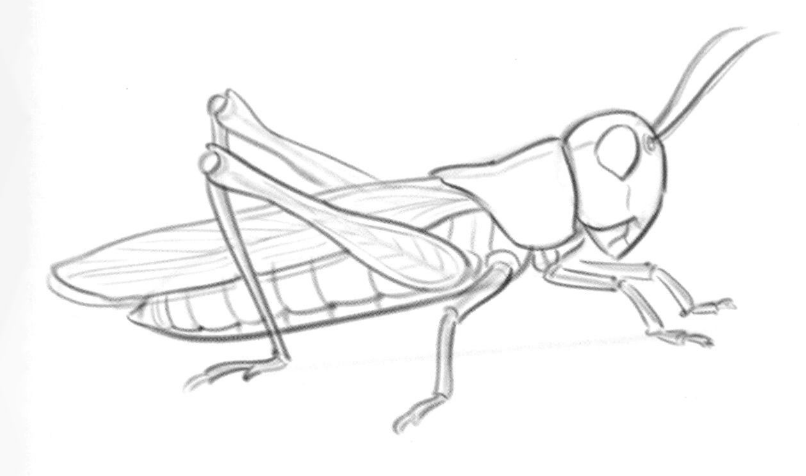

Step 3

Add the pattern to the grasshopper's thorax and the leaf-like details on the legs and wing. Sketch the fine details on the face and draw the antennae.

Step 4

Where needed, darken the line work. The shading is important as it will help the body look more rounded. Pay special attention to the eye and the underside of the body.

Draw the leaf the grasshopper is perching on using the baseline from step one. Make sure the leaf is larger than the plant in the background. This will give your picture perspective. Sketch in the vertical plant and finally add shading. Your grasshopper is ready to jump!

DRAWING TIP

Always begin your drawing by pressing lightly with the pencil so you can rub out any mistakes or marks that you are unhappy with.

INTERESTING FACTS

- A grasshopper's blood is green because it doesn't carry oxygen.
- In some countries, people eat grasshoppers. They are a good source of protein!

HONEYBEE

Honeybees are fascinating insects because of their ability to make honey from the nectar of flowers. They also play a very important role in pollinating flowering plants, as they carry pollen from one plant to another on their legs. Bees defend their hives from predators by using their stingers. During summer, hives can contain up to 20,000 bees!

Before you begin

Shape, line and texture are art elements that will help you construct this image. It is important to pay attention to the construction line for the backbone of the bee and the curved and rounded shapes that make up the bee's form. Also be aware of the texture used for the bee's hair and the organic pattern on the wings and abdomen.

Step 1

It is important to start by drawing the construction line for the centre of the bee. Next, draw a circle for the thorax and add upside-down teardrop shapes for the head and the abdomen. Add three pointy lines for the legs.

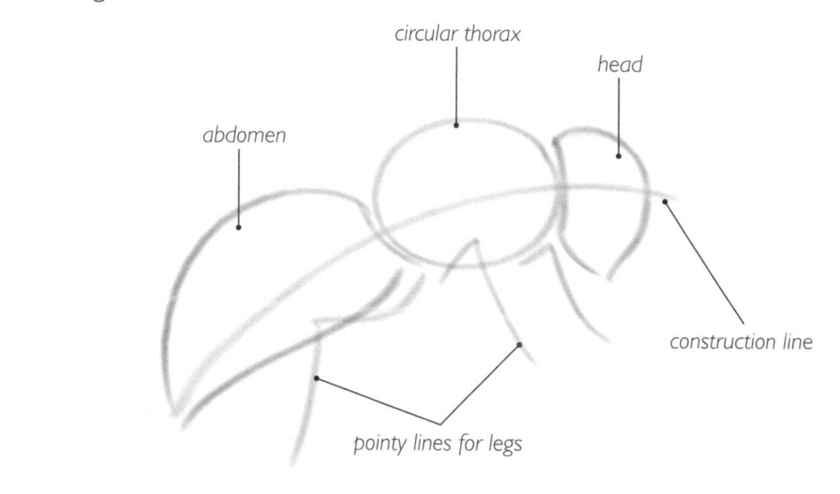

Step 2

Add wavy lines to construct the wing and a squashed oval for the eye. Use line work to build the shapes for the legs. Add more line work for the antennae, tongue and stinger.

Step 3

Sketch the cracked line work for the veins on the wing. Working from the top of the abdomen down, draw a wavy leaf pattern. Define the jagged edges of the abdomen and add a sharp stinger. Focusing on the thorax and head, add a pattern of fine soft lines to show hair. Lastly, add feathery details to the feet.

Step 4

Pay special attention to the shading. Shade between the patterns on the abdomen and add tone to the middle of the legs, the bottom of the eye and the mouth area.

Add details to the background. Behind the wing, faintly sketch a second wing. Add faint movement lines that mirror the edge of the wings. Add in faint legs on the other side of the body. When drawing the flower, begin with the stem using medium pressure with your pencil. Add the petal shapes from the bottom upward. Ensure that they change in size. You can also try to draw a different flower for your bee to drink from.

DRAWING TIP

Get to know your pencil. You can create your own practice page of patterns, shapes, lines and different levels of shading. Explore ways to use your pencil by lightly pressing it to the paper and then harder.

INTERESTING FACTS

- A queen bee can use her curved stinger many times.
- A female worker bee can only uses her stinger once, then she dies!

LADYBIRD

Ladybirds (also known as ladybugs or ladybeetles) are brightly coloured beetles with yellow, orange and red wing cases and black spots. When they see these bright colours, predators are warned that ladybirds taste awful. Gardeners are happy to find ladybirds as they eat aphids and fruit flies, which can destroy crops. It is thought to be a sign of good luck if a ladybird lands on you.

Before you begin

The following steps focus on shape, pattern and observation. All of these elements are important when constructing an image. Be aware of the circular shapes that help create the ladybird's form and the repeated patterns on the ladybird's wings. Pay attention to the types of line work used for the drawing.

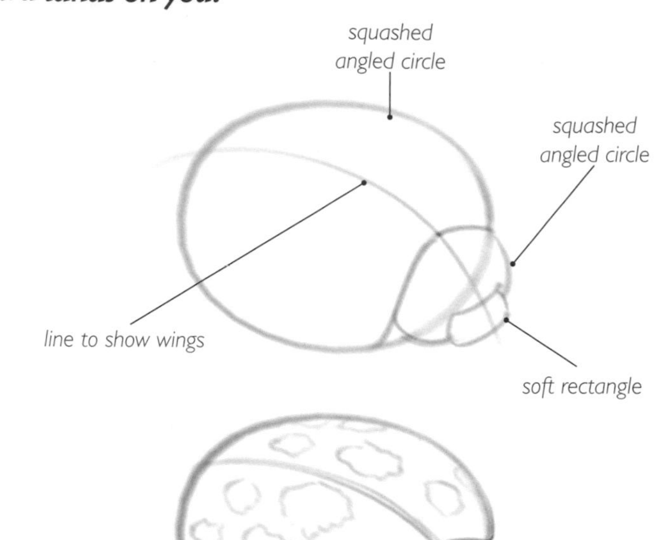

Step 1

Remember, use your pencil lightly at first. Sketch a slightly squashed circle on an angle. Place a curved line through the circle for the wings. Connect another curved line to the right side of the circle and add an oval shape for the head. Add a rectangular shape to the oval.

Step 2

Add detail to the ladybird. Draw three small oval shapes at the base of the head. Add the lines that make up the antennae and legs. Finally, sketch a fuzzy circular pattern over the ladybird's wing cases.

Step 3

Using darker pencil work, add shading to the pattern on the wings and the eyes. Softly draw a wavy pattern for the veins of the leaf in the background. Lastly, draw a shadow under the belly and add extra shading to the leaf.

INTERESTING FACTS

- In winter, ladybirds cluster on twigs and enter into a deep sleep to survive the cold.
- Adult ladybirds release an oily yellow toxin with a strong smell from their leg joints when handled roughly.

MOUSE

Mice have poor eyesight and can only see in black and white, so they use their sensitive whiskers to detect things. They can be kept as pets but they can also cause a lot of damage, as they eat crops and spread disease. Mice are found in almost every country in the world.

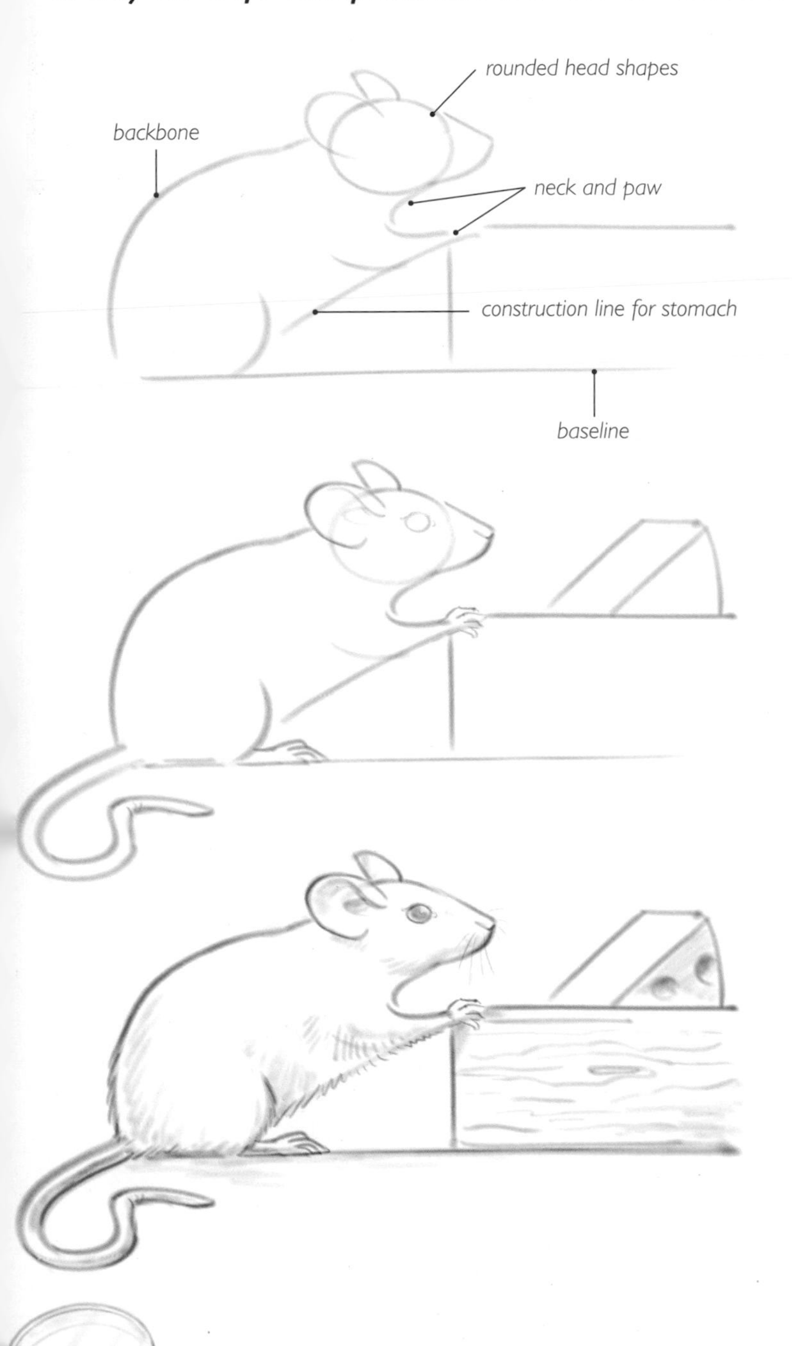

Before you begin

The following steps focus on shape, line work, texture and observation. Pay attention to the curved lines that form the body, the different shapes that make the head and the patterns that show texture on the body and the wood.

Step 1

Using light pencil work, draw a baseline for the mouse to sit on and draw the straight edges of the wood. Add a construction line for the stomach so it looks like the mouse is sitting on the wood. Add curved lines for the hip, paws and neck. Sketch a circle for the head, just above the neck. Connect the ear shapes and the curved tip of the nose. Add the backbone running from the ear to the baseline.

Step 2

Define and smooth the outline. Add a squiggly tail and draw a wedge shape for the cheese. Develop the inside line work of the front ear. Use curved lines to create the details for the claws and draw the round eye with pointed corners and the mouse's nostril.

Step 3

Darken the mouse's outline. Using a light pressure with your pencil, create the pattern and texture of the fur. Add shading to the eye, ears and tail. Lastly, shade the ground and add the texture of the wood. Don't forget the details of the cheese!

INTERESTING FACT → Egyptians discovered many centuries ago that cats are the most efficient way of getting rid of mice!

RABBIT

Rabbits are much-loved, fluffy creatures that have been illustrated in children's books and cartoons for many generations. Even though rabbits make wonderful pets, and can be house-trained like cats, in the wild they destroy farmers' crops. Rabbits live underground in a burrow and build interconnecting tunnels, called warrens, to help them escape from predators.

Before you begin

This drawing explores the use of shapes. Much of the rabbit's form is rounded. When creating the initial structure in the first step, you will notice that it consists of a series of circles, ovals and curves. Shapes are elements that are often used in drawing to help construct a picture.
You can also see shapes used in different types of patterns.

Step 1

Using light pencil work, sketch a baseline for the rabbit to sit on, which will help make the rabbit's feet point in the right direction. Draw an egg shape for the body and rest it on the middle of the line. Draw a circle that slightly overlaps the right side of the body for the head.

Step 2

Draw a curved shape for the front ear. See how it sits at the back of the head. Draw the second ear behind the first. Add a brush shape for the tail and a curve for the hip. Sketch the front paws, sitting them on the baseline. Draw the rear front paw above the baseline.

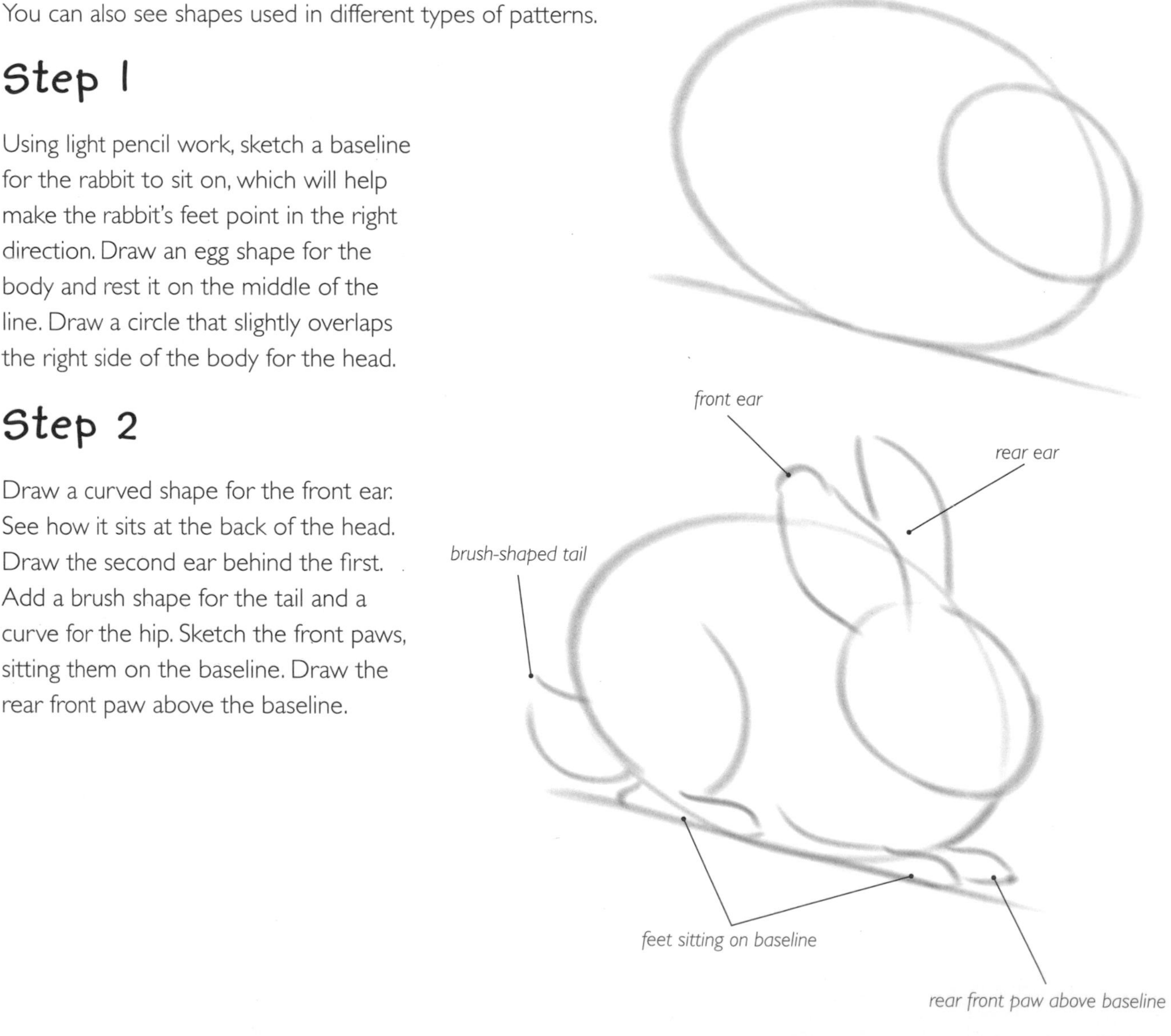

Step 3

Define the outline of the rabbit, using darker line work. Draw the line work in the shape of a 'Y' for the nose, adding a curve for the mouth. Sketch a round eye with pointy corners lined up with the top of the nose. Draw a wavy line inside the ear and another line to show the neck. Create a slight dip in the line work at the top of the back. Next, add marks to create the paws and any other details.

Step 4

Start by adding fuzzy line work inside the ear and under the jaw. Carefully sketch a fine pattern to show texture on the tail, hip area, belly and chest. Add medium grey shading to the outside edge of the eye. Lightly add strokes for the whiskers and any other necessary shading.

Draw the rabbit's habitat, beginning with vertical fence posts, and then the beams that run across. Add in line work to show the texture of the fence. Sketch leaf shapes for the plants and spiky grass pattern. Your rabbit is complete and is relaxing at the bottom of the garden!

DRAWING TIP

Practise by drawing a page of different sized circles and ovals. Try relaxing your pencil grip and drawing each shape quickly. This will help improve your technique.

INTERESTING FACT → Rabbits should only a eat small amount of carrots each day and their diets should be rich in leafy vegetables.

SQUIRREL

Squirrels are a type of rodent and are closely related to mice. Like mice, they are cheeky little guests around the home as they hunt for food. They are known for their love of raw nuts and will 'squirrel' them away for winter in hiding spots throughout the garden. Squirrels will nibble on anything to wear down their sharp teeth when they grow too long.

Before you begin

The most important elements when drawing the squirrel are shape and texture. Check the details of each step before you begin. Pay attention to the circle shapes for the head and body, the direction of the feet on the baseline and the texture and detail of the fur.

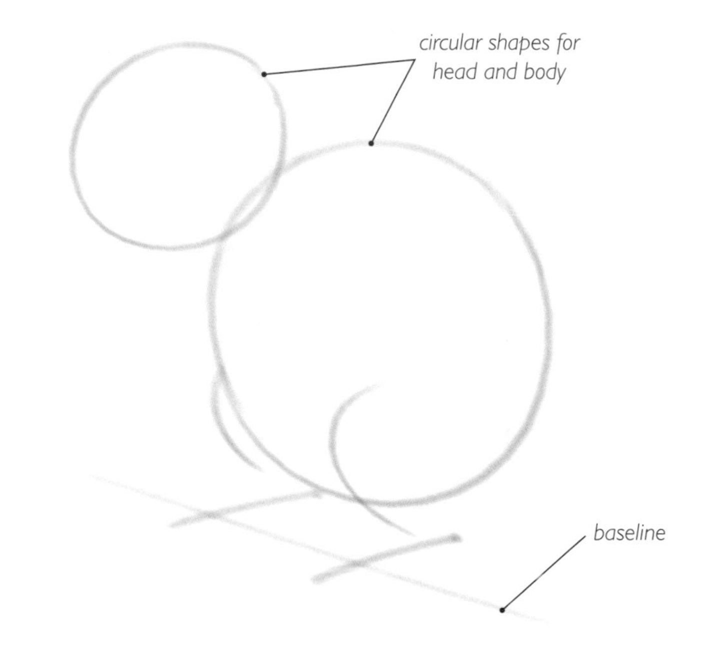

Step 1

Begin by drawing the baseline on an angle. Next, draw a circle for the body sitting just above the baseline. Attach a smaller circle to the top left corner of the body for the head. Draw curved lines for the hips and straight lines for the feet. Make sure the feet are on the correct angle so the squirrel is facing the right direction.

Step 2

Develop the outside form of your squirrel. Add curves to either side of the neck and a point for the nose. Draw a circle for the eye below the triangle shapes for the ears. Sketch the sweeping line work for the shape of the arm. Connect the square-shaped paws by drawing a nut between them. Build the form of the feet by adding a line on top. Finally, draw a wave shape for the tail, beginning with the bottom line first, and then adding the top line.

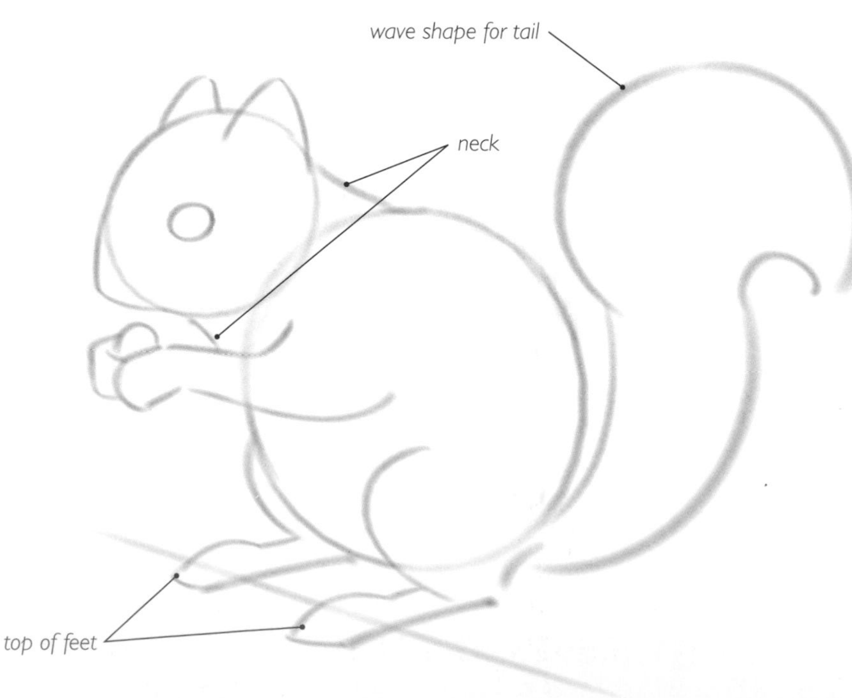

Step 3

With a clean eraser, rub out any unneeded line work inside the body. Add details for the four paws and arm and wavy marks inside the ear. Next, draw faint texture marks under the jaw and at the corner of the eye. Define the shape of the nose and mouth and draw a line for the nostril.

Step 4

Using darker line work, smooth the curves of the body. Add fine texture for all of the fur (see the texture sample box above). Draw the grey tone inside the eye and ear. Shade the neck and feet area and the nut. Add fine whiskers and any other necessary marks.

Now create the squirrel's habitat. The squirrel has been nibbling on many snacks, so scatter leaf and nut shapes all around it. Don't forget the soft shading to show the ground. Your friendly squirrel is complete and waiting for more food!

DRAWING TIP

It is important to be confident when developing your drawing skills. If you doubt yourself, the results will show it! Keep a positive attitude and know that your drawing will improve with time.

INTERESTING FACT

Squirrels make a loud screeching sound to warn other squirrels of danger.

ROBIN

Robins are small birds with bright red breasts. They sing sweet melodies, even near streetlights at night. Robins are often associated with Christmas, as some people say their song is more passionate around that time. They enjoy snacking on worms and bugs, but will also eat fruitcake and pastry. You can also see robins eating the hearts of sunflowers.

Before you begin

You will explore shape, line and texture art elements in this drawing. Shape creates the basic form of your bird (form refers to the whole shape). Line helps create the direction in which the bird is facing and is also used to explore texture. The texture of the robin's feathers is made up of a series of lines.

Step 1

Remember to sketch lightly for this step. Draw a construction line for the branch that the robin will rest on. Next, draw a curve for the robin's breast just above the branch. Add a circle for the head and line work for the wing and tail, and draw the hooks for the legs and claws.

Step 2

Define the outside form of the robin's body. Attach pointy shapes to the end of the wing and tail, as well as details for feathers. Draw a circle for the eye and add a triangle shape for the beak. Notice that the line for the beak is drawn across the head.

Step 3

Use darker pencil work for this step. Begin by adding an extra line for the beak and fine details for the feather pattern on the chest. Develop the legs of the robin, using curved line work for the claws. Extend and widen the branch, adding the bumps.

DRAWING TIP

Texture is seen on the surface of an object. It is the look and feel of something. In drawing, it is represented by a series of marks. For example, if you were drawing carpet, you could draw a collection of bumps close together. Fur could be drawn using a pattern of fine soft lines.

Step 4

Now focus on the texture of the feathers. Start by drawing a fan pattern on the wing and shading to the tail. Build up the texture for the feathers using a series of soft lines. Darken your pencil work for the breast, remembering to leave the white areas clear.

Add shading to the underside of the branch and draw the wavy shaped leaves with the veins inside. Your robin is happily sitting in a tree, ready to break into song!

INTERESTING FACT → Robins have been known to nest in some strange places, like kettles and coat pockets!

SPIDER

Spiders are not insects, but arachnids, because they have two body sections and eight legs. Spiders also have 6–8 eyes. Even though a lot of people fear them, spiders are very useful because they eat insects and pests. Spiders produce silk through spinning glands called spinnerets. All spiders make some venom, but only a few produce enough to harm humans.

Before you begin

Size plays an important role in this drawing. Practise drawing the spider at a large size first, so that you learn to construct the drawing with the correct shapes, lines and shading. In the final step of this lesson, the spider will be smaller and the web larger. Organic line and shape, which is all around us in nature, is used when drawing the cobweb pattern.

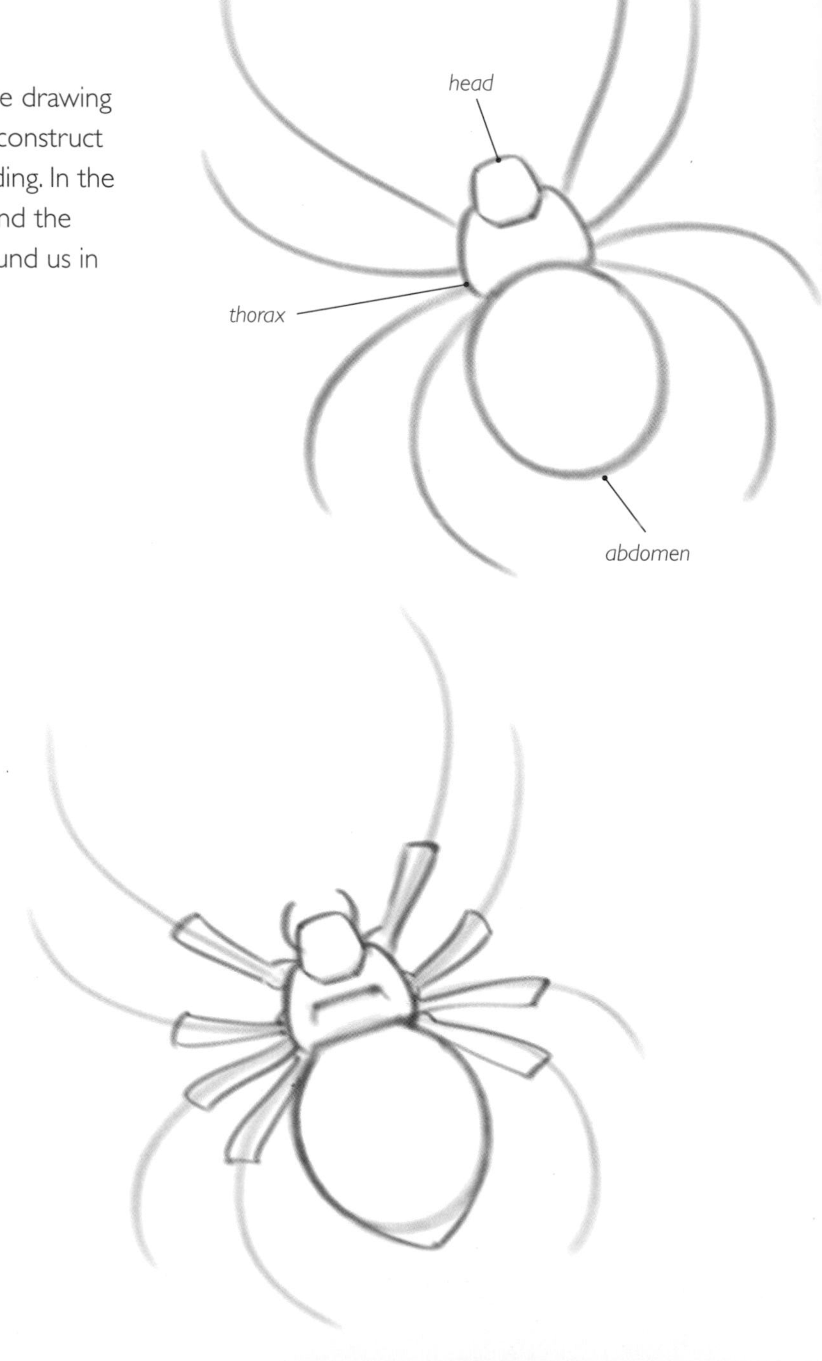

Step 1

Remember to use light pencil work at this stage. Draw a circle shape for the abdomen and attach shapes for the thorax and head. Add four legs to both sides of the thorax, beginning with the top legs first. The spider is symmetrical, which means that it should be equal on both sides.

Step 2

Define the spider's abdomen with smooth line work and add a tip at the bottom. Add fangs on either side of the head, and a line in the middle of the thorax. Build the curved rectangular shapes around the top of the legs.

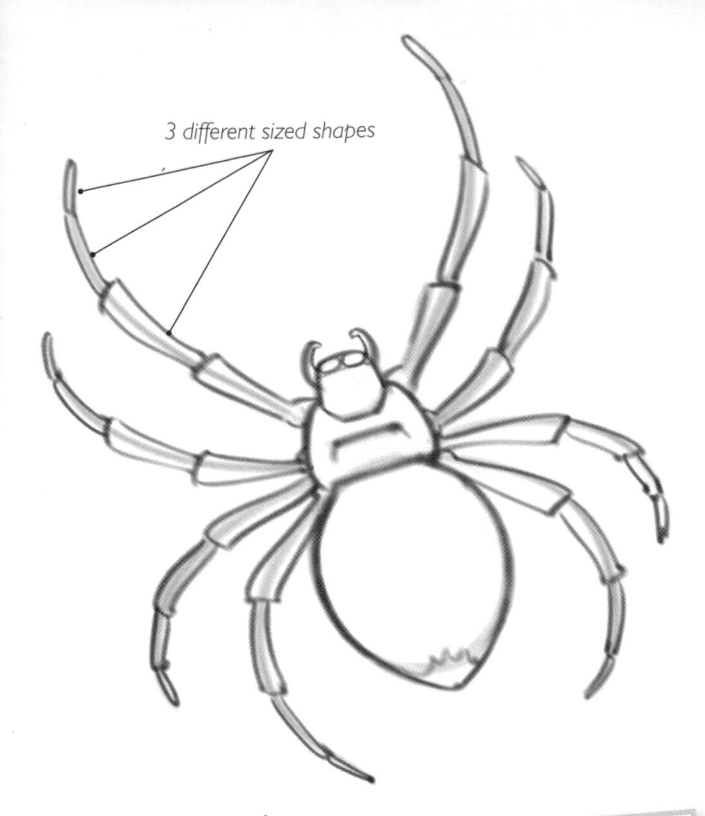

Step 3

Construct the rest of the shapes around the legs. Make sure that they get smaller in size as you add them. Add a line to the inside of the fangs, ovals for the eyes and a wavy line at the bottom of the abdomen.

DRAWING TIP

Organic patterns can be found all around us in nature. The spiral in a cobweb can also be found on a snail's shell in the garden, or on seashells at the beach.

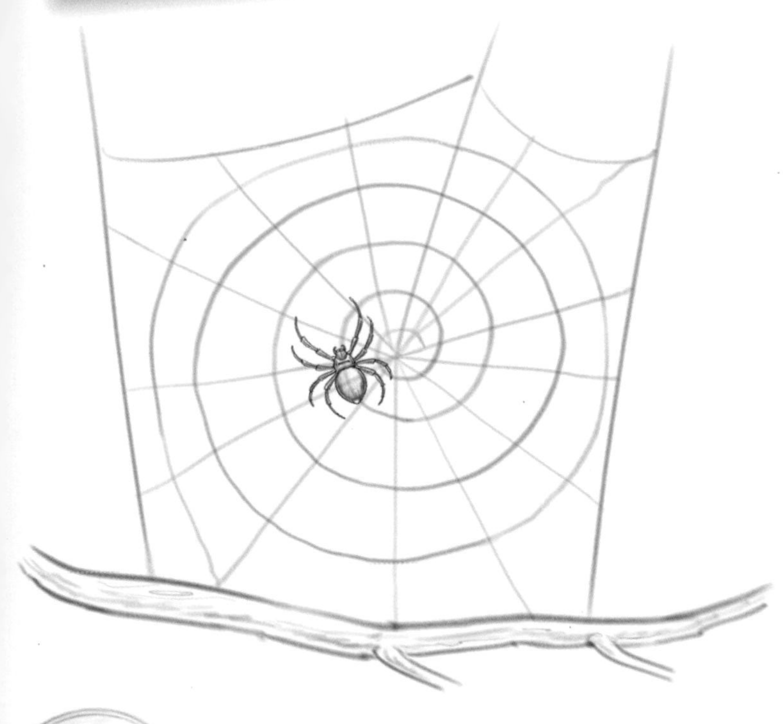

Step 4

Define the spider's outline with darker pencil work. Shading the body is important, as it makes it look rounder. Focus on the abdomen, starting with a darker shade just in from the edges of the abdomen. Lighten the shading as you move in towards the middle. Leave the tip white. Work your way up to the thorax and head. Finish by shading the edges of the legs.

Step 5

Draw a branch and connect the straight edges of the cobweb. Add a wavy line at the top. Starting at the branch, draw the spiral centre of the web. Finally, add the lines that travel out from the centre of the cobweb. You can now sketch your small spider. Its habitat is complete and ready for it to capture its prey!

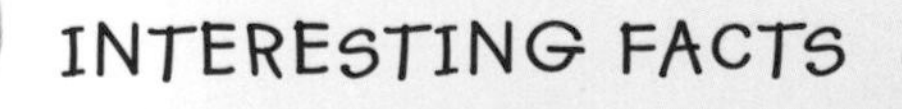

- Spiders are near-sighted. They use the hair on their body to sense predators.
- Spiders never waste a torn, dirty web, because they roll it into a ball and eat it!

GECKO

Geckos live in warm climates all over the world. They are helpful because they rid homes of troublesome insects. Geckos defy gravity by using special toe pads to crawl upside down across ceilings and walls. They make a noticeable chirping sound when calling other geckos. Perhaps one of their most impressive traits is their ability to drop their tail when attacked by predators. Amazingly, the tail grows back!

Before you begin

The gecko's form is made up of simple lines and shapes. This basic structure will help you build the outside shape of the gecko. Focus on sketching the lines for the legs in the right direction and ensure you carefully copy the shapes for the body. This will help you create the correct perspective, so it seems like you are looking down at the gecko.

Step 1

Lightly draw an oval shape for the body. Next, add a curved triangle for the head, and then the bent lines for the legs. Finish drawing the form by adding circles for the eyes and feet. Don't forget a line for the tail.

Step 2

Using line work, add a smooth outline. Add the shapes around the legs and tail. Carefully draw the toes in the right positions. Add a line across the front of the eye and rub out any lines inside your gecko that you don't need. Before using your eraser, clean it by rubbing off any dirty marks on a clean piece of paper.

Step 3

Define the outline using darker pencil work. Connect the line work from the toes to the feet. Add an extra circle for the eye. Draw a line for the nostril and any other marks you see. Now the gecko's form is taking shape.

Step 4

Add a fuzzy circle pattern on the body and a band of stripes on the tail. Draw wavy marks on the head and side. Softly add shading under the belly and tail, and to the front of the legs.

Finally, sketch the background. Draw the edge of the dirt between the beetle and gecko. Next, draw line work to show cracks in the ground. Try drawing the beetle and add the shading next it. Your gecko is ready to hunt his prey!

DRAWING TIP

Take your time when sketching detailed pictures. Remember, your skills will improve over time with patience and effort.

INTERESTING FACTS

- Geckos lick their faces clean like cats.
- Geckos can change colour like a chameleon.

Funky Things to Draw horses

INTRODUCTION

Horses have been admired for centuries for their beauty, strength, intelligence and speed. They have played an important role throughout human history. Horses have been essential for transport, farming, industry and even sport!

The horse has also been a popular subject for artists through the ages. To help draw this muscular animal, visualise its features. Imagine the way its muscles move when running. Picture its flowing mane and tail as it jumps over a fence. Visualise a trained horse standing on its hind legs during a performance.

THINGS YOU WILL NEED

- An HB or 2B pencil (they are light and won't smudge too easily)
- A pencil sharpener and a small dish for shavings
- A4 cartridge paper or copy paper and some scrap paper for experiments
- A clean eraser
- Confidence: a positive attitude will help improve your skills
- Imagination: don't be afraid to explore your own style or ideas

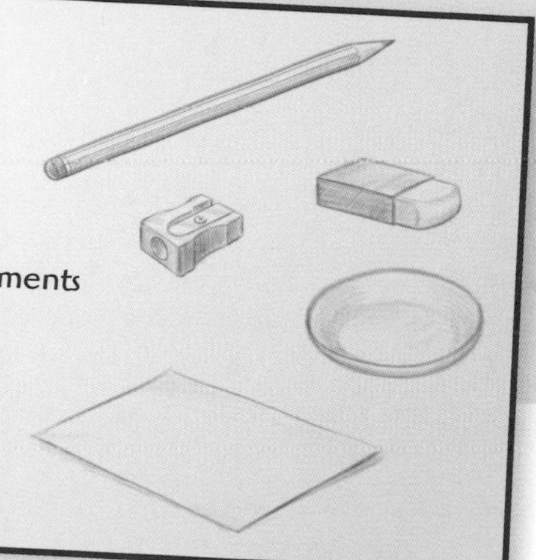

Drawing guidelines

There are a few things you should be aware of when drawing your horses.

1 The body of the horse is built around a series of rounded shapes, creating a muscular form.
2 The shape of the horses' legs is constructed using lines and circles for the legs, joints and hooves.
3 Be careful to position the head and legs of each horse and rider so that they face in the right direction.
4 Parts of the pictures, such as wheels, hooves, riders' shoulders or carriages, are drawn on a specific angle. Pay attention to the direction of each angle so that the perspective of your drawing is correct.
5 Begin the first step by drawing your horse lightly so the construction lines won't be too obvious as you progress. If you want to erase any pencil lines, use a clean eraser.

Stages of drawing

Drawing horses takes patience, as there are many elements you will need to sketch to create each picture. You will see that a style of curved, smooth line work is explored in the drawings. Before you begin, read all the instructions and carefully study the images for each step so you will be confident throughout the drawing process.

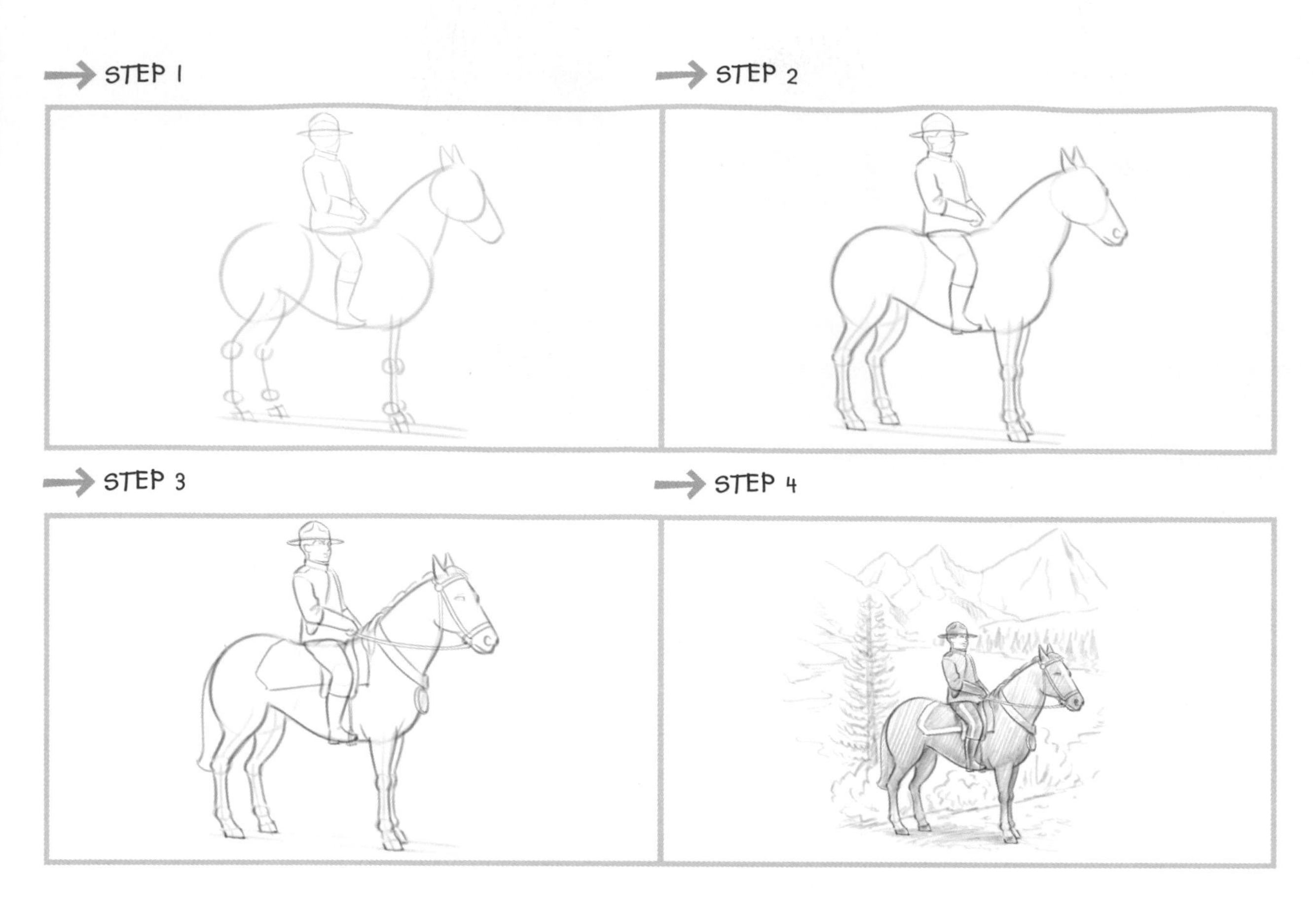

Each step will give you direction on the levels of shading and the types of line and shape that are explored. Study how the horses are shaded and how light or dark the tone is. Look at the type and length of the lines and how they give the horse a sense of movement. Also, pay attention to the shapes used for the rider and horse. How large are the shapes for the rider compared to the shapes for the horse?

Skills and techniques

Here are some examples of the different techniques and art elements you will learn about.

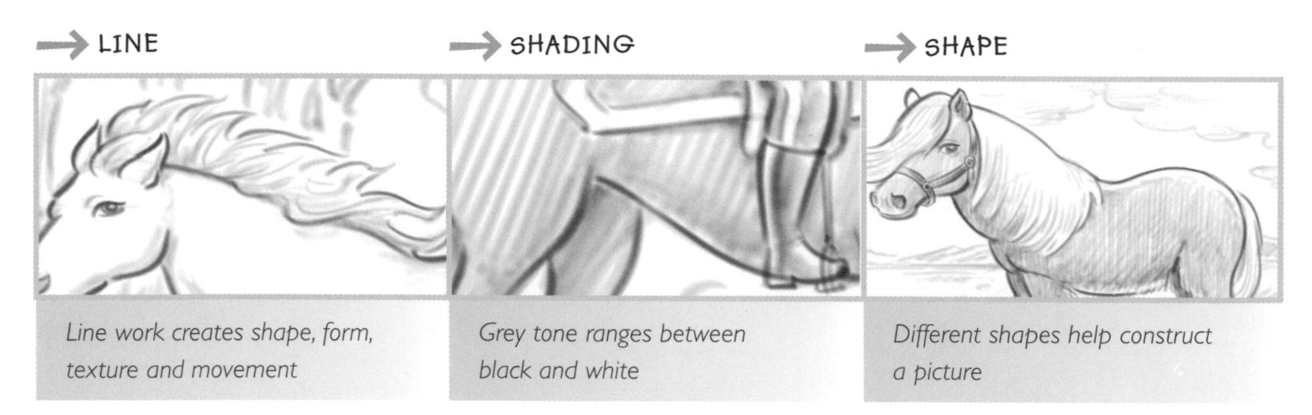

Line work creates shape, form, texture and movement

Grey tone ranges between black and white

Different shapes help construct a picture

Horses can be difficult to draw. To draw them well, you need to finetune your observation skills and trust your sense of judgement. Most of all, you need to have faith that, with practice, you will learn to draw them beautifully!

STALLION

A stallion is a male horse that is used for breeding purposes. Stallions tend to be more aggressive than other horses. They are known for their dominating behaviour and will protect their territory using threatening body language. Most herds of horses will only have one stallion, as he will fight with other males who he sees as a threat to his mares. Stallions are popular competition horses, but should be handled by an experienced rider.

Before you begin

The stallion is drawn from a front perspective. To ensure it is seen from the correct perspective, study the angle at which the horse is galloping and the positioning of the legs. Observe the types of line used to construct the legs and the direction the head faces. Pay attention to the curved line work used to draw the whole body.

Step 1

Lightly draw a baseline on a slight angle. Add a curved body shape above it on the same angle, paying attention to the chest area. Draw construction lines for the legs and sketch all joints and hooves. Build the shape of the legs around the construction lines. Draw a thick neck shape and add a circle for the head. Add a rounded muzzle, the brow line and the ears.

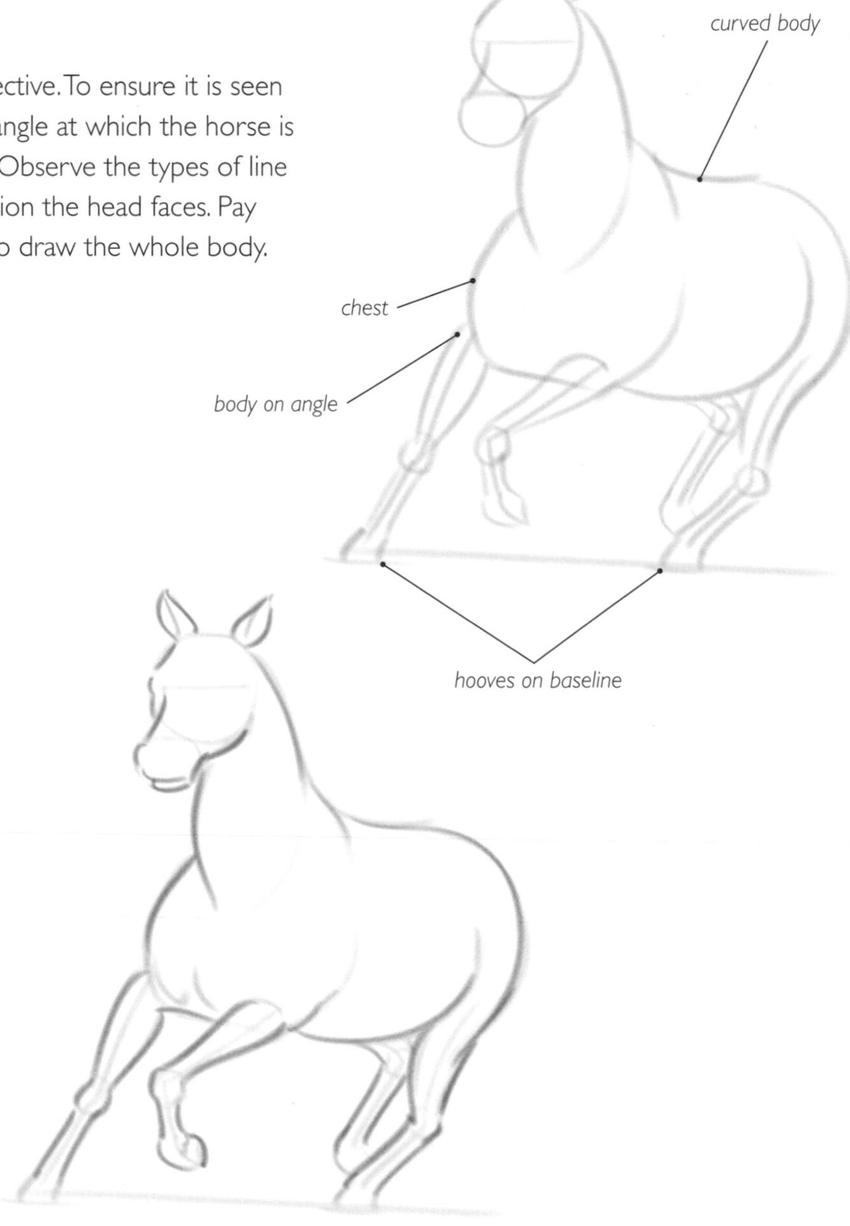

Step 2

Define and smooth the curves of the horse's form. Define the marks around the chest area and the shape of the brow, muzzle and jaw. Add a mouth and the details inside the ears.

Step 3

Darken the outline. Draw eyes on either side of the brow and nostrils on the muzzle, making sure they face in the right direction. Draw a wavy mane flowing behind the horse's head. Add a tail curving above the hindquarters.

DRAWING TIP

Develop your technique by creating a practice page of lines, shapes and patterns. Try sketching your marks loosely and quickly, and then try a slower, controlled pencil technique.

Step 4

Create soft line work to add texture to the mane and tail. Using a light pressure with your pencil, gently shade the edges of the horse's body. Define the nostrils, eyes and ears.

Create the background, using faint line work to draw the texture of the grass. Once you sketch the trees and mountain peaks, your stallion will be ready to gallop through the field!

INTERESTING FACT → Stallions tend to be more muscular than other horses and their neck is usually thicker.

ANDALUSIAN

The Spanish Andalusian horse developed when the invading Moor's Arabian horses bred with the Iberian horses in the 700s. Cave paintings of the Iberian horse that date back 20,000 years have been found. Andalusians (named after a region in Spain) were bred by Carthusian monks in the Middle Ages. They were favoured by European kings and their cavalries because of their agility and speed. Most Andalusians have a white or light grey coat.

Before you begin

The Andalusian is drawn from a side-on perspective. Pay close attention to the angles of all the horse's body parts and to the direction the rider is facing. The horse's and rider's eyes must be looking in the right direction to achieve this. Pay attention to how the curves of the horse are drawn and the positioning of the rider.

Step 1

Lightly draw two parallel angled baselines. Sketch a curved line for the chest above the baselines and add a curve for the hindquarters and back. Build the shape of the neck, add a circle for the head and draw a muzzle. Add construction lines touching the baselines for hind legs. Draw the front legs and sketch all joints and hooves. Draw the rider's leg, chest and arms. Add the rider's head and hat. Add the horse's ears.

Step 2

Define and smooth the curved outline of the horse, paying attention to the brow and chest. Build shapes around the construction lines for the back legs. Create the shapes of the front legs, one pointing out and the other behind it.

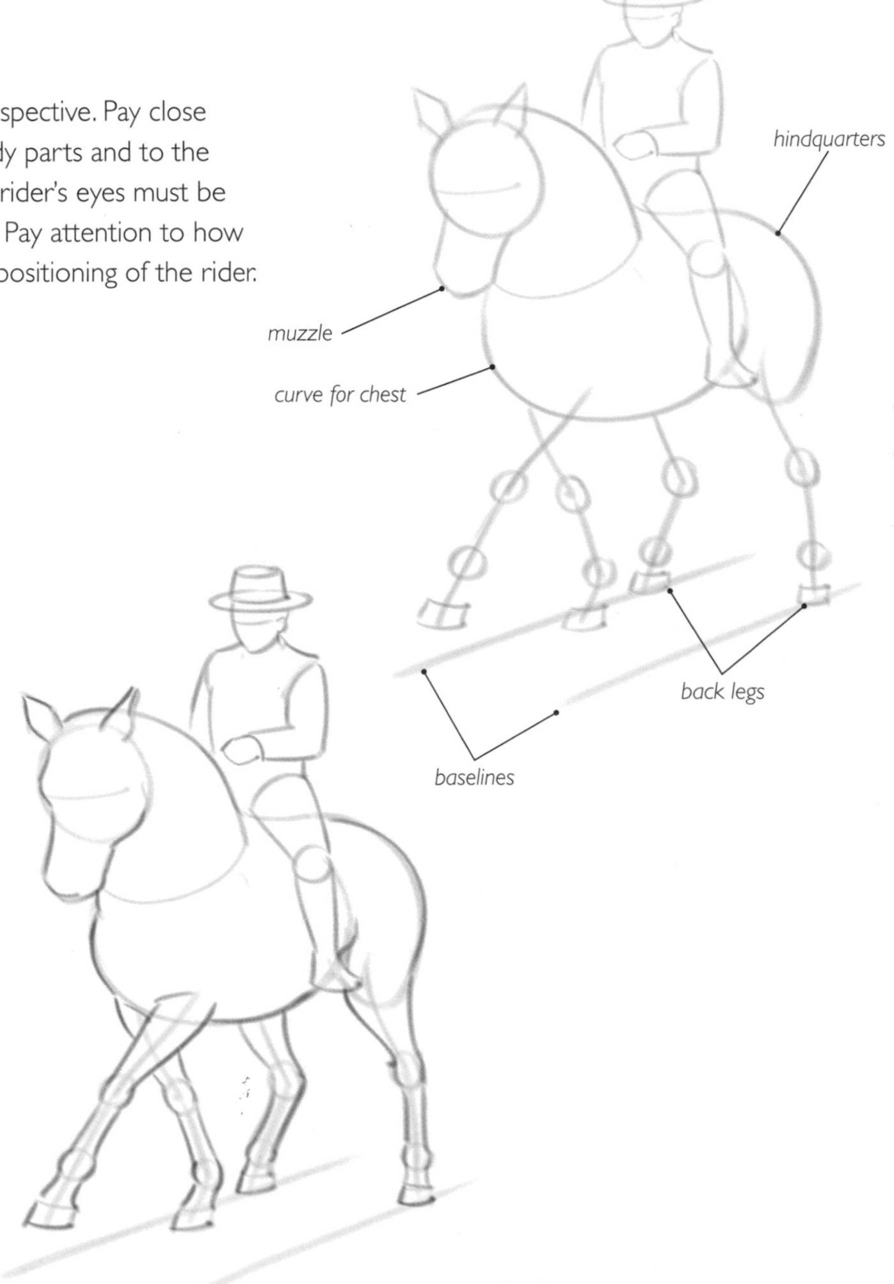

Step 3

Add a nostril to the horse's muzzle, an almond-shaped eye over its brow and a crinkly mane over its head. Draw a flame-shaped, flowing tail. Create the line work for the harness over the head and chest area. Add a saddle and marks for hooves. Sketch the line work for the rider's jacket, shirt and boot.

DRAWING TIP

Horses can be difficult to draw. Be patient and confident when drawing detailed pictures. Don't worry if your picture isn't perfect on your first try. Your skills will improve with practice.

Step 4

Shade a mid-grey tone with medium pencil pressure across the horse's body and the rider's clothes, paying attention to the darker areas. Add faint line work to the horse's tail to show texture. Draw the rider's eyes on either side of the face and add a nose and mouth. Shade the rider's hair and sketch the fingers.

Add bumpy marks and shading to the ground beneath the hooves. Once you draw the stadium in the background, your Andalusian is ready to perform!

INTERESTING FACT → Andalusians excel at classical dressage and show jumping because they learn very quickly and are elegant.

APPALOOSA

A hardy and gentle horse, the Appaloosa's most noticeable feature is its distinctive spotted coat. Cave paintings of spotted horses that date back 20,000 years have been found in France. The Spanish introduced horses to North America during the 1600s. The Nez Perce Native Americans, who lived in the Washington state area, bred the descendents of these original horses to create the Appaloosa's distinctive spotted colouring.

Before you begin

The bean-shaped body is the most important part of this picture because all elements of the drawing connect to it. Observe how the rider sits over the middle of the body. The hindquarters and head are connected to either side of the bean shape. Pay attention to how high the rider sits on the horse and where his body is positioned. Also, note the levels and types of shading used.

Step 1

Lightly draw a bean-shaped body. Add a thick neck in the top right corner. Sketch a head, brow, muzzle and jaw, and add a shape for the hindquarters. Draw curved construction lines for the hind legs and straight ones for front legs, and add joints and angled hooves. Add shapes for the rider's legs, chest, angled shoulders and arms. Draw the rider's head and hair and a cross for the face.

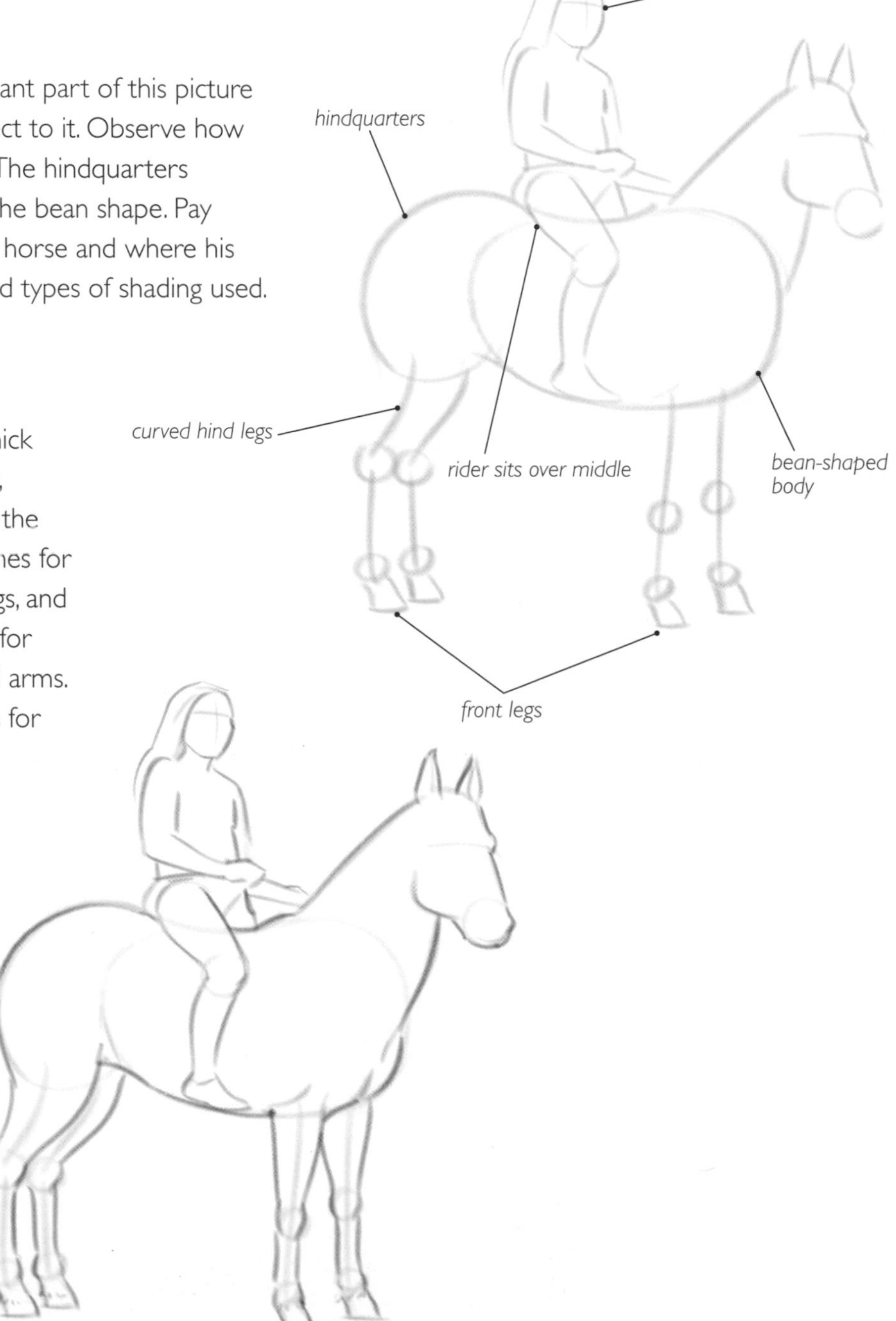

Step 2

Define and smooth the curved outline of the horse and rider. Build shapes for the front legs around the construction lines and joints. Add the shapes for the legs behind. Sketch marks around the chest and hooves, and draw the details inside the ears.

Step 3

Draw a shape for the horse's left eye on the brow line. Add a mouth and nostrils on the muzzle. Draw a fuzzy outline for the stripe on the head and curved shapes for the tail. Draw the rider's eyes on either side of the face and add a nose and mouth. Define the details of the rider's hair, neck and chest, and shade the rider's clothes. Add a spear in the front hand and the reins reaching to the rear hand.

DRAWING TIP

To draw light, medium and dark tones and explore shading techniques, create different levels of tone by changing the pressure you exert with your pencil.

Step 4

Study the levels of shading over the horse. Using a right to left motion, shade a mid-tone around the edges, leaving the white areas clear. Darken the eye, ears, nostrils, hooves and back leg. Create the mane and tail's texture using soft line work. Add a faint spotty pattern over the hindquarters and shade and define the rider's body.

Once you add shadows beneath the horse and jagged line work for the background, your rider will be ready to hunt!

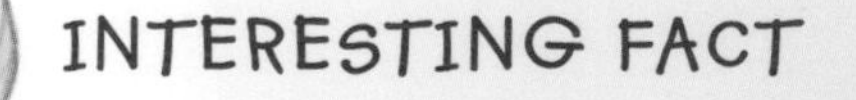

INTERESTING FACT

The word *Appaloosa* comes from the name of the Palouse river, where the Nez Perce tribe lived. It means 'something sticking down in the water' and is thought to be a reference to a large rock formation on the river where the tribe lived.

ARABIAN HORSE

The Arabian horse is an ancient breed of horse known for its stamina, speed, intelligence and alertness. For centuries, the nomadic Bedouin people of the Middle East developed these qualities in the Arabian, as they were essential for a desert warhorse. The Arabian is known for its good disposition and relationship with humans. Most modern breeds of horse are connected to the Arabian through their bloodlines.

Before you begin

The most important art element in this drawing is shape, as it gives the Arabian horse its muscular, rounded form. Observe the sizes and types of shapes used and how they connect together. Pay attention to the perspective from which the horse is seen and ensure that the head and legs are positioned correctly.

Step 1

Lightly draw a circle for the chest and the line work for the thick neck shape. Add a circle for the head and a curved shape for the muzzle. Sketch a line for the brow and leaf-shaped ears. Draw construction lines for the front legs. Add the joints and draw hoof shapes on a slight angle. Sketch the shape for the hind legs, with one in front and the other behind. Add the construction lines, joints and hooves for the hind legs.

Step 2

Define the curved shape of the horse's muscular form, paying attention to the outline of the brow, ears and muzzle. Add the mouth and build the shape of the legs around the construction lines, starting with the front legs.

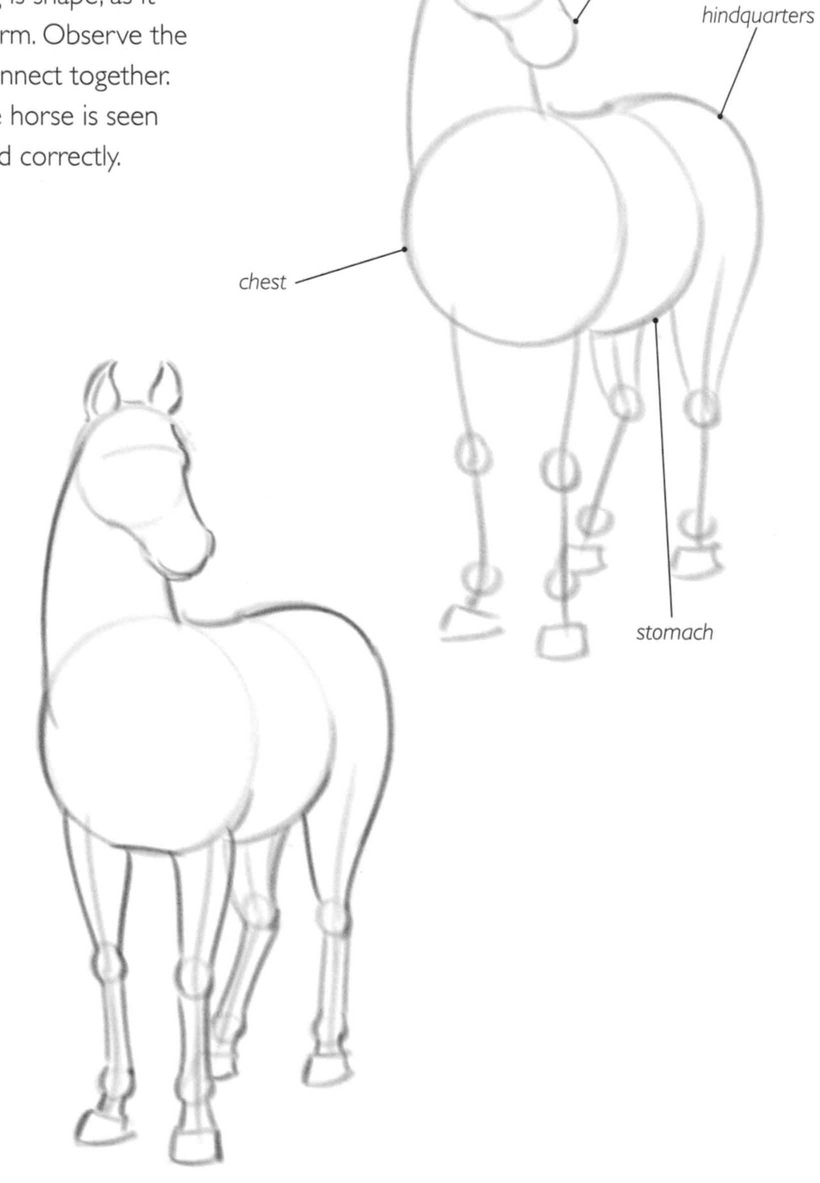

Step 3

Draw a curved palm tree trunk with a slightly irregular outline to the left of the horse. Draw an eye on the brow and nostrils on the muzzle. Add curved line work for the tail and an outline of the harness around the face and chest. Add decorative tassels to the harness and a lead curving from the muzzle to the tree trunk. Draw a mane flowing down from the head to the back.

DRAWING TIP

When you follow drawing instructions, carefully read through the changes between each step before you start drawing. Study the level of shading, the type of detailing and where the background is positioned.

Step 4

Darken the outline. Shade the edges of the horse's body with light pencil pressure. Add texture to the mane, tail and tassels using faint line work. Shade the ears, hooves and back leg using a mid-grey tone. Darken the eye and nostrils and add shadows beneath the hooves. Define the details of the harness and create a zigzag pattern on the trunk.

Once you faintly draw an oasis in the background, your Arabian horse will be ready to ride into the desert sun!

INTERESTING FACT → **Regardless of their coat colour, all Arabian horses have black skin as protection against the hot desert sun.**

RACEHORSE

Horse racing is an ancient sport that originated around 4500 BC, when horses were first domesticated in Central Asia. The most common type of horse used for horse racing is the 'thoroughbred'. This breed of horse stands at over 16 hands (1.63 cm or 64 in) tall and is agile and fast. Thoroughbreds are known for their superior racing abilities and extreme speed on the racetrack.

Before you begin

The racehorse is drawn from a side-on perspective. To achieve a sense of movement, draw the bent hind legs kicking out behind the horse. Also, pay attention to the way the horse's head sits forward and how the ears flow back.

Step 1

Lightly draw two parallel baselines. Draw an angled body shape and a thick neck shape. Sketch a circle for the head and a muzzle. Add a brow line and ears flowing back from the head. Draw the construction lines, joints, outlines and hooves for the legs, with the crossed front legs on the baselines and the back legs kicking behind. Add the jockey's leg shape over the horse's back. Sketch the jockey's chest, arms and rear leg. Draw the head pointing forward and the helmet.

Step 2

Define the outline of the horse, paying attention to the brow, muzzle and chest area. Draw the eye on the brow line and the nostrils on the muzzle. Add the mouth. Develop the jockey's hand, facial features and outline.

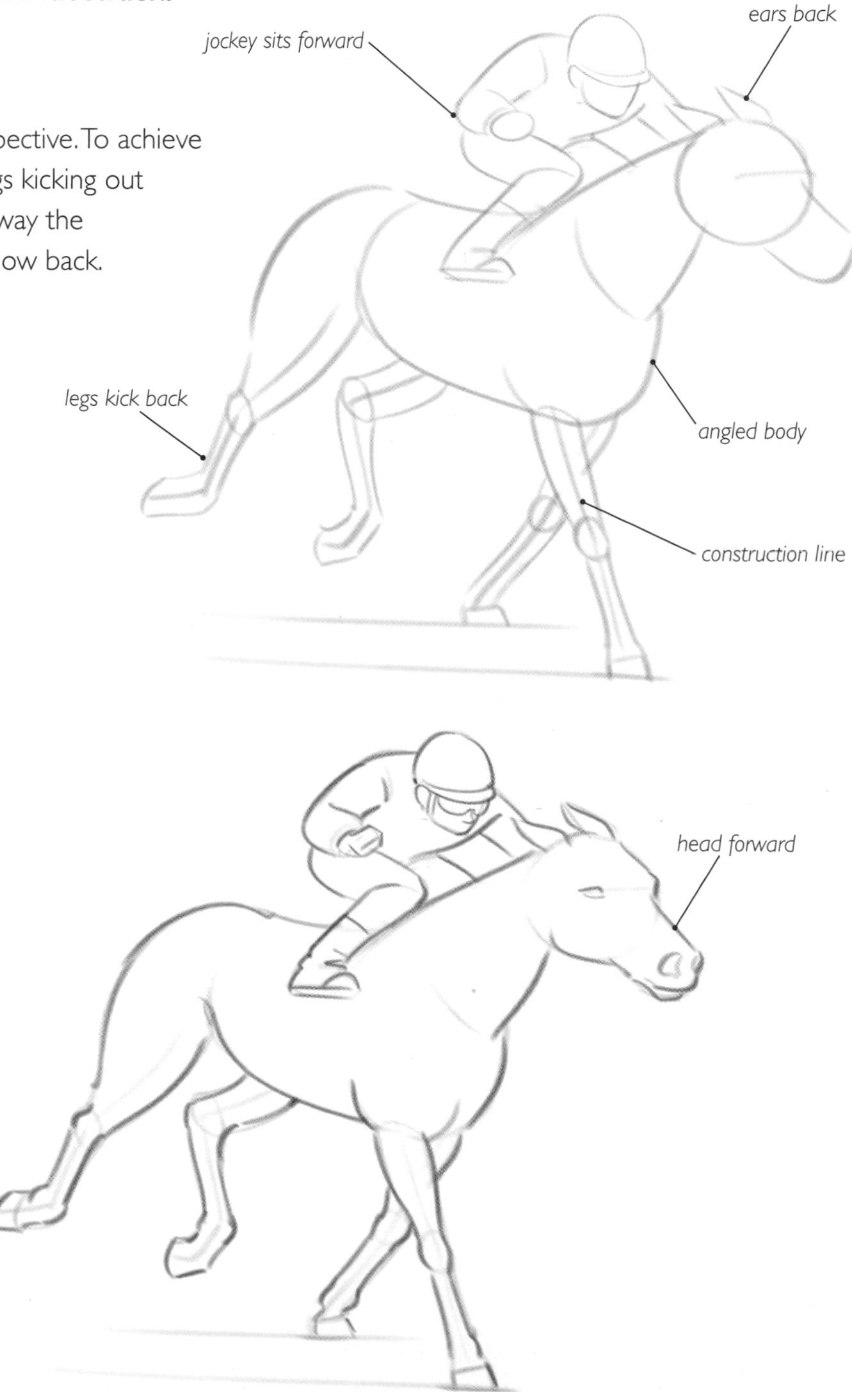

Step 3

Darken the outline and draw the harness around the horse's head and neck. Add shapes for the saddle and strap under the jockey's leg. Draw a wavy mane and tail flowing back. Develop the details of the jockey's helmet and mouth, and sketch the whip and helmet.

Step 4

Shade open line work across the horse's body with light pencil pressure. Darken the harness, saddle, hooves and legs. Shade a faint number four on the saddle. Use soft line work to add texture to the mane and tail. Apply a mid-grey tone to parts of the jockey's clothing.

Draw the racetrack, with the straight edge of the fence lined up with the top of the horse's body. Draw the fence poles on the same angle as the front leg. Once you add the texture of the ground, the jockey can race your horse to the finish line!

DRAWING TIP

Each time you sharpen your pencil it becomes shorter. Check your pencil when it shortens to see whether or not it is easy to draw with. If is difficult to sketch with, it is time for new pencil.

INTERESTING FACT → Horse racing became a professional sport in England during the reign of Queen Anne, in the early part of the 17th century.

SHOW JUMPING

Show jumping involves riding a horse through a series of jumps and obstacles. It is judged by whether the horse attempts each jump and clears it, and the time taken to complete a course. A show jumping horse needs to be strong and agile to manage the many jumps and sharp turns. The horse should also be fast, so the course can be completed quickly. Most successful show jumpers are large horses, but some exceptional pony-sized horses have been excellent show jumpers.

Before you begin

The horse and rider are constructed from a series of solid shapes. Carefully study the sizes and types of shapes use in the first step. The horse and rider are drawn from a side perspective. To achieve this, it is important to correctly position the bar and all the horse's legs.

Step 1

Start by drawing the bar on an angle. Draw the horse's stomach shape above the bar. Add a curved neck shape in the left corner and a circle for the head. Sketch the muzzle shape, a brow line and pointy ears above the head. Add an oval for the hindquarters and draw the curved back legs. Starting at the top, build the shape of the front leg and then the leg behind. Draw the shape of the rider's foot and leg over the hindquarters. Add the chest and the arm resting on the horse's neck. Sketch the rider's head, hat and other limbs.

Step 2

Define and smooth the outline of the horse's form. Add a nostril to the muzzle and a saddle. Sketch a block to the right of the bar. Draw a strap on the rider's hat and develop the face and hand. Add the coattail and details to the coat.

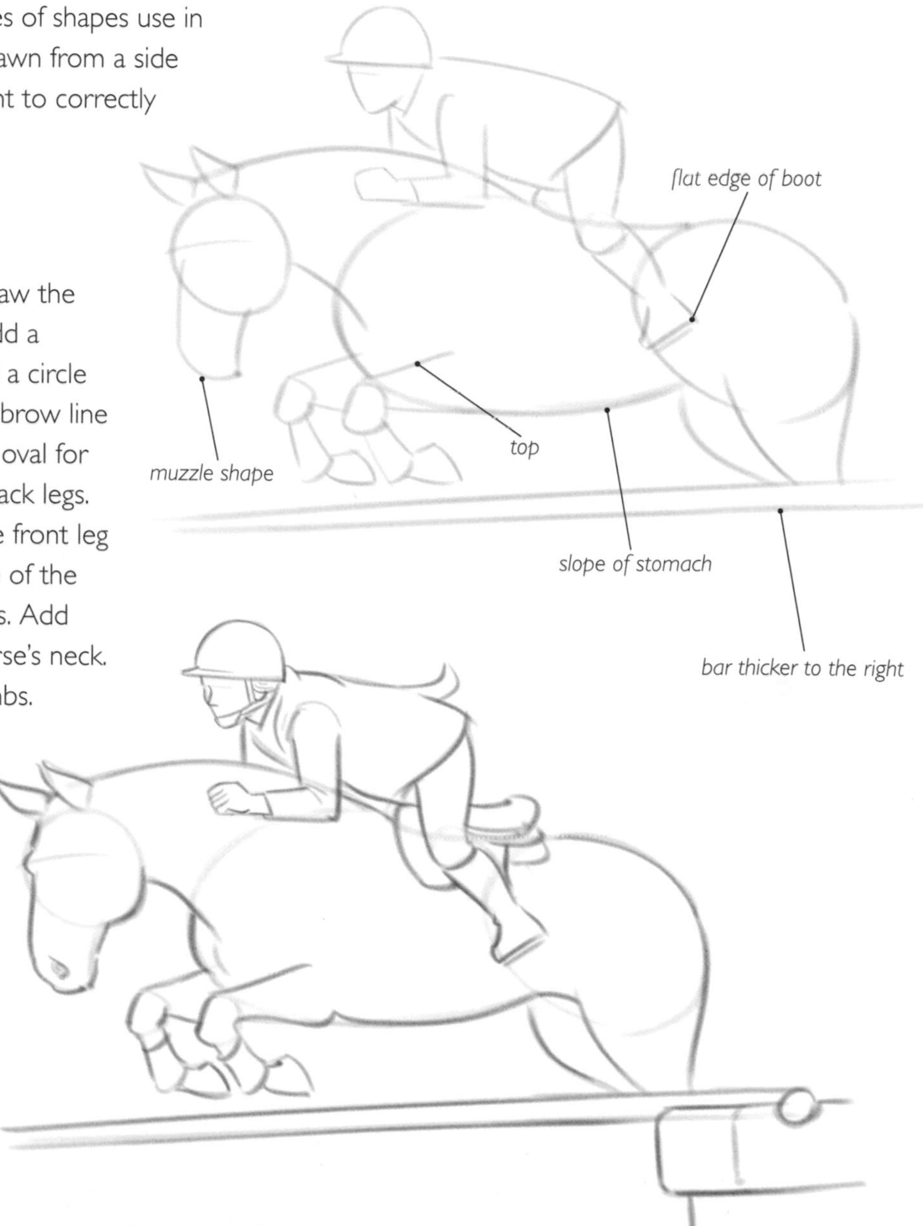

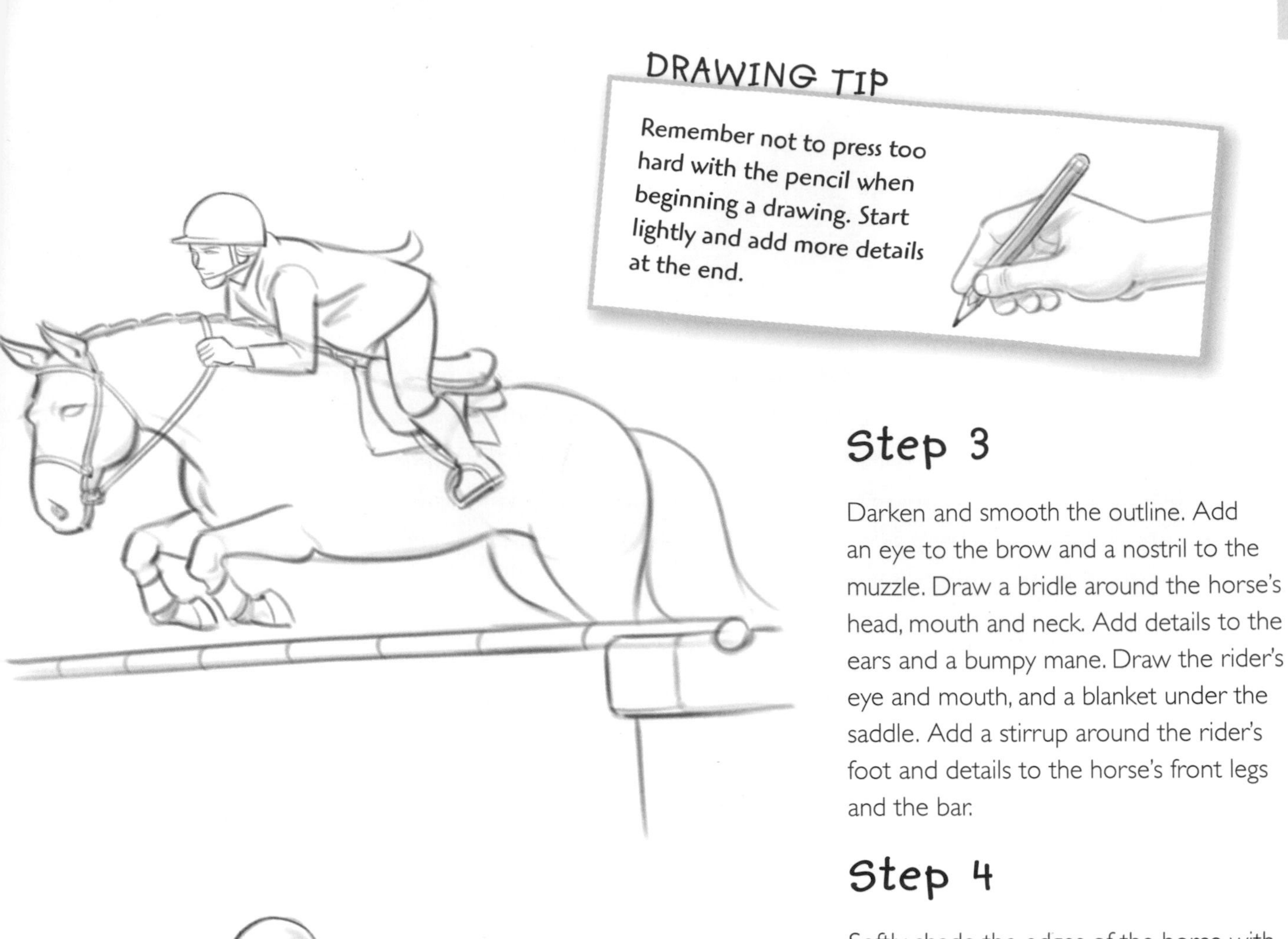

DRAWING TIP

Remember not to press too hard with the pencil when beginning a drawing. Start lightly and add more details at the end.

Step 3

Darken and smooth the outline. Add an eye to the brow and a nostril to the muzzle. Draw a bridle around the horse's head, mouth and neck. Add details to the ears and a bumpy mane. Draw the rider's eye and mouth, and a blanket under the saddle. Add a stirrup around the rider's foot and details to the horse's front legs and the bar.

Step 4

Softly shade the edges of the horse with light pencil pressure. Apply a medium grey tone to the rider and saddle. Darken the horse's mane, eye, nostril, hooves and rear leg.

Once you add details to the bar, your horse is ready to win its equestrian event!

INTERESTING FACT → Some of the jumps and obstacles include the vertical, the oxer, the Swedish oxer, the triple bar, the Liverpool, the wall, the hogsback, the fan and the joker.

MUSTANG

Horses were introduced to North America when the Spanish Conquistadors arrived in the 1500s. Over the next 200 years, many horses were taken in by Native American tribes, who were quick to adopt the horse into their way of life. With the settlement of the west, many horses escaped from ranches and farms. These horses have developed into a strong, hardy animal that can survive harsh conditions. The word 'mustang' comes from the Spanish word 'mesteño', meaning mixed breed or feral animal.

Before you begin

The form of the mustang is made up of a series of rounded muscular shapes. Observe the curved line work used to create these shapes. Study the size of the shapes and the types of line work used to create its structure. It is important the legs are drawn correctly to give the mustang a sense of movement. The way the mane and tail flows out behind the horse also helps to achieve this.

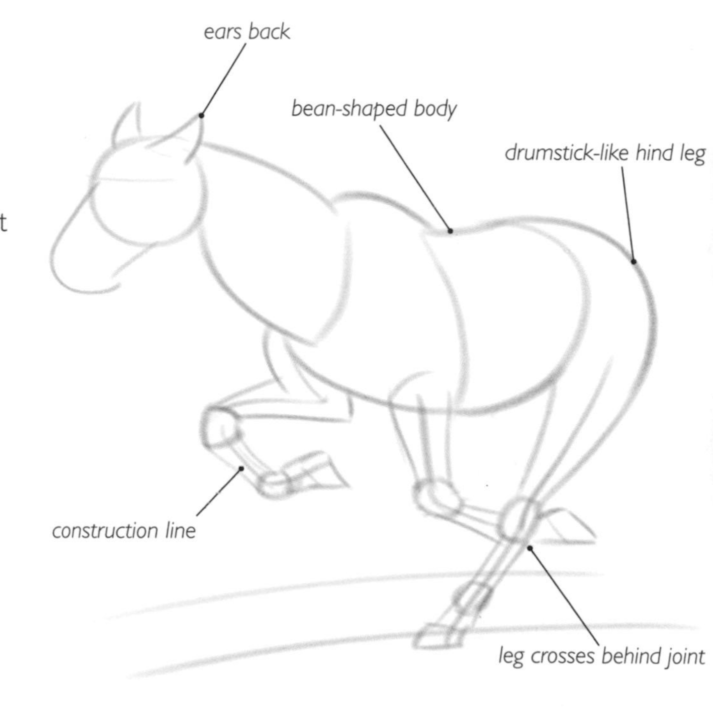

Step 1

Lightly draw two slightly angled baselines and a bean-shaped body above them. Sketch the construction lines, joints and hooves for the legs, sitting the back hind leg on the baseline. Cross the bent middle leg behind the rear leg and add the bent front leg. Build the shapes of the legs around the construction lines. Add a thick neck shape, a circle for the head, a muzzle shape and the ears pointing back.

Step 2

Define and smooth the outline of the mustang, paying attention to the brow, muzzle and chest. Sketch the shape of the fourth leg. Start at the top of the leg and sit the hoof on the baseline. Add the horse's mouth.

Step 3

Sketch a flame-shaped mane and tail flowing out behind. Draw an eye on the brow and a nostril on the muzzle. Add in details for hooves.

DRAWING TIP

Don't be afraid to experiment by drawing your own backgrounds for your subjects. If you are unsure what to draw, look up reference in books or on the internet! Try colouring in your picture with coloured pencils as well.

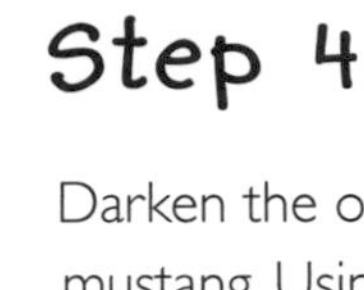

Step 4

Darken the outline of the mustang. Using a right to left drawing motion, shade a light grey tone around the edges of the horse. Darken the eye, nostril, hooves and rear leg. Use soft line work to add texture to the mane and tail.

When drawing the faint line work of the background, sketch the ground first and then the trees. Now your mustang is ready to gallop through the wild!

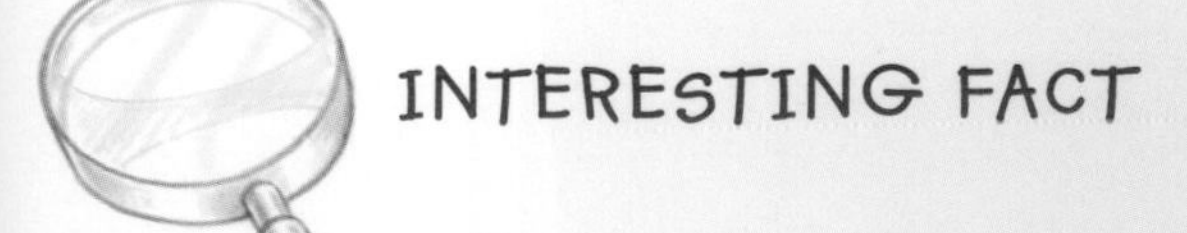

INTERESTING FACT

Many other countries also have feral horses (horses not native to the area but descended from domesticated horses). In Australia, these horses are known as brumbies. In New Zealand, they are Kaimanawa horses and in Spain they are called Sorraia horses.

CANADIAN MOUNTIE

Perhaps the most famous mounted police force is the Royal Canadian Mounted Police (founded in 1873), who wear a dress uniform of red tunics, wide-brimmed hats, black boots and bright banners. The RCMP is known for the role they played in Canada's settlement when they patrolled mountainous frontiers and borders. These days, the Mounties' horses and red uniform are primarily used for ceremonial occasions.

Before you begin

This drawing is constructed using a series of curved lines and rounded shapes. Pay attention to the size of the shapes and the types of line used to create this picture. The placement of the horse's legs on the baselines is also important so you achieve the correct pose.

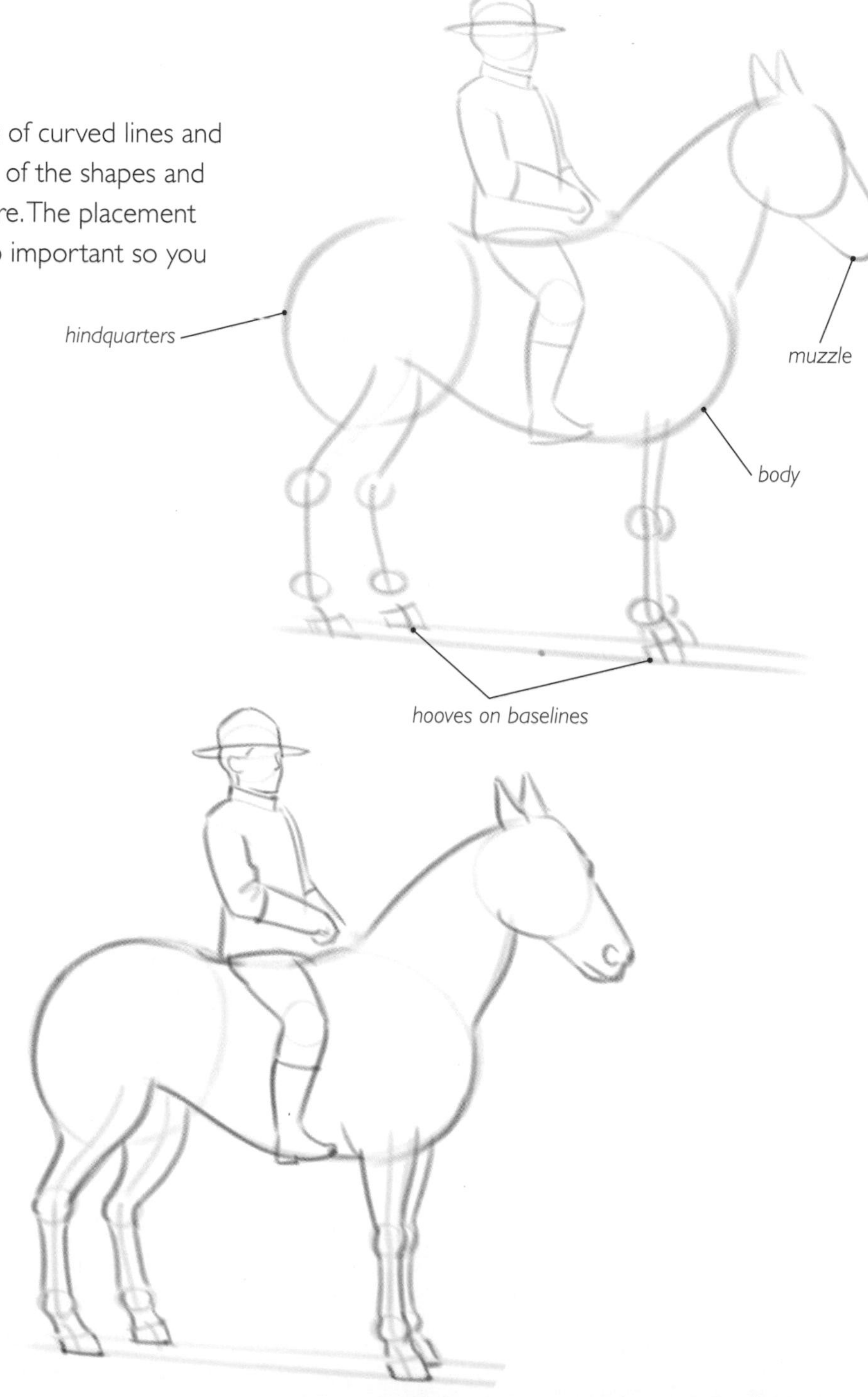

Step 1

Lightly draw parallel baselines on a slight angle. Draw a curved shape above the baseline for the body and add an oval for the hindquarters. Create a thick neck shape, a circle for the head and a muzzle. Add triangles for ears and construction lines for legs. Draw the joints and place the hooves on the baselines. Draw a shape for the Mountie's leg over the horse's back. Build the shape of the Mountie's chest, shoulders and arm. Add the head and hat.

Step 2

Define and smooth the curves of the horse's form and the Mountie's body. Pay attention to the horse's brow and muzzle. Add a nostril and mouth, and build the shape of the horse's legs around the construction lines.

DRAWING TIP

There are many different types of line used in creating a drawing. For example, lines are bent, straight and curly. There are spirals, wavy, loopy and curvy lines. See how many types of line you can draw!

Step 3

Draw the horse's eye on the brow line and add a harness around its face and chest. Sketch solid shapes for the tail and the bumpy mane. Add a medallion and reins. Draw a blanket under the Mountie's leg, add a saddle and sketch a stirrup around the boot. Define the Mountie's facial features and his clothing.

Step 4

Using a right-to-left drawing motion, shade the horse with soft open line work. Darken the eye, nostril and back legs. Apply a darker tone to the body of the policeman.

Use a light pencil pressure when creating the background. Draw the ground first, and then the bushes and the tree. Once you sketch the tiny pine trees and the large mountain peaks, your Mountie is ready for duty!

INTERESTING FACT → **The official motto of the Mounties is 'uphold the law', but a more famous saying is 'a Mountie always gets his man', a reference to the stereotype of the Mounties as tough, determined, tenacious lawmen.**

CLYDESDALE

Clydesdale horses are a breed of draft horse developed in Scotland around 300 years ago for their power, strength and agility. This gentle, tough breed stands around 16 to 19 hands (1.8 metres or 6 feet) in height. They were originally used in the early nineteenth century to perform heavy hauling work. With the dawn of the mechanical age, Clydesdale numbers dwindled dramatically when machinery such as the tractor was introduced.

Before you begin

The drawing of the Clydesdale horse and carriage is very detailed. Start by observing how the drawing changes between each step. This picture is created using a series of shapes. Study the type and size of shapes used. To achieve the correct perspective, study the angle that the horse's legs and the carriage are drawn on.

Step 1

Lightly draw two parallel, angled baselines. Draw the horse's chest area and a thick neck curving forward. Add a circle for the head and a muzzle shape. Draw a brow line, ears sitting forward, a curved stomach and hindquarters. Draw construction lines on the baseline for front legs and add the bent hind legs. Add joints and leg shapes. Draw the carriage's wheels on the same angle as the baselines, making the back wheel smaller. Add the base of the carriage and the pole attached to the horse. Sketch the front of the carriage and the cabin.

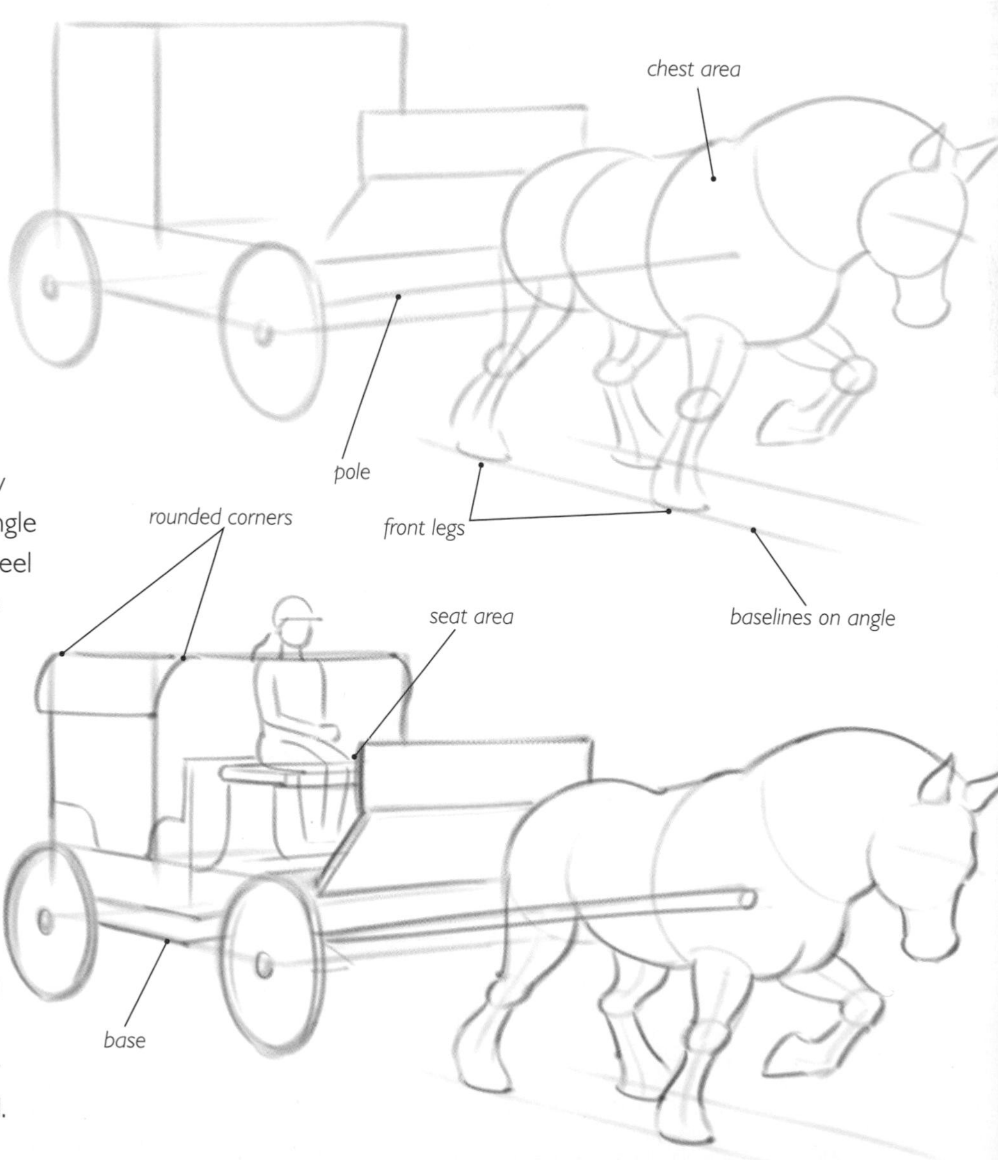

Step 2

Define and smooth the curves of the horse's form. Thicken the line work of the carriage's pole and wheels and develop the base. Round the corners of the cabin and draw the seat. Sketch the driver's legs over the seat and the chest, arm and head.

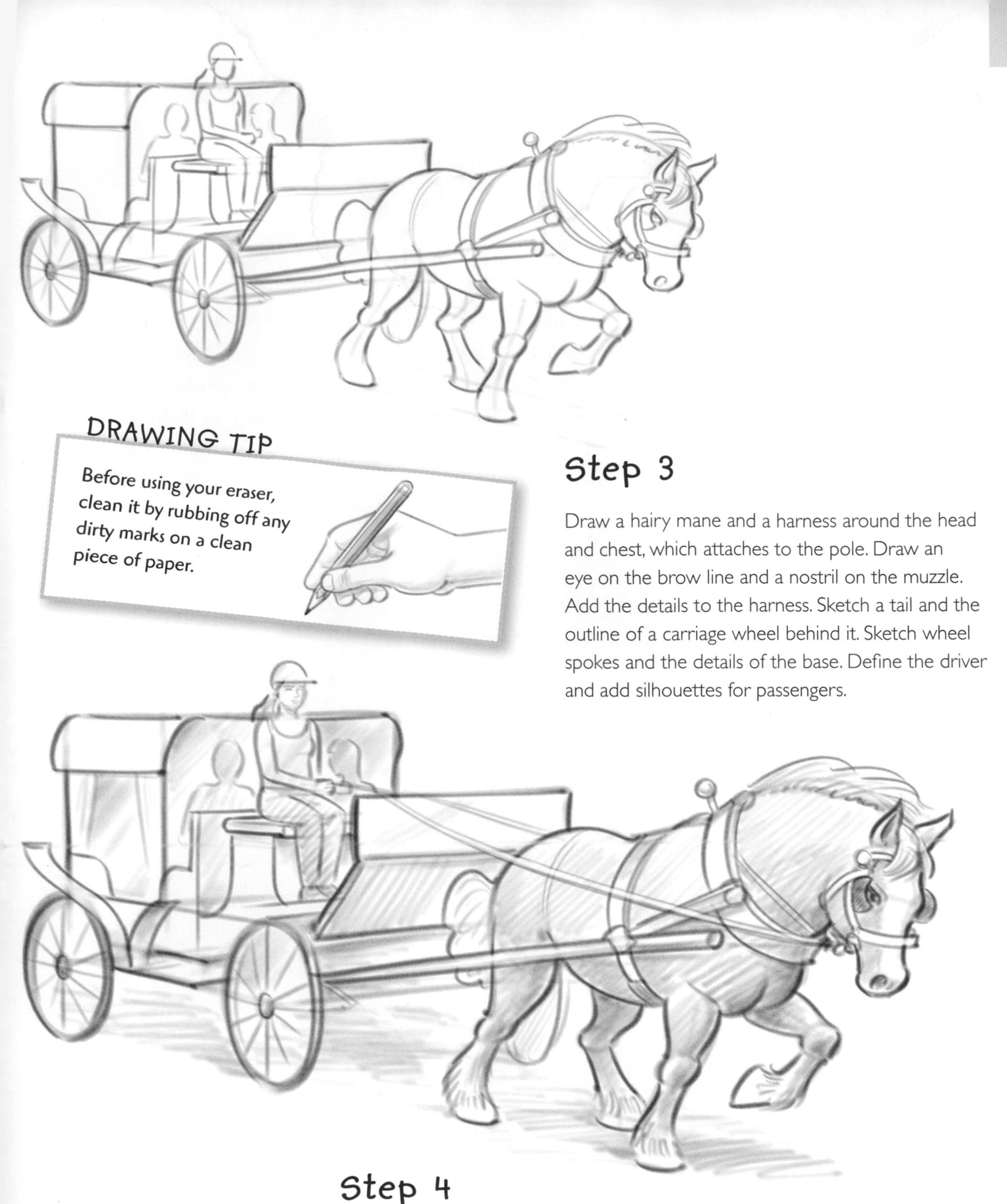

DRAWING TIP

Before using your eraser, clean it by rubbing off any dirty marks on a clean piece of paper.

Step 3

Draw a hairy mane and a harness around the head and chest, which attaches to the pole. Draw an eye on the brow line and a nostril on the muzzle. Add the details to the harness. Sketch a tail and the outline of a carriage wheel behind it. Sketch wheel spokes and the details of the base. Define the driver and add silhouettes for passengers.

Step 4

Darken and smooth the outline. Shade open line work across the carriage and horse with a light pencil pressure. Add darker shading where required and sketch soft line work for texture of the mane and tail. Define the hooves. Once you add a faint shadow under the horse and carriage, your Clydesdale is ready to pull its load!

INTERESTING FACT → There are around 5000 registered Clydesdale horses around the world today, with the breed gaining popularity in the USA.

SHETLAND PONY

Shetland ponies come from the Shetland Islands, which are located to the north east of Scotland. It is estimated that they have been living there since the Bronze Age. They developed into strong, tough, hardy animals due to the cold, wet climate of the islands. Shetland ponies have long, heavy manes and tails. They develop a thick coat to help them stay warm in winter. The official maximum height of a Shetland pony is 107 cm or 42 in.

Before you begin

The most important art element in this drawing is shape. A series of solid shapes are used to construct the pony's bulky form. Observe the curved and rounded shapes used for the body and the line work drawn for the mane and hair. Study the level of shading covering the pony's form.

Step 1

Lightly draw two parallel baselines. Above the baseline, draw a bean-shape for the body and a curved shape for the hindquarters. Add a thick shape for the neck and a circle for the head. Draw the muzzle shape and the ears on the head circle. Drawing the front legs first, sketch solid shapes for the legs, sitting them on the baselines.

Step 2

Darken and smooth the outline of the pony's form. Define the curves of the outline, paying attention to the brow, muzzle, chest and back. Draw nostril shapes on the muzzle.

Step 3

Develop curved pointy line work for the edges of the mane. Draw a curved tail down behind the pony's back legs. Add an eye in the brow area and the line work for the harness around the head. Sketch a mouth and add a mark to the inside of the ear.

Step 4

Using a right-to-left drawing motion, apply a medium grey over the pony's form. Add furry marks around the legs and hooves. Create soft line work for the texture of the pony's mane and tail. Darken the eye, nostrils, harness and front ear.

Once you add the details of the field in the background, your pony will be ready to ride!

DRAWING TIP

If you're worried about smudging your drawing, place a clean piece of paper under your hand where you're not drawing to prevent your sketch from getting dirty.

INTERESTING FACT → Shetland ponies make perfect children's ponies because of their gentle, intelligent nature and good temperament.

Published in 2008 by Hinkler Books Pty Ltd
45–55 Fairchild Street
Heatherton, Victoria 3202 Australia
www.hinklerbooks.com

Illustrated by Paul Könye
Written by Kate Ashforth
Internal design by Leigh Ashforth
Edited by Hinkler Studio
Cover design by Hinkler Studio
Prepress by Graphic Print Group

15 14 13 12 11 10
14 13 12 11

ISBN 978 1 7418 2937 2

Printed and bound in China

Photo Credits

Cover
Flower © Wael Hamdan/iStockphoto.com
Eraser © David Russell/iStockphoto.com
Hand holding pencil © Kelvin Wright/iStockphoto.com

Fairies
Flower © Kuleczka/Dreamstime.com
Hand holding pencil © Kelvin Wright/iStockphoto.com

Fairytale Princesses
Flower © Erikreis/Dreamstime.com
Hand holding pencil © Kelvin Wright/iStockphoto.com

Baby Animals
Gerberas © Caramaria/Dreamstime.com
Hand holding pencil © Kelvin Wright/iStockphoto.com

In the Ocean
Shell © Stepanjezek/Dreamstime.com
Starfish © Kuleczka/Dreamstime.com
Pink hibiscus © Fotonomy/Dreamstime.com
Hand holding pencil © Kelvin Wright/iStockphoto.com

Costumes & Fashions
Red lipstick © Sonja_inselmann/Dreamstime.com
Gerbera daisy flowers © Maxfx/Dreamstime.com
Hand holding pencil © Kelvin Wright/iStockphoto.com

Fantasy
Genie's lamp © Cre8tive_studios/Dreamstime.com
Exotic flower © Lepas/Dreamstime.com
Hand holding pencil © Kelvin Wright/iStockphoto.com

In the Garden
Ladybug © Milosluz/Dreamstime.com
Flower © Shahinkia/Dreamstime.com
Hand holding pencil © Kelvin Wright/iStockphoto.com

Horses
Horseshoe © Christine Balderas/iStockphoto.com
Daisy © Broker/Dreamstime.com
Hand holding pencil © Kelvin Wright/iStockphoto.com